WALKING WITH THE FULL ASSURANCE OF UNDERSTANDING

Walking with the Full Assurance of Understanding

Sterling Merritt Durgy

WIPF & STOCK · Eugene, Oregon

WALKING WITH THE FULL ASSURANCE OF UNDERSTANDING

Copyright © 2019 Sterling Merritt Durgy. All rights reserved. Except for brief quotations in critical publications or reviews, no part of this book may be reproduced in any manner without prior written permission from the publisher. Write: Permissions, Wipf and Stock Publishers, 199 W. 8th Ave., Suite 3, Eugene, OR 97401.

Wipf & Stock
An Imprint of Wipf and Stock Publishers
199 W. 8th Ave., Suite 3
Eugene, OR 97401

www.wipfandstock.com

PAPERBACK ISBN: 978-1-5326-9377-9
HARDCOVER ISBN: 978-1-5326-9378-6
EBOOK ISBN: 978-1-5326-9379-3

Manufactured in the U.S.A.   OCTOBER 14, 2019

Unless otherwise noted, Scripture quotations are taken from the *New American Standard Bible*®, Copyright © 1960, 1962, 1963, 1968, 1971, 1972, 1973, 1975, 1977, 1995 by The Lockman Foundation Used by permission. www.Lockman.org. Words in italics are not in the original text, but deemed necessary to complete the meaning in the English translation.

Scripture quotations in Greek are taken from *The Greek New Testament*, Fourth Revised Edition, edited by Barbara Aland, Kurt Aland, Johannes Karavidopoulos, Carlo M. Martini, and Bruce M. Metzger in cooperation with the Institute for New Testament Textual Research, Münster/Westphalia, © 1993 Deutsche Bibelgesellschaft, Stuttgart. Used by permission.

Scripture quotations in Hebrew are taken from *Biblia Hebraica Stuttgartensia*, edited by Karl Elliger and Wilhelm Rudolph, Fifth Revised Edition, edited by Adrian Schenker, © 1977 and 1997 Deutsche Bibelgesellschaft, Stuttgart. Used by permission.

Scripture quotations marked KJV are taken from the King James Version of the Holy Bible.

Scripture quotations marked NIV are taken from the Holy Bible, New International Version®, NIV®. Copyright © 1973, 1978, 1984, 2011 by Biblica, Inc.™ Used by permission of Zondervan. All rights reserved worldwide. www.zondervan.com The "NIV" and "New International Version" are trademarks registered in the United States Patent and Trademark Office by Biblica, Inc.™

Scripture quotations marked NRSV are taken from the New Revised Standard Version Bible, copyright © 1989, National Council of the Churches of Christ in the United States of America. Used by permission. All rights reserved worldwide.

Quotations from *Theological Wordbook of the Old Testament*, 2 vols., edited by R. Laird Harris, Gleason L. Archer, and Bruce K. Waltke, Chicago: Moody, 1980 used by permission.

To the memory of
Delbert R. Rose and Susan Schultz Rose,
who exemplified scriptural holiness
both in their personal lives
and in their lifetimes of service
devoted to promoting the understanding of God's Word.

Contents

Preface | ix
Acknowledgments | xi
Abbreviations | xiii
Transliteration | xv

1. Holding the Pattern of Sound Words | 1
2. Looking to the Creator | 14
3. Maintaining the Biblical Perspective | 24
4. Building on the Cornerstone | 38
5. Following Jesus | 48
6. Receiving the Witness | 59
7. Receiving the Teaching | 71
8. Understanding God | 84
9. Seeing the Need | 100
10. Making It Personal | 113
11. Comprehending the Triumph | 127
12. Recognizing the Provision | 141
13. Responding to Grace | 158
14. Bearing Fruit | 175
15. Living Redemptively | 192
16. Looking Expectantly | 210

Recommended Reading | 227
Bibliography | 231
Index | 233

Preface

Far from what its detractors may argue, Christianity based on the teachings of the Bible is neither antiquated nor narrow-minded. Scriptural Christianity is always relevant, always timely, always more than helpful—it is life-giving to those who live by it because Scripture is the Word of the living God.

We live in a time when the larger culture works against understanding Christianity, giving the false impression that it is a relic of the past. The educational system today, from preschool through graduate schools, all too often promotes a way of thinking that precludes even the consideration of Christian concepts.

Unfortunately, we also live in a time when the understanding of Christianity in the Christian community is often shallow, governed more by whim than by fact. It is all too common for popularizers of Christianity to peddle beliefs that reflect more of contemporary culture than Christianity. At the same time, many are tempted to think that their quick, personal impression of what Scripture teaches is what God meant for them to understand. In both cases, people are robbed of the true guidance, assurance, and joy of walking with God in the light of his Word.

A stable, confident walk with God requires a correct understanding of the central truths, logic, and promise of Christianity. This book has been written to provide this understanding. The discussion is geared to the needs of contemporary Christians, bringing in, where appropriate, information not commonly found in other writings of this type. Each chapter discusses a practice with the knowledge and insights that support it. The combination of these practices creates a strong groundwork for a close, fruitful, and confident walk with the Lord.

Some knowledge of the background of contemporary culture is necessary to understand how modern thought steers away from an accurate understanding of the biblical text. Therefore, where helpful, there is a discussion of history and philosophy to explain where and why a true understanding of Christianity differs from some of the common opinions of our time.

To accommodate a range of readers, I have attempted to balance the need for readability with the need for sufficient reference information.

Scripture verses in English are taken from the New American Standard Bible. Greek and Hebrew words, where provided, are transliterated into the Latin character set more familiar to readers of English. This enables those who cannot read the original characters to see them as more than just squiggles on a page and to have a good idea how to pronounce them. The transliteration is specific enough to enable those with a knowledge of Greek and Hebrew to comprehend the words and to do their own research on the original words and text.

For those concerned about the theological orientation of the writer, you will want to know that while this book largely discusses truths that are generally agreed upon by the wider Christian community, the interpretation of Scripture is from the Wesleyan-Arminian perspective. This is the same as the founder of Methodism: John Wesley. The goal of this writing is the same as Wesley's—to promote scriptural Christianity. Nevertheless, this book is not largely a presentation of Wesley's views and theology, but scriptural teaching interpreted in a manner that is consistent with Wesley's views.

My sincere hope is that this book builds the same confidence in you that I have: that God seeks to bless each one of us for eternity and that we can have that blessing through Jesus Christ. Further, one of the joys God has for us is to serve him in this age. I hope that in addition to whatever personal blessing may come to you as a result of reading this book, you are encouraged to serve him, confident that God can use each and every Christian in some way to build his kingdom to his glory through Jesus Christ our Lord.

Acknowledgments

A BOOK such as this could not be written without the insights communicated to me by many teachers through the years, including relatives, Sunday School teachers, pastors, professors, and authors. Too numerous to mention, whatever is of value in this work must, nevertheless, be seen as the product of their labors as well as my own.

I would like to express my appreciation for those at Asbury Theological Seminary, Wilmore, Kentucky, who increased my understanding and appreciation of Wesleyan theology, especially (in alphabetical order): William M. Arnett, Anthony Cassurella Jr., Robert E. Coleman, Donald E. Demaray, Harold B. Kuhn, John N Oswalt, Delbert R. Rose, Susan Schultz Rose, George A. Turner, and Joseph Wang. My appreciation for their ministry to me while a seminary student has only increased throughout the years.

I would be remiss if I did not also express appreciation for those who taught and supported me while working on my doctoral degree at Trinity Theological Seminary, Newburgh, Indiana, especially (in alphabetical order): Ronald T. Clutter, Rodger W. Dalman, Edward N. Martin, David P. Meyer, and Frank J. Smith.

I would also like to express my deep appreciation for those whose reviews and suggestions helped me prepare this manuscript: my wife, Dorothy, my sister-in-law, Judith Chamberlin, and my dear brothers-in-Christ: Rev. Joe Hoover and Rev. Edward Marks.

Last, but certainly not least, I want to express my sincere gratitude to Matt Wimer and all the folks at Wipf and Stock Publishers for publishing this work and for providing valuable assistance in its preparation.

My hope and prayer is that the prayers and labors of so many others flows through me to bless others through this book to the glory of God through Jesus Christ.

Abbreviations

Old Testament Books

Gen	Genesis	2 Chr	2 Chronicles	Dan	Daniel
Exod	Exodus	Ezra	Ezra	Hos	Hosea
Lev	Leviticus	Neh	Nehemiah	Joel	Joel
Num	Numbers	Esth	Esther	Amos	Amos
Deut	Deuteronomy	Job	Job	Obad	Obadiah
Josh	Joshua	Ps	Psalms	Jonah	Jonah
Judg	Judges	Prov	Proverbs	Mic	Micah
Ruth	Ruth	Eccl	Ecclesiastes	Nah	Nahum
1 Sam	1 Samuel	Song	Song of Solomon	Hab	Habakkuk
2 Sam	2 Samuel	Isa	Isaiah	Zeph	Zephaniah
1 Kgs	1 Kings	Jer	Jeremiah	Hag	Haggai
2 Kgs	2 Kings	Lam	Lamentations	Zech	Zechariah
1 Chr	1 Chronicles	Ezek	Ezekiel	Mal	Malachi

New Testament Books

Matt	Matthew	Eph	Ephesians	Heb	Hebrews
Mark	Mark	Phil	Philippians	Jas	James
Luke	Luke	Col	Colossians	1 Pet	1 Peter
John	John	1 Thess	1 Thessalonians	2 Pet	2 Peter
Acts	Acts	2 Thess	2 Thessalonians	1 John	1 John
Rom	Romans	1 Tim	1 Timothy	2 John	2 John
1 Cor	1 Corinthians	2 Tim	2 Timothy	3 John	3 John
2 Cor	2 Corinthians	Titus	Titus	Jude	Jude
Gal	Galatians	Phlm	Philemon	Rev	Revelation

General Abbreviations

ca.	*circa*
cf.	*confer*, compare
e.g.	*exempli gratia*, for example
Gk.	Greek
Hebr.	Hebrew
i.e.	*id est*, that is

Reference Works

CNTUOT	*Commentary on the New Testament Use of the Old Testament: Exegesis and Interpretation.* Edited by G. K. Beale and D. A. Carson. Grand Rapids: Baker Academic, 2012.
KJV	King James Version of the Holy Bible
NASB	New American Standard Bible
NIV	Holy Bible; New International Version
NRSV	New Revised Standard Version Bible
TDNT	*Theological Dictionary of the New Testament.* Edited by Gerhard Kittel and Gerhard Friedrich. Translated by Geoffrey W Bromiley. 10 vols. Grand Rapids: Eerdmans, 1964–76.
TLNT	Spicq, Ceslas Spicq. *Theological Lexicon of the New Testament.* Edited and Translated by James D Ernest. 3 vols. Peabody: Hendrickson, 1994.
TWOT	*Theological Wordbook of the Old Testament*

Transliteration

Greek Letters

Letter	Transliteration		Letter	Transliteration
α	alpha	a	ν	nu	n
β	beta	b	ξ	xi	x
γ	gamma	g	ο	omicron	o
δ	delta	d	π	pi	p
ε	epsilon	e	ρ	rho	r
ζ	zeta	z	σ ς	sigma	s
η	eta	ē	τ	tau	t
θ	theta	th	υ	upsilon	y
ι	iota	i	φ	phi	ph
κ	kappa	k	χ	chi	ch
λ	lambda	l	ψ	psi	ps
μ	mu	m	ω	omega	ō

Notes on Greek Transliteration:
1. Accents are not preserved.
2. The letter *h* is added to the beginning of a word to represent a rough breathing mark.
3. The letter *i* is added after a vowel when necessary to represent an iota subscript.
4. The first γ in γγ, γκ, γξ, γχ is transliterated *n* (i.e., ng, nk, nx, nch).

5. ρ (rho) is transliterated *rh* when it appears at the beginning of a word and when it is the second rho immediately following a rho (i.e., rrh for ρρ).

6. υ (upsilon) is represented by the letter *y* when it appears alone and by the letter *u* when it is part of a dipthong (au, eu, ēu, ou, ui).

7. A diaeresis indicates that a letter is to be pronounced as a separate syllable rather than with a preceding vowel (e.g., Mōüsēs).

Hebrew Consonants

Letter		Transliteration	Letter		Transliteration
א	aleph	ʼ (silent)	ם מ	mem	m
ב	bet	b	ן נ	nun	n
ג	gimel	g	ס	samek	s
ד	dalet	d	ע	ayin	ʻ (silent)
ה	he	h	ף פ	pe	p
ו	waw	w	ץ צ	tsade	ṣ (ts)
ז	zayin	z	ק	qoph	q
ח	khet	ḥ (kh)	ר	resh	r
ט	tet	ṭ (t)	שׂ	sin	ś (s)
י	yod	y	שׁ	shin	š (sh)
ך כ	kaph	k	ת	tav	t
ל	lamed	l			

Hebrew Vowels

Vowel		Transliteration	Vowel		Transliteration
בַ	patakh	a (a as in bat)	בֹ	holem	ō (o as in mole)
בָ	qamets	ā (a as in father)	בוֹ	full holem	ô (o as in mole)
בָה	final qamets he	â (a as in father)	בֻ	short qibbuts	u (u as in bull)
בֶ	segol	e (as in get)	בֻ	long qibbuts	ū (u as in rule)
בֵ	tsere	ē (e as in grey)	בוּ	shureq	û (u as in rule)
בֵי	tsere yod	ê (e as in grey)	בֳ	khatef qamets	ŏ (o as in hot)
בִ	short hireq	i (i as in hit)	בֲ	khatef patakh	ă (a as in ascent)
בִ	long hireq	ī (i as in marine)	בֱ	khatef segol	ĕ (e as in methodical)
בִי	hireq yod	î (i as in marine)	בְ	vocal shewa	ᵉ (o as in hot)
בָ	qamets khatuf	o (o as in hot)			

1

Holding the Pattern of Sound Words

Retain the standard of sound words . . . in the faith and love which are in Christ Jesus.

2 TIMOTHY 1:13

I testify about them that they have a zeal for God, but not in accordance with knowledge.

ROMANS 10:2

In his journal, John Wesley provides a revealing account of his perilous journey across the Atlantic Ocean. Setting sail October 21, 1735, his vessel encountered powerful storms starting January 17, 1736. Towering waves pounded the wooden vessel, sometimes making it impossible to control, often threatening to break it apart. More than a few waves crashed over the ship, drenching anyone on deck. Sometimes ocean water poured between the deck planks, also soaking those below. At one point, a wave crashed through the windows of the main cabin, rolling over Wesley and others who were trying to sleep. The storms terrified Wesley. Although he was on a missionary voyage to the colonies in America, he confessed that he was afraid to die.

Wesley noticed that the same was not true of twenty-six German Christians traveling on the same ship. He had already observed that they were happy to do menial tasks without pay and that they were not upset when things went wrong. In other words, they were happy to serve others for the sake of Christ—which set them apart from the other Christians onboard. After a wave crashed over the ship, splitting the mainsail, Wesley learned that every one of these Christians, including the children, were unafraid to die. Wesley, however, would endure another voyage before he found peace.

After his return to England, Wesley himself was transformed into a fearless servant of Christ, facing angry mobs with calmness and grace. This followed a meeting in 1738 where, listening to Martin Luther's discussion of salvation by faith alone, Wesley understood and accepted that Christ's atonement was sufficient for the forgiveness of *his* sins. Interestingly, his transformation has similarities to that of Simon Peter. Peter was afraid to confess that he was a disciple of Jesus the night of Jesus' trial; but after Pentecost, he testified boldly even to his enemies.

The experiences of both men testify to the importance of the presence of God working in a person's life. They also demonstrate something that may not be as evident: the importance of not only the knowledge of but also the correct understanding of Scripture. As a young man, John Wesley attained a thorough knowledge of Scripture, but had not given sufficient attention to the role of faith, especially with regard to his own relationship with God. Once he recognized what the Scriptures meant and exercised faith in Christ, he was open to the witness of the Spirit that he was a child of God (Rom 8:16).

The New Testament is clear that before the resurrection of Christ, the disciples, including Peter, knew but did not understand the teachings of Scripture regarding Christ's atonement and resurrection. After Jesus' resurrection, Jesus instructed them and opened their minds to understand his teaching (Luke 9:44-45; 24:6-8, 25-27, 44-48; John 2:18-22; Mark 9:30-32). At Pentecost, they received the indwelling Holy Spirit to aid them in their walk and testimony (John 7:39; 14:25-26). The Spirit's presence led to increased understanding, as when Peter's mind was opened to understand that the work of Christ applies to Gentiles as well as to Jews (Acts 10:34-35).

In his writings, John recognizes truth as a body of sacred teaching that must be correctly understood as well as truth manifested by the Holy Spirit—the Spirit of Truth—in the life of a believer. Both aspects are essential in what John called "walking in truth" (2 John 4; 3 John 3-4). It is the knowledge of God's Word, especially through Jesus Christ, that lays the groundwork for the work of the Holy Spirit in a person's life (cf. 1 John 1:5-6; 2:3; 3:11, 23-24; 5:1-13; 2 John 6-10). However, the misunderstanding of Scripture can deprive a person of a close walk with God, and sometimes deprive of salvation itself.

After his resurrection, Jesus commanded his disciples to teach others all that he taught them. The Apostle Paul recognized the importance of this when he told the elders of the church at Ephesus that he had not withheld any of God's counsel from them (Acts 20:24-27). However, Paul also warned the elders to be prepared to oppose false teachings (Acts 20:28). Even among those who value God's Word, there is still the potential for those who desire to remain faithful to go astray if they are not careful (2 John 7). Indeed, Jesus taught his followers to judge correctly, not just by appearance (John 7:24). For this reason, John warned, "Watch yourselves" (2 John 8).

The Tendency to Go Astray

If you're like people I know, there were times when the sky not only grabbed your attention, it lifted your spirits. I recall times when after a long day working in an office, I walked into a parking lot where the stars, moon, and planets shone brightly in the night sky, often against the beautiful deep blue that follows sundown. On some occasions Venus, the evening star, shone especially bright in the evening sky; sometimes other planets were in view. It was all very refreshing. I felt as if I was coming alive again as the closed-in "world" of office rooms and halls gave way to the expansive beauty of the heavens above.

It seems people have always been fascinated by the sky—especially the night sky. The ancients—who had a much darker sky than most of us have today—probably noticed very early that some stars stayed in the same position relative to one another, forming constellations. They would also have noticed that certain night objects moved against the background of the constellations: certainly the moon, but also the objects we know as Venus, Mars, Jupiter, and Saturn. The Greek word for these heavenly objects thus means "wanderer," and the English word "planet" comes from this Greek word. In the New Testament (which was originally written in Greek) the noun and verb forms of this word are used to describe the kinds of wandering that, unlike the wandering of the planets, is cause for concern.

For example, it is a cause for concern when sheep wander from their fold and the safety of their shepherd's watchful eye. They may do so quite innocently as they graze in a meadow, absentmindedly munching their way apart from the flock, or they may stubbornly decide to leave the flock to go off on their own. Either way, they place themselves in danger of becoming lost or of falling victim to predators such as lions or wolves. It is also cause for concern when Christians depart from the true faith and wander into falsehood, whether they do so innocently in search of more spiritual knowledge or they do so deliberately because they consider themselves too smart to be fooled. John used a form of the Greek word for wanderer in 2 John 7 when he warned of deceivers—those who could influence Christians to wander from the truth. In letters written with great pastoral concern, the Apostle Paul—mature, experienced, and guided by the Holy Spirit—warned his readers about certain beliefs that would lead astray from a true understanding of biblical teaching. Paul had personal experience with this problem before his conversion.

As a "Hebrew of Hebrews," Paul took seriously the fact that the Hebrews were "entrusted with the oracles of God" (Phil 3:5; Rom 3:2). In the time that he lived, Jewish life and worship were totally focused on the Old Testament Scriptures. All adult men were expected to be competent enough to bring the sabbath message in their synagogue using Old Testament texts. As a young man, Paul made the correct interpretation of those Scriptures his life's work, seeking education from the finest minds in the Jewish religious leadership. He was so zealous for the purity of the faith that he persecuted those he believed were undermining it—the followers of Jesus of Nazareth. Under his leadership, men and women were put in prison, and some, like Stephen, were martyred. Yet, after coming to Christ, Paul realized that his zeal, and the zeal of many of his fellow Jews, stemmed from a serious misinterpretation of the Old Testament writings. Their understanding was so flawed that they were actually opposing the work of the God they thought they were serving. While it strengthened his faith in God's mercy and saving grace, Paul always regretted that he had acted "ignorantly in unbelief" (1 Tim 1:12–17; cf. 1 Cor 15:9). As an apostle of Christ, an evangelist, a teacher, and a missionary, Paul came to know that this problem wasn't limited to the Jews; Christians, too, can become confused and wander from the Truth.

It is for this reason that Paul advised Timothy to pay attention to the way Timothy lived his life and to what Timothy's taught, so that both Timothy and those Timothy pastored would find salvation (1 Tim 4:16). In the context of this advice, in his Second Letter to Timothy, Paul exhorted Timothy to "retain the standard (Gk. *hypotypōsin eche*) of sound words" (2 Tim 1:13). Paul's other letters reflect this concern that those who follow Christ would grow in both knowledge and discernment (1 Thess 4:13; Phil 1:9–11; Col 1:9–12; cf. 1 Cor 2:1–13). He told the Colossians that he labored so that those under his ministry would have "the full assurance of understanding" (Col 2:1–4).

What kind of things would cause Christians to lose hold of the Truth? The Scriptures constantly warn against false prophets and self-serving religious teachers. They also warn that people close to us may promote popular teachings that do not promote godliness (cf. 1 Tim 1:3–4; 2 Tim 3:13). Whatever the source, Paul warned that this kind of talk can spread like gangrene, bringing decay and death. In this case, the death of godliness, the ruin of the spiritual life of a person, a family, or a local church.

With this as his concern, the Apostle Paul wrote to the Christians in Corinth: "I, brethren, could not speak to you as to spiritual men, but as to men of flesh, as to infants in Christ. I gave you milk to drink, not solid food; for you were not yet able *to receive it*. Indeed, even now you are not yet able" (1 Cor 3:1–2). The author of Hebrews made a similar statement in his letter, telling his readers they should have become mature enough in the faith to become teachers, but instead, they were forgetting the basic teachings of the faith; so he was forced to give them "milk"—in other words: "baby food"—instead of "solid food" (Heb 5:12). The problem that follows when people are stuck on spiritual milk rather than spiritual food is that they aren't well-grounded enough to resist teachings that seem right, but instead are intrinsically wrong. In Ephesians 4, Paul encourages his readers to grow in the faith so that they are not, like children, easily led astray by false teachings.

The mishandling of anything that is powerful can result in great destruction—fire, water, electricity, and drugs to be sure—but also the Holy Scriptures. Jesus taught that those who build their lives on his teachings are building their lives on solid rock. Surely those who mishandle his teachings are just like those who ignore his teachings, the foolish who build their lives on sand (Matt 7:24–29). At the heart of resistance to false teachings is a discipline that seeks out the true meaning of God's Word, not just the popular or comfortable interpretation. It is handling God's Word in a reverent manner, the manner of a learner, a disciple. The bottom line is that those who don't wander from God are those who focus their attention on being faithful.

God's plan is for his people to shine like the stars in a world that is spiritually dark (Phil 2:14–15). When that happens, people around them are drawn to the Christ who can give them a refreshment much deeper than I received when I emerged from the office to look at the night sky (John 7:37–38; cf. 4:13–14). But that only happens if God's people are true to his Word and his ways.

Two Major Movements That Can Lead Astray

It is helpful to take a step back before continuing to consider what is happening with regard to Christian teaching in general. The Christian message is being undermined from both outside and within the Christian community in our time.

A rather large community of individuals believes it is their duty to do everything within their power to discourage traditional Christianity. This group traces its roots to the Deists of the 1600s and the philosophies of David Hume, Immanuel Kant, and others. Their core belief is that the Bible is largely a collection of falsehoods, and thus traditional Christianity is destructive of human progress. Essentially unbelievers, some nevertheless adopt the language of Christianity to work within the Christian church. In our time, these people are known as liberal progressives—often just liberal, progressive, humanist, or "the left."

There *are* certainly liberals who are truly liberal—willing to give opposing views a hearing and to debate different points of view even though they reject many traditional Christian beliefs. However, given their conviction that traditional Christianity is an impediment to progress, most progressives are impatient to see traditional Christianity relegated to the past. Wherever the members of this group have gained power, they have used it to eliminate traditional Christians from positions of leadership throughout society, but especially in the church. Since entering the leadership of Christian churches in the 1800s, liberals have chipped away at the message of many "mainline" churches until little, if anything, remains of what was historically considered the bedrock beliefs and practices of Christianity.

Progressives believe that history is on their side. They expect opposition to the progressive movement will inevitably wither and die. Confident in the righteousness of their cause, the problems of the world always seem to progressives to be "out there," not within themselves. Not only does this cause them to be dismissive of arguments that expose the weaknesses in their views, it tends to prevent them from any form of serious self-criticism. Too often, this results in their being closed-minded, elitist, legalistic, dictatorial, derisive, divisive, intolerant, and oppressive—the very behaviors they say they exist to oppose.

To be sure, traditional Christians strongly oppose many progressive beliefs. However, from the perspective of traditional Christianity, the major problem with liberal progressives is not that they hold contrary beliefs, which, of course, progressives have every right to do; the problem is that they don't extend the same consideration to traditional Christians that they demand for themselves—the freedom for all people to think things through for themselves, and to express and to live by their convictions. Further, it is a problem when progressives claim to be Christians while promoting positions that are the opposite of traditional Christianity. It would seem that honesty would require them to join or to start churches that hold their beliefs, not to join traditional Christian churches and then work to undermine their teachings.

On the other hand, there is also a movement within the traditional Christian community in our time that is undermining a true understanding of Christianity. This movement results from an overemphasis on individualism. Unlike liberal progressives, the people in this group truly believe they are promoting traditional Christianity. Many believe they are directly guided by the Holy Spirit. Nevertheless, it is this group more than any group outside Christianity that is responsible for the erosion of Christian teaching. It has resulted in the two greatest problems in the Christian community today: ignorance and unbelief. How can this be?

When individuals believe that they can understand everything about Christianity completely on their own, they cut off the opportunity to learn from others. When there was serious disagreement on teaching in the early church, the apostles and elders came together in Jerusalem to discuss the matter and seek a common understanding of true doctrine; each person did not decide on their own. The Scriptures provide the letters of Paul, Peter, and John as they instruct others in the faith. These letters do not stand alone, however, but often followed face-to-face teaching by the apostles. We also have the example of Priscilla and Aquila correcting Apollos. Apollos was knowledgeable and persuasive, but needed the help of Priscilla and Aquila to understand the faith correctly (Acts 18:24–28). The prophets who spoke for God in both testaments did not invent their own message, they received a message from the Lord that they were to deliver faithfully to others (2 Pet 1:20–21). If the prophets did not have the freedom to invent what they said, surely we do not have the freedom to interpret their words any way that we please.

The ability to learn requires humility. We must be teachable as well as firm in our convictions; otherwise, we are limited by our own understanding—and too often misunderstanding—of Christianity. If we do everything on our own, we deprive ourselves of the support of the community of faith, not only the community of faith in our time, but the community that includes all Christians who have gone before us.

There is, of course, an important place for individualism. Every person is unique, and should relate directly to God as an individual. God's design is for each person to have a unique personality, interests, and gifts. Christianity is not a religion in which, like Hinduism, people strive to lose their identity. But when individualism means accepting only our own private judgments, or only the judgments of a small group, or what is merely popular, we have lost the ability to learn and to grow. This is especially troublesome when beliefs are judged by how comfortable they feel. Feelings are affected by so many factors within and without that feelings, alone, can never serve to determine what is true. Feelings alone cannot determine whether we are in step with the Holy Spirit.

Both progressive liberalism and excessive individualism promote beliefs that send people in unhelpful directions. For example, some in both communities promote the belief that Christianity has to be rescued from the outside or it will die. An early form of this belief was held by the Anglican bishop George Berkeley (1685–1753), who believed that his philosophy made Christianity totally secure from modern attacks. His optimism proved completely unfounded. He was followed by the philosopher David Hume (1711–76), who used Berkeley's general approach to question all beliefs, including Christianity.

The philosopher Immanuel Kant (1724–1804) was horrified when he read Hume's writings, believing that Hume's total skepticism endangered both science and religion. Kant developed a sophisticated philosophy, convinced that he had rescued both science and religion from Hume's approach. However, Kant argued that we can never know reality, only our impression of it, preserving a large part of Hume's skepticism. Kant also argued that religion is unnecessary in an age of reason. Like other thinkers of the Enlightenment, he reduced religion to morality, and thought that all other aspects of religion were outmoded and would soon pass away. Berkeley's arrogant belief that Christianity needed to be rescued by his novel approach thus undercut rather than supported Christianity. Any scheme to "rescue" Christianity from itself is likely to lead to similar ends. This is not to disparage philosophy itself, because right thinking is an aid to Christianity, not a threat. Christian philosophers serve an important purpose in supporting a Christian worldview and defending it against competing religions and philosophies.

Recent history also shows that wrongheaded philosophers are not to be outdone by those in the Christian community whose determination to "keep up with the times" sacrifices traditional faith and practice in the attempt to win new converts to Christianity. Some are progressive liberals, but many are believing Christians who, nevertheless, think the continuation of Christianity rests on their shoulders. It does not.

Christianity is not a collection of ideas that, like a helium balloon, leaks over time and eventually falls out of the air. The future of Christianity rests today, as in the past, in the reality of the living God, his Word, and his work in the past, present, and future. Christians do not initiate God's work, they enter into the work he is already doing. He would not be doing this work if he knew it wouldn't succeed in accomplishing his purposes! This is not an argument against updating language and styles to better communicate and practice the faith, but against thinking that the Christian faith itself needs "updating."

When it comes to ignorance, neither progressives nor individualists have a "corner on the market," so to speak. Progressive liberals are ignorant of the message of Scripture because they think anything from the past must be harmful, and so generally cherry-pick Scriptures they feel support their beliefs and ignore everything else. Many who value Scripture, on the other hand, are ignorant because they would rather go by their inward feelings than study the text adequately, incorrectly assuming that all education leads to liberalism. For too many in both camps, Christianity is a faith of catchy slogans and popular opinions. The corrective to all counterproductive beliefs, from whatever their source, is a zeal that is *according* to knowledge. As Paul counseled Timothy, it is those who labor to understand God's Word of Truth accurately who have no reason to be ashamed (2 Tim 2:15). Today as in the time of Paul, those who truly seek to serve the Lord Jesus preserve the pattern of sound words.

Removing Blinders

One of the unfortunate aspects of modernism has been the tendency to eliminate certain words that had meaning in the past. Language always changes to some degree over time. But the elimination of certain words from the vocabulary makes it impossible to discuss or even think about some important concepts. Some within the Christian community have also tried to "cleanse" the faith by defining some terms too narrowly. God is big enough to be Lord of all of life. We should not allow people with an agenda to control our thinking by controlling the words we use. Let's take off the intellectual straightjackets so we can think about words from a solidly Christian perspective.

"Theology" is often disparaged today. The word "theology" doesn't appear in the Bible, but it is a useful term that has a straightforward meaning. A theology is simply a collection of beliefs about God and all things in relation to God. Yes, there are theologies that ignore biblical teaching, and thus are contrary to the true practice of Christianity. But that does not disqualify theology that is based upon a correct understanding of biblical teaching.

There are theologies written by Christian scholars, but it isn't necessary to be a learned scholar to have a theology. Just about everyone has a collection of beliefs about God and spiritual things that constitute *their* theology, *their* understanding of God and all things in relation to God. It is also helpful, at times, to separate beliefs by topic. If you were asked to tell your theology of God, or Jesus, or the church, all you would need to do is to state your beliefs on that subject based on your understanding of what Scripture tells us. It is an achievable goal for all Christians to have an adequate knowledge of Christian theology, even though only some need to seek academic degrees. Sound theology is important, because what we believe governs how we live.

The word "doctrine," while commonly used in the past, makes some people grimace today. However, there is nothing dark or menacing communicated by this word. The Greek word translated "doctrine" in the New Testament is *didaskalia*, which simply means "teaching." There are a number of Christian teachings—doctrines—that comprise Christian theology, and thus communicate the Christian faith. The teaching of sound doctrines corrects false ones, preserving the standard Paul called for in 2 Timothy 1:13.

There are many examples in Christian history of theologians wasting time on useless issues such as "how many angels can dance on the head of a pin." However, the best Christian theologians in history, represented by such individuals as Irenaeus, Augustine, Athanasius, Anselm, Philip Melancthon, Heinrich Bullinger, John Wesley, John Fletcher, and many others were pastorally oriented—fully focused upon the real-life needs of those under their spiritual care. The major doctrines of the Christian faith, even those about supernatural subjects and deity, not only affect our theology, they directly affect how we think and how we live our lives.

The word "religion" is another word that has fallen out of favor in some quarters. It has become fashionable in some circles today to say: "Christianity is not a religion." If that were true, however, "freedom of religion" guaranteed under the United States Constitution would not apply to Christians. It is doubtful most American Christians would agree to do away with that protection! There is, therefore, a practical problem here if we dismiss the concept of religion altogether. Beyond this, if religion is correctly understood, Christianity is, indeed, a religion.

Certainly in the past Christians had no problem speaking of Christianity as a religion. For example, John Calvin, a leader of the Protestant Reformation, gave his great work on Christian theology the Latin title: *Institutio Christianae Religionis*, which is, in English, *Institutes of the Christian Religion*. The preamble to the *Thirty-Nine Articles* of the Church of England, the English version of which was published in 1571, states that the purpose of the articles is to bring common agreement on "true Religion."[1] John Wesley, an Anglican minister and founder of Methodism, edited the Anglican Articles for American Methodists in 1784, calling them: "Articles of Religion."[2] Methodists in America made some changes, then included them in the governing documents of the new Methodist Episcopal Church as, again, "Articles of Religion."[3]

---

1. Schaff, *Creeds*, 3:487.
2. Schaff, *Creeds*, 3:807.
3. Schaff, *Creeds*, 3:807.

Some might argue that the Scriptures themselves never speak of "religion"; however, that is not strictly correct. In Acts 26:5, Paul testifies that when he lived as a Jew, he "lived *as* a Pharisee, according to the strictest sect of our religion." The word translated "religion" here is the Greek word *thrēskeia*, which refers to worship and morality that is associated with the worship of a deity; in this case, the one, true God. It was certainly sufficient to communicate to the readers of Acts that Paul was distinguishing Judaism from other religious groups of his time. The same Greek word is used in James 1:26–27 to distinguish correct Christian practice from that which is false.

People often mean different things by the word "religion." For those who study the philosophy of religion formally, belief in a deity or deities is an essential part of religion. With this in mind, the definition of religion that best fits the way "religion" has been thought of through the years is: Religion is a belief or a collection of beliefs regarding deity or deities that results in a particular way of life.

Christianity has a basic theology—and thus a basic set of beliefs (i.e., doctrines, teachings) concerning God—that results in a particular way of life. Christians treat the Scriptures of the Old and New Testaments as sacred, worship Jesus Christ, set aside one day a week for corporate worship—usually Sunday to celebrate the resurrection of Christ on the first day of the week, practice baptism and celebrate the Lord's Supper, and have a specific morality. Therefore, Christianity qualifies as a religion according to the definition given here. Rather than say "Christianity is not a religion," it is more accurate to say that Christianity is "true religion versus false religion." It is also accurate to say that Christianity is a different *kind* of religion because of its central emphasis on a personal relationship with God through Jesus Christ versus outward ceremonies, and because of its roots in actual historical events. A proper understanding of the concept of religion helps us to understand both the uniqueness of Christianity and its practical demands on our lives.

Finally, our attitude toward philosophy requires careful consideration. In Paul's letters to the church at Corinth and the church at Colossae, he warns against being misled by philosophers, and with good reason (1 Cor 1:18–25; Col 2:8). The pagan philosophers Paul warned against had no respect for and were ignorant of the Hebrew Scriptures. The philosopher known as Philo Judaeus (or simply, Philo), was a contemporary of Jesus. He was part of an active community of Jewish scholars in Alexandria, Egypt. Philo tried to mix Old Testament theology with Greek philosophy. The goal was to make Judaism more acceptable to the Gentiles; but the result was to lower the Old Testament to the level of human thought and cleverness.

None of this helped lead people to Jesus Christ nor to God's saving grace. Diluting Christian theology with secular philosophy is no less damaging today.

Nevertheless, philosophy has more impact upon people's thought and lives than many contemporary Christians would like to recognize. Philosophy is the search for wisdom, the search for right thinking. It is hard to see why any Christian would oppose right thinking. The truths revealed by God through his prophets have priority over human thought, of course. But the Scriptures do not cover everything. Where Scripture does not speak, Christians need to use the resources available to them to develop sound thinking. Even when it comes to reading the Scriptures, a defective philosophy undercuts a correct understanding of what God is saying. In his "Address to the Clergy," given in 1756, John Wesley recommended a knowledge of philosophy as helpful to the correct interpretation of Scripture.[4]

The Apostle Paul was well-schooled in pagan philosophy. He learned it first to help him promote an accurate understanding of Judaism; later, he put this knowledge to good use in promoting Christianity. One evidence of this is found in 1 Corinthians 13:12, where Paul uses a metaphor based on the thought of Plato. Another is Acts 17:22–34, where Paul's speech to the snooty philosophers at Athens won converts. Apollos, who was from Alexandria, Egypt, a center of Jewish as well as Greek scholarship, may well have become a powerfully persuasive preacher because of what he learned in this center of intellectual activity. If so, this would also explain why he needed additional education regarding Christianity from Priscilla and Aquila (Acts 18:24–28).

Most of the more prominent and influential Christian leaders throughout history had a good knowledge of philosophy in addition to a thorough knowledge of Scripture. Among these were Irenaeus, Augustine, Athanasius, Gregory Nazianzen, Thomas Aquinas, Martin Luther, John Calvin, John Wesley, and C. S. Lewis. The Christian community needs Christian philosophers to guide them in right thinking. Without them, Christians are liable to engage unknowingly in thinking that is governed by non-Christian philosophies—which is all too common in our time. In addition, some who are outside the faith need to have their philosophies challenged before they are open to receiving the gospel. When this is true, studying philosophy serves the same purpose as studying a foreign culture to know how best to do missionary work.

The bottom line is that while all Christians are not expected to be scholars, Christianity is a faith that requires all of us to give careful thought

---

4. Wesley, *Works*, 10:483–84.

to our beliefs and practices, and to exercise care in choosing which Christian leaders we follow. This requires fidelity, as best we are able, to the Christian faith set down by the life and teachings of Jesus Christ.

2

Looking to the Creator

By the word of the Lord the heavens were made,
And by the breath of His mouth all their host.

PSALM 33:6

For us there is *but* one God, the Father, from whom are all things.

1 CORINTHIANS 8:6

As a man approached death, a small group of his closest friends gathered around him for one final talk. They were determined to discuss the things that matter most in life before he died. Their discussion turned to the human soul, the possibility of life after death, and the judgment of the wicked. One friend offered this advice about how to approach spiritual subjects:

1. Do everything you can to figure out the truth for yourself.
2. If you can't figure out the truth, find someone whose wisdom seems greater than everyone else's, and cling to his judgments.
3. Value divine revelation above human wisdom; however, divine revelation is hard to come by.

These words seem to summarize the thinking of many people today, whose first choice is to try to figure things out for themselves, second choice is to believe the opinion of someone they like (perhaps a friend or a celebrity), and if all else fails—almost as an afterthought—to seek the counsel of God. However, these words summarize the argument of Simmias, a character in a book written by the ancient philosopher Plato almost four hundred years before the birth of Jesus Christ.[1]

---

1. Plato, *Phaedo*, 85C–85D.

Simmias was one of a small body of men gathered for a final discussion with the philosopher Socrates on the day Socrates was sentenced to die. You may recall that Socrates was sentenced by a Greek court to die by drinking hemlock juice—a deadly poison. The subjects Socrates and his friends chose to discuss are timeless ones that affect all people in all times. However, the solution Simmias proposed is backward. If we can have the counsel of God, why start with our own thoughts or the thoughts of another mortal?

The ideas in Plato's writings were limited by the thought of his place and time. The gods the ancient Greeks worshipped never inspired full confidence. They believed their gods were concerned primarily with their own lives, not with human affairs. Although deities, these gods were believed to be part of the universe rather than its creators, so there were definite limitations to their knowledge. They were certainly not all-knowing. They were also far from trustworthy. Even if the ancient Greeks believed their gods knew more than human beings, no one could be certain that their gods would care enough about human beings to share their insights with them or to tell the truth when they spoke. On the other hand, Plato also believed that people exist as spirits before they are born as human beings, and therefore are born with some knowledge of the realities of the universe. Under these circumstances, it seemed to make more sense to Plato for people to look inward and think things through for themselves rather than to look to a deity for answers.

Few people today hold Plato's view that we are born with a deep, inner knowledge of reality. Nevertheless, there is now a strong tendency for people to trust their own judgments regarding spiritual things or to accept whatever views are most popular. Unbeknownst to many, it is the influence of contemporary philosophies, rather than ancient ones, that convince people today to look to themselves or to follow the crowd rather than to "look upward" for answers. Clearly, however, if the universe has a Creator, it makes better sense to seek the knowledge he can give us. We should follow the best thinking we can find or fall back on our own judgments *only* on matters about which our Creator has not spoken.

Two Views of the Origin

Of course, not everyone believes that a divine Creator actually exists. Broadly speaking, there have been two general views of the origin of the universe throughout history.

Natural Stuff as Creator

In one view, nature inherently orders itself. The "stuff" of which the universe is made is believed to exist eternally and to develop naturally into complex forms, including life forms. Such a view grows out of the cycles of nature (day and night, the seasons, birth-growth-reproduction-death, etc.) and for some, the universe is believed to be cyclic as well.

The concept of a cyclic universe is essentially a pagan concept. Not only is everything within the universe believed to decay and die at some time, the universe itself is believed to end as well, returning to the original form of the "stuff" the universe is made of; then, somehow, the universe is believed to develop into a complex, life-sustaining universe all over again.[2] There are many variations of this view. All, however, are eternal, with this process continuing forever. Variations notwithstanding, this is the basic view of the religions of the world that are referred to as "pagan." In the past, some scientists also held this view, which they referred to as an "oscillating universe."[3] Recent findings do not support the oscillating universe theory, causing scientists to reject this theory—at least for now.

In modern times, many scholars and scientists followed Aristotle in maintaining that the universe as a whole never really changes. Within the universe, objects arise, exist, and die. Life evolves, and dies. The universe doesn't cycle, but everything in the universe does. However, the universe itself remains essentially the same. One such view is called the "Steady-State Universe."

By the latter half of the twentieth century, most scientists adopted the "big bang" theory that the universe came into being suddenly and explosively. Whatever their position, secular scientists take a viewpoint that is essentially that of the ancient pagan religions in the sense that everything is the result of natural processes. The stuff of the universe is not referred to as deity or deities, but is still believed to generate all that is. The belief that matter and energy are all that exist is called "secular materialism" or "physicalism." While the orderly, collaborative investigation of the physical universe is called "science," the belief that all there is to the universe is what can be discovered by science is called "scientism." The belief that life is generated without a Creator by the material of the universe is called "hylozoism." These terms reflect a determination to limit reality to the natural universe.

---

2. Eliade, *Myth of the Eternal Return*, 86–90.
3. Jastrow, *God and the Astronomers*, 109–10.

A Supernatural Creator

The other view of the origin of the universe is that a divine Creator originated, orders, and controls the universe. In this view, the Creator stands separate from and above the universe, which exists because it is the will of the Creator for it to do so. Accordingly, all things in the universe had a point of origin and continue toward some definite goal established by its Creator. This is the Hebrew or Judeo-Christian view.[4] The Creator is, therefore, necessarily intelligent and all-knowing, otherwise the Creator would not have the ability to create what exists. The Creator is truly "supernatural" because the Creator, though accessible in the universe, is not part of the universe, and would continue to exist even if the universe ceased to exist. Cycles take place within nature, but do not govern the movement of the universe toward the goals the Creator established for it. The "stuff" of the universe is not alive, but under the control of the Creator. The Creator grants the physical universe the ability to cause various effects in uniform ways. We think of these as natural laws. Human beings are part of this creation. Human beings have been given a spiritual nature as well, that, like God, transcends physical creation; nevertheless, as created beings, this spiritual nature exists only because God wills it to be so.

The gods and goddesses of most religions, in biblical times and even today, are associated with the universe in some manner. They are, therefore, not truly *super*natural because they are not separate from nature. Some, like the ancient Egyptian god Nun, represent the primal material of the universe from which everything else is thought to have come. For Hindus, the Brahman is the ultimate reality from which all else is created and of which everything is a part. The gods and goddesses that do not fall into this category are generated in some manner from the universe and remain part of it. They generally represent a portion of life or nature. These "lesser" gods have characteristics and needs that are similar to animals or people, are often dependent upon the service of human beings, and are subject to the cycles of nature.

The merging of deities with the natural world makes it easier to imagine that human beings may be or may become "gods." The belief that the Egyptian Pharaoh was considered a type of god is common knowledge. Some Buddhists today believe that under the right circumstances they might be reborn in beautiful worlds in which they have godlike abilities for a long time, though not forever. Because pagan gods are not separate from the universe, they are not greater than the universe. Therefore, they are not immortal, and their knowledge and power are strictly limited.

4. Eliade, *Myth of the Eternal Return*, 104–7, 137, 143, 160–62.

Perhaps the biggest problem with the pagan viewpoint is trying to explain why anything exists at all. Clever theories have been offered by highly intelligent people to explain how the universe we see, including human life and culture, developed the way that it has without intervention from a supreme deity. However, since there is no definite way to investigate what existed before the origin of the universe, these theories do not explain why the universe should develop with any order or consistency.

Some have tried to resolve this problem by theorizing that there are an enormous number of universes. They argue that due to random processes, these universes would develop in every way imaginable, and perhaps in ways beyond what we can imagine. Statistically, they argue, at least a small number of these universes would develop like ours. However, this theory depends on concepts of randomness and probability drawn from the nature of our universe. The idea that these concepts may be applied to a hypothetical infinite number of other universes is an assumption that cannot be confirmed. It does not answer the question why anything like our universe should ever exist. Given the need for the substance of a universe like ours to be created, organized, and regulated, it seems most likely that without a Creator nothing would develop in any of a large number of these universe "compartments."

The ancient Greek word for the universe is *cosmos* (Gk. *kosmos*). It is related to the word "cosmetics" because it has to do not just with what exists, but with the ordering of what exists. Consistency is essential to our universe. There is no orderliness unless certain events follow other events in a predictable manner. If atoms and molecules change unpredictably, for example, no regular chemical processes can take place. Suppose, for example, an atom of carbon could change back and forth into an atom of silver, sulfur, or oxygen at any moment, just by itself without a consistent cause. Absurd? Of course. But why should atoms and molecules follow any rules at all—or even exist? Or consider what would happen if gravity were to suddenly vary widely at unpredictable times. Or if some of the energy from the sun just disappeared from the universe without a trace before reaching the earth. That which holds our solar system together and makes life on earth possible would make the existence of any life problematic at best, and more likely, impossible. Of course, any such irregularity would likely not exist because there needs to be some underlying order for atoms, gravity, and energy themselves to exist.

Some refer to the oddities of the subatomic world to argue that the underlying reality of the universe isn't uniform. This, however, is to focus on the wrong level. However bizarre the subatomic world may be, it resolves itself at a higher level into the regularity we see and experience.

The high level of orderliness we see in our universe is absolutely necessary for the universe to be what it is and for scientists to be able to study the universe in a meaningful way. If there is no consistency in the universe, and thus no orderliness, scientists cannot draw any conclusions from their observations and experiments since everything may change at any time. The philosopher David Hume (1711–1776) argued that we cannot know for certain that the universe *is* uniform.[5] He thought, however, that we had to *act* as if there is consistency and predictability in events in order to live our lives.[6]

The scientist/philosopher Charles Sanders Peirce (1839–1914), on the other hand, argued that scientific investigation is based upon the assumption that there is regularity in the universe.[7] Astronomer Robert Jastrow (1925–2008), first head of NASA's Jet Propulsion Laboratory, wrote, "There is a kind of religion in science; it is the religion of a person who believes there is order and harmony in the Universe."[8]

The goal of science is to learn what is true about the universe, and the application of that knowledge is called "technology." Technology is only possible because we can be certain that if we do some things, other things will happen consistently and predictably. The success of contemporary science and technology demonstrates the orderliness and consistency of nature. In suggesting that we must *act* as if there is orderliness in order to live our lives, Hume acknowledged that the universe *does* have orderliness, because if there is none, pretending doesn't make it so; soon enough, the inconsistencies of nature would undermine any planning we might do.

A Complete Explanation for What Is

The issue regarding creation, then, is that even if someone is clever enough to explain how the basic stuff of the universe developed into the universe we have now, it is also necessary to explain how this stuff had the ability to develop into the complex, diverse, and well-ordered cosmos we live in—one that supports sophisticated life forms.

This issue is larger than it may first appear. The philosopher Immanuel Kant acknowledged this when he wrote that there are two great wonders: "the starry heavens above and the moral law within."[9] Kant knew that both require an explanation. It isn't enough just to explain that the cosmos is

---

5. Copleston, *History of Philosophy*, 5:282, 288.
6. Copleston, *History of Philosophy*, 5:282, 291–92.
7. Turrisi, *Pragmatism as a Principle*, 59–62.
8. Jastrow, *God and the Astronomers*, 103.
9. Kant, *Critique of Practical Reason*, 170.

complex and wonderful, there is also the mystery of why human beings are the way they are, why human beings have a spiritual dimension that goes beyond the material stuff of the universe: matter and energy.

The world we live in is more than a world of biochemical machines. Even if that were true, the complexity of life at the cellular level and above is sophisticated beyond anything human beings can currently design and build from scratch. Many an engineer has become stressed out trying to get comparatively simple products to function. However, let's assume for a moment, just for the sake of argument, that it is possible for a complex life form to evolve from an unorganized batch of chemicals without any outside guidance or assistance. This would still not explain human culture.

Human beings are both intelligent and aware of their own existence. This self-awareness is more than simple responses to stimuli. Further, human beings do more than just seek to sustain their existence. Human beings develop cultures with morality, religion, and various artistic endeavors—things that hardly seem to be the by-products of mechanical beings. If the universe developed all by itself, with no divine Creator, the potential for all of this had to be in whatever stuff the universe sprang from.

If the development of human culture from the material universe without divine intervention seems likely to you, I suggest that you try a thought experiment. Put together a large jar of whatever chemicals you can think of, close it tight, and set it on your desk (or near your desk if it doesn't fit). At least once every day, look at it and think: "Everything the world is, everything that I am and will ever be, came out of that." The more you consider this, the more likely you'll realize that it isn't likely at all.

Scientists are correct to seek natural explanations for things in nature whenever what happens is purely natural. On the other hand, sometimes the existence of a Creator is the very best explanation we have for why things are the way they are. This is certainly true of the universe as a whole, of the orderliness of the universe, and of the existence of life—especially human life. To do otherwise is to ignore reality. This is not just "throwing God in" because we don't have a better explanation. Good science and good engineering require a great deal of intelligent effort. It is absurd to think that the complexity of life, and especially human life, is just a happenstance. Those who claim that the stuff of the universe was able to create everything we see in the universe—including human life and culture—have some holes in their arguments that cry out for miracles; but they have no deity to provide them.

In fact, the effort to avoid seeing the universe as the product of a Creator can be detrimental to scientific investigation. In his book *God and the Astronomers*, Robert Jastrow, an agnostic, relates how most scientists vehemently opposed the big bang theory simply because they believed it would point to a Creator, but finally accepted the theory because the evidence in favor of it was so strong.[10] The lesson that follows Jastrow's account is that scientists should not be affected one way or the other by whether a theory seems to support or deny belief in a Creator; they should follow the facts. I think we can go beyond this, however, to say that if the existence of an intelligent, divine Creator is the best explanation for the way things are, it should not be off limits to credit a deity with the creation of the universe. This is especially true when paganism and secular science have no better explanation for the way things are than to say, "It just happened."

The Good News about Creation

Many scientists, scholars, and journalists in the modern world embrace the belief that the Bible, Christian theology, and traditional Christianity are the enemies of science. Nothing could be farther from the truth. Believing Christians have no argument with scientific investigation. The physical universe has the ability to cause events. Therefore, scientific investigation through observation and experimentation is entirely compatible with the theology of both the Old and New Testaments. However, there is a strong objection to the position that the findings of science alone tell us everything we would like to know about life and the cosmos we live in.

The universe that science alone describes is largely cold and dark. Science fiction often makes space travel seem attractive. Science reality, on the other hand, shows us a universe apart from earth that is often strikingly beautiful, but just as often is completely hostile to human life—a universe filled with forbidding places that exhibit extreme temperatures, dangerous chemicals, noxious fumes, harmful radiation, and, at best, a complete absence of that which sustains life—and even in the absence of such dangers, an untold number of planets and planetoids with boring landscapes devoid of life and beauty. While a universe vacant of a true deity might seem attractive in allowing us to chart whatever destiny we might choose in life without divine interference, inwardly, most reject this notion. Most recognize that if the physical universe is all there is, there is nothing to provide meaning to what we do, nothing to provide purpose or hope in life. We are entitled to look for more than science alone provides us.

No human being with normal faculties thinks of himself or herself as simply a bag of sophisticated chemical reactions. We are certain that we are more than that. This is not just the instinct to survive seen in insects

---

10. Jastrow, *God and the Astronomers*, 17, 102–4.

and other lowly life forms. When human beings are treated poorly, they know they are being treated unjustly. The need to be treated justly is felt and expressed by the youngest children. Unless traumatized or indoctrinated otherwise, human beings clearly believe they are special and deserve to be treated as such. They differ greatly as to where this concept of justice comes from—a deity, spiritual beings, the physical universe, human nature, or some deep universal mystery. In any case, people value themselves and other people in ways that have no significance for survival or evolutionary advancement. They also sense that their personal existence is meant for an ongoing existence without end.

Throughout human culture, human accomplishments that are strictly artistic, moral, or religious are preserved and passed down to future generations purely for their aesthetic or spiritual value. This is different from the transmission of patterns of behavior; it is not in the same category with animal instinct. Of all the events we know of in the universe, the handing down of aesthetic and spiritual values is characteristic only of human beings. This verifies that human beings are, in fact, unquestionably unique. Human beings and culture thus present the primary evidence that the physical universe is not all there is. We carry this evidence with us.

The teachings of Scripture are consistent with our intuition that the universe had a Designer, that human life has special significance, and that there are spiritual forces at work here on earth. Intuition, of course, is not proof. However, we are under no obligation to accept the bias against seeing the evidence of a divine Creator just because there are scientists and scholars who demand that we do so. There are scientists and scholars who are open to recognizing evidence of a divine Creator in the natural universe that those biased against it may miss. Moreover, we do not have to be limited to scientific study. After all, life is more than scientific facts. We can learn from human experience—ours and the experiences of others. We can learn from history. This opens us up to information that tells a fuller story than science alone can provide.

The good news is that the universe has a divine Creator who promises more than the physical universe can offer—a Creator who answers deep and very human needs for importance, purpose, and eternal life. Our Creator is the basic reality of our universe. Everything taught in Scripture rests on this foundational truth.

This truth is underscored in the Revelation to John chapters 4 and 5, which recount the praise given to God in the great throne room of heaven. Reginald Heber (1783–1826) had these chapters as well as Isaiah 6:1–5 in mind when he composed the beloved hymn "Holy, Holy, Holy." In John's vision, various beings represent the advanced creatures of earth, including human beings. Praise begins by celebrating God himself: his holiness, supreme power, and eternal existence. God is then praised as the Creator of all things that exist. Finally, God is praised as Savior, the ultimate achievement of God the Creator that confirms both his power and his love for humankind.

We can draw the following conclusions from the fact of a divine Creator:

- As the reality behind our universe, our Creator does not change in his essential nature and character; therefore, reality, truth, and purpose are settled, not open to change.
- Everything apart from the Creator exists because of the will, creative intelligence, and creative power of the Creator.
- Order in creation is established by and maintained by the Creator.
- There is no force greater than the Creator, the Almighty (Gk. *ho Pantokratōr*); there is no dualism—evil cannot ultimately win over the righteousness of the Creator.
- Human life is not an accident; there is a purpose for people beyond what is seen in physical creation.
- Our Creator is moving all things toward the goals he has planned for creation and human beings.
- It is reasonable to believe that our Creator will communicate with us, and to expect him to provide a perspective beyond what the physical universe provides.

The Scriptures are part of this fuller story that assures us that our existence has great significance. Written across many centuries by many authors in different cultures, the Scriptures echo the affirmation of Genesis that we were created with a special purpose.

In Psalm 8, David recognizes the insignificance of human beings in relation to the majesty of God and the universe we live in. He goes on, however, to recognize that our importance comes from the God who created us, and for this David offers further praise to God. This same assurance comes to all who look at creation and envision the Creator who stands behind it.

3

Maintaining the Biblical Perspective

> By the word of the Lord the heavens were made,
> And by the breath of His mouth all their host....
> For He spoke, and it was done;
> He commanded, and it stood fast.
>
> PSALM 33:6, 9

> Where were you when I laid the foundation of the earth?...
> When the morning stars sang together
> And all the sons of God shouted for joy?
>
> JOB 38:4, 7

The Teaching of Genesis

THE book of Genesis has become a battleground in the last century-and-a-half, especially the first chapter. Those who oppose Christianity would like everyone to believe that it should be tossed aside as mere myth. It is important to realize, however, that issues reconciling the first two chapters of Genesis with what is known about the universe did not just arise in modern times. St. Augustine, who lived from AD 354 to 430, tried three times to find the correct interpretation of Genesis. So, this is by no means an issue of just the modern world. Nevertheless, the first two chapters of Genesis are not myth. The truths taught there are foundational to Judaism and Christianity, and these truths are not at all unreasonable for thinking people. Here, as well as with other Scripture, however, it is essential to ferret out the truths and to separate them from false understandings of what God intends to communicate to us.

Finding the Correct Perspective

If St. Augustine's interpretations of Genesis weren't always well-founded, his approach to the interpretation of Genesis is refreshingly contemporary. He was deeply concerned that Christians approach Genesis with both reverence and care. He warned that when a Christian speaks about things that pagans know a great deal about and the Christian is wrong, it causes pagans to question the entire Christian faith, not just the particular point that Christian is wrong about.[1] Not that Augustine thought Christians should be reluctant to speak to pagans about the clear teachings of Scripture.[2] However, he believed it is essential for Christians to determine what Scripture really teaches. He did not believe Christians should try to make Scripture support preconceived ideas nor speculate carelessly where Scripture does not clearly support a particular interpretation.[3]

Augustine observed that Christians who are careless often use Scripture inappropriately to back up their positions. He said those who do so are accurately described by Paul's words in 1 Timothy 1:7: "not understanding either what they are saying, or the matters on which they are asserting themselves."[4] Such carelessness is more likely to push people away from the gospel than to lead them to faith. In Augustine's view, if we care about convincing unbelievers of the truth of the gospel and strengthening the faith of our brethren, we will be careful about what we say when we speak in areas that touch both Scripture and the natural world.

With Augustine's concerns in mind, there are a couple of approaches to the first two chapters of Genesis that Christians need to be careful of today. The first is to say that the Bible exists to teach spiritual truths, not to give us a detailed description of the creation of all things. This is true as far as it goes. It is fairly obvious that the brief accounts in Genesis 1 and 2 are not comprehensive descriptions of the origins of the natural universe in terms of contemporary science. Nevertheless, we must be careful to maintain that when God intended to teach us about the universe, what Scripture teaches is always factually correct when correctly understood.

Even if we confess that there are some issues reconciling Genesis with current scientific knowledge that we cannot resolve, there are three foundational teachings in Genesis that are certain and clear—teachings that only those most prejudiced against Christianity would claim conflict with natural science. First, God existed before the universe. Second, everything that

---

1. Augustine, *Literal Meaning of Genesis*, 1.19.39 in *On Genesis*.
2. Augustine, *Literal Meaning of Genesis*, 1.21.41 in *On Genesis*.
3. Augustine, *Literal Meaning of Genesis*, 1.18.37 in *On Genesis*.
4. Augustine, *Literal Meaning of Genesis*, 1.19.39 in *On Genesis*.

exists other than God was created by God. Third, the universe is entirely separate from God, but not from his influences.

The other approach we need to be careful of is to treat Genesis as if it were written in our own time. Genesis was written some three thousand years ago. One of the most basic rules guiding the interpretation of any Scripture is to understand what it meant (what should have been understood) by the people to whom the Scripture was originally given *before* determining what it means to those of us who live long after. To interpret the Scriptures as if they were written in our time risks attributing ideas to Scripture that were never actually there.

The First Role of Genesis

We tend to think of Genesis as the first book of the entire Bible. However, when it was authored, most if not all of the books of the Bible did not yet exist. The Israelites had just escaped slavery in Egypt and become a nation in their own right (Exod 19). Genesis provided the background to the exodus, telling the Hebrew people who they were and how they came to be slaves in Egypt. Of course, who they were and the fact that they became a nation was the result of God's work in their past. So, to understand themselves, their lives, and their futures, they needed to understand God and his relationship with their forbears.

Most of the Hebrews who followed Moses probably could not read or write. Their knowledge of Genesis came when it was read to them. Whether heard or read, these people knew nothing of the universe as we know it now. They did not know that the earth is one of a number of planets that orbit the sun in what we call a "solar system," that this solar system is part of a galaxy, and that there are many galaxies in the universe. Their point of view was standing on the earth looking up at the sky and stars.

Further, having spent hundreds of years in Egypt, their view of the universe was strongly affected by Egyptian understandings of the universe. As has been discussed, for people in the ancient world, and in some religions even today, everything that exists, including their gods, develops naturally from some kind of original, primal stuff. The Egyptians believed that everything that exists came out of the primal waters of Nun. They believed this developed into the world they knew, with the land floating on top of the primal waters of Nun and the sky a kind of canopy above the land.

It would have been possible for God to show the Hebrew people illustrations or a model of the solar system and the universe to correct their misunderstandings; however, to what purpose? It wasn't important that they learn astronomy at that time. Learning the structure of the universe was not of paramount importance, learning about God and his relationship to the universe *was*. The immediate, practical need was replacing the Egyptian worldview with a worldview centered upon the one, true God, orienting the Hebrews in their faith and lives. This was more than enough for them to comprehend.

"In the beginning, God created the heavens and the earth" (Gen 1:1). These words are so familiar to us that it seems strange to think of this as a radical statement; but it was. It was a blockbuster statement in the ancient world because it started with the existence of supernatural God and made all things dependent on his creative will. By declaring a supernatural Creator, Genesis 1:1 contradicted all the religions of the ancient Near East at that time in one sentence. Further, everything that follows in Genesis and beyond is dependent upon what is said here. All Christian theology, including salvation through Jesus Christ, stems from this one concept.

Creator of All

The concept that all things were non-existent until God willed them into existence is called "creation from nothing," which is often referred to by the Latin: *creatio ex nihilo*. It is true that the clearest teaching of *creatio ex nihilo* is made and reinforced elsewhere in the Old and New Testaments. However, Genesis 1:1 strongly supports this. The Hebrew word used for "create" in Genesis 1:1 and elsewhere in the Old Testament is *bārā'*. Thomas McComiskey observes that this word is only used in the Bible concerning acts of God, indicating that the ability to do these creative acts is uniquely his. McComiskey further notes, "Since the word never occurs with the object of the material, and since the primary emphasis of the word is on the newness of the created object, the word lends itself well to the concept of creation *ex nihilo*, although that concept is not necessarily inherent within the meaning of the word."[5]

Even if the ancient readers or hearers didn't understand *creatio ex nihilo* from Genesis 1:1, the force of the statement is the same: all things apart from God were created by God, *he* was not created *by or as part of them*. There is really no way to turn this around.

While the people of the ancient Near East and elsewhere at the time Genesis was written believed that everything came from some primal stuff that they often conceived of as a god, some Greek philosophers in the six centuries before Christ came up with other ideas. In Plato's *Timaeus*, he described the material of the universe as eternal and chaotic. He suggested

---

5. McComiskey, "*bārā'*," in *TWOT*, 1:127.

that there was a divine being that he called the *Demiurge* (Gk. *dēmiourgos*; literally "people's craftsman" or "worker for the people"). The *Demiurge* knew of eternally perfect ideas, or forms, that defined various objects (e.g., rocks, rivers, mountains, plants, trees, birds, mammals, fish, human beings, and so forth). Using these perfect ideas, the *Demiurge* ordered the material of the universe to make the objects that make up the cosmos. It is impossible to make perfect objects with the material of which the universe is made. The *Demiurge* did the best he could, but given the material he had to work with, each object he crafted is imperfect and changeable.[6]

The exact identity of the *Demiurge* as Plato conceived it, and whether Plato meant this as a suggestion or a statement of fact, are matters of scholarly debate.[7] Nevertheless, some in our time would prefer to think that the God of the Bible is very much like Plato's *Demiurge*. They can't accept that even God could create something from nothing. Finding the idea of creation from nothing unpalatable, they return to the view that the material of the universe, like God, is eternal. This position is called "dualism." The God of the Bible, they believe, did not create the universe; rather, God manipulated the chaotic, raw material of the universe to craft it into the universe we have now.

Still another view preferred by some scholars today goes by the name "panentheism"—a name designed, it seems, to make just about everyone's eyes glaze over even though it makes sense in Greek. In this view, God is greater than the universe, but the universe is part of God. Here again, God creates out of something, but in this case, that something is God, himself. This isn't the usual pagan pantheism, which is the view that everything is god. Panentheism recognizes the eternal existence of God and that the universe is somehow different. It also provides a rationale for God's omnipresence and sovereignty. It is still, nonetheless, a compromise with pagan pantheism that, like dualism, has no biblical support whatsoever.

The authors of the New Testament are in agreement with the Old Testament that God our Creator is responsible for the origin of all other things that exist. In 1 Corinthians 8:5–6, Paul contrasts the faith of pagans and the faith of Christians by observing that the pagans worship many gods, but Christians worship "*but* one God, the Father, from whom are all things." "All things" here is the Greek *ta panta*, which is used elsewhere in the same manner. In Ephesians 3:9, Paul refers to "God who created all things." When Paul preached to pagans in Lystra and Athens, he emphasized from the start that the God he proclaimed created everything (Acts 14:15; 17:24–26). In

---

6. Plato, *Timaeus*, 28A–28B.
7. Bury, "Introduction to the *Timaeus*," in Plato, *Timaeus*, 7–8.

Romans, Paul praises both "the wisdom and knowledge of God. . . . For from Him and through Him and to Him are all things" (Rom 11:33, 36). John picks up the same thought in Revelation 4:11, saying that God is worshipped in heaven as worthy of all praise because: "You created all things, and because of Your will they existed, and were created."

The same language is used of Christ as the one through whom all things were made in 1 Corinthians 8:6 as Paul furthers his contrast with pagan belief: "and one Lord, Jesus Christ, by whom are all things, and we *exist* through Him." In Colossians 1:16, Paul says of Jesus: "For by Him all things were created, *both* in the heavens and on earth, visible and invisible . . . all things have been created through Him and for Him." In John 1:3, John wrote: "All things came into being through Him, and apart from Him nothing came into being that has come into being." The author of Hebrews refers to God's Son as the one "through whom also He made the world," the one "for whom are all things, and through whom are all things" (Heb 1:2; 2:10).

The Sole "I AM"

New Testament references to God as Creator of "all" are too frequent and too clear to be considered anything other than essential information. Their foundation is in the Old Testament, where the Creator of Genesis manifests himself as the God of the Israelites.

Raised by Egyptian royalty, Moses refused to abandon the Hebrew people or their God (Heb 11:24-27). His overzealous efforts to help them caused him to commit murder, then to flee into the wilderness, where he found a home and a life as a shepherd. Up to that point, Moses had no personal encounters with God; he was simply proceeding with faith in the God of his Hebrew forbears. Moses' encounter with God at a bush with a flame that did not consume the bush was the beginning of his direct communication with the God of Abraham, Isaac, and Jacob (Exod 3). Like Genesis, this was an important part of the background to the exodus.

At the burning bush, God revealed that he would work through Moses to deliver the Israelites from Egypt. But the exodus was much more than an escape from slavery. As important and dramatic as this deliverance was, it was the beginning of a more intimate relationship of God with the Israelites—a relationship central to the story of the five books of Moses (Exod 19:1-6). It would result in the dwelling of God among the people in a carefully prepared tabernacle (Exod 24-31, 35-40; esp. 40:34-38).

"God said to Moses, 'I AM WHO I AM' (Hebr. *'ehyeh 'ăšer 'ehyeh*); and He said, 'Thus you shall say to the sons of Israel, "I AM (Hebr. *'ehyeh*) has sent me to you"'" (Exod 3:14). The Hebrew word *'ehyeh* is an ancient

Hebrew form of the verb "to be"; the name *Yahweh*, used in the very next verse, is derived from it. The Lord told Moses that under his eternal name, *Yahweh*, he was the God of Abraham, Isaac, and Jacob. This is also the name he would be known by in the future.

Yahweh's first reference to himself is translated somewhat differently by different translators: "I AM WHO I AM" (NASB, NIV), "I AM THAT I AM" (KJV), or "I WILL BE WHAT I WILL BE" (alternate reading, NIV and NRSV). There is more uniformity on the shorter name by which Moses was to identify the God to the Israelites, "I AM," for which the third person form used in speaking *of* God, "He is," became *Yahweh*.[8] It is certainly true, as many commentators note, that this name emphasizes the continual presence of God with the Israelites going forward. *Yahweh's* presence is seen first in the miracles that brought deliverance from Egypt, then in protection from Pharaoh's army and in provision for food and water in the wilderness, next in divine manifestations at Mt. Sinai, and finally in the tabernacle—and later in the temple—as the God of the Israelites. However, it seems there is another factor at work that makes the promise of God's presence all the more meaningful.

Because his name refers to existence, *Yahweh* emphasizes the presence of the one whose being and character are never in question because *he has always been* and *he will always be*. This side of the name *Yahweh* should not be lost. It is the affirmation of a Creator who is existent in himself and therefore is in no way dependent upon creation or any part of it; *this* is the God who sends and promises to stand with Moses—a God who cannot fail because there is nothing and no one greater. The miracles and miraculous manifestations of God's presence seen throughout the exodus, the travels in the wilderness, and the conquest of Palestine are confirmation that this one is, indeed, the Creator he claims to be. It is on this basis that Moses assured the people, "The Lord your God is the one who goes with you. He will not fail you or forsake you" (Deut 31:6; Heb 13:5). Much later, when Jesus used "I am" (Gk. *egō eimi*) to refer to himself, the Jews immediately sought to stone him for blasphemy. They knew that this indicated his complete identification with the God who manifested himself to Moses (John 8:58–59).

Though certainly not the only name used to identify God as Creator in the Old Testament, beginning with Genesis 2:4, the name *Yahweh* is often used when referring to the Creator. In Psalm 33, it is *Yahweh* who spoke creation into existence. In Psalm 104 and in Hannah's prayer in 1 Samuel 2:8, it is *Yahweh* who firmly established the earth. When God corrects Job by pointing to his mastery over creation, it is *Yahweh* who speaks (Job 38:1).

---

8. Payne, "*yāh*," in *TWOT*, 1:211.

And in Isaiah, it is *Yahweh* who challenges his readers to understand that he is uniquely exalted as Creator (Isa 40:28). This is a cause for *Yahweh's* enemies to fear and for his people to rejoice and find comfort.

Learning from Ancient Books

Since God is greater than the universe, God is not subject to limitations of knowledge. It is also reasonable to believe that an intelligent Creator will communicate in some manner with the intelligent beings he has created. The question then becomes: How does God communicate?

For many today, there seems to be no easy answer. The writings of Søren Kierkegaard (1813–1855) became popular in the twentieth century. In agreement with the gnostics of the early Christian centuries, Kierkegaard suggested that God makes himself hard to find because he only wants those who are truly determined to know him to find him. The truth is much better than Kierkegaard knew: God wants to be found and to have fellowship with everyone who desires to know him. Any impediments to that relationship are on our side, not God's.

In his High Priestly Prayer of John 17, Jesus prayed to God the Father on behalf of his followers: "Sanctify them in the truth; Your word is truth" (John 17:17). The repository for this truth is the Bible. The Bible is, of course, not just one book, but thirty-nine ancient writings comprising the Old Testament coupled with twenty-seven first-century writings comprising the New Testament: sixty-six documents in all. When skeptics suggest that Christianity has only one source, it is important to recognize that these were originally separate documents. Some strongly question whether such ancient texts can be genuinely helpful to people who live in a world in which science and technology reign. The answer to this question rests on whether there are things about God and things about human beings that do not change.

It is common in our time to focus on change, and for certain, change is a constant part of life. All living things—human beings no exception—come into being, grow, age, and die. Circumstances change the world we live and work in. Yet, there are also things that do not change.

When Jesus spoke of the end of the world, he said that people would be: eating, drinking, buying, selling, planting, building, marrying, and given in marriage—specific activities that took place in the ancient world, take place now, and will certainly continue to take place throughout the world even if we should pass away (Luke 17:26–30). In a more personal sense, there are certain things about human nature that have not changed since ancient times. Human plans and emotions have not changed, as evidenced by the constant attempt to create, build, and find recognition and love. On the negative side, the greed, jealousies, abuses of power, and violence so common in today's world troubled people in the past as well.

It is also true that there are things about God that have changed and things that have not changed. God is a supreme being, able to make and execute plans. The universe we know did not always exist; God became its Creator when he brought it into being. He has acted in many ways throughout human history. The coming of God in Christ and the coming of the Holy Spirit marked changes in God's relationship with his creation in general and with human beings in particular. And yet, we can see common factors in the way God relates to the universe and to people. His essential nature and character do not change.

Certainly there is much about the ancient world that has little or no relevance to contemporary life. However, if there are things about human beings that do not change and things about our Creator that do not change, then it is reasonable to believe that ancient writings can contain information and insights that can benefit people today.

There is only so much time for each of us to learn and there is much to learn. If we can benefit from lessons learned in the past, then it seems foolish to ignore insights we would otherwise have to find out for ourselves. Further, if God spoke to people in the past about things important for all people in all times, it is even more foolish to ignore what was said.

During the period known as the Renaissance, scholars such as Petrarch (1304–1374) believed that it was important to recover insights gained in the ancient world. This led to the study of all ancient writings in the language in which they were originally written, including the documents of the Old and New Testaments. The Protestant Reformation resulted, to a large degree, from insights gained by studying the biblical documents in the languages in which they were originally written.

The Misrepresentation of the Past

By the eighteenth century, resentment against the church was growing. This was largely because the state churches of Europe imposed Christianity on all citizens. Paganism was reemerging in the thought of many people; but it was the forcible imposition of Christian belief and practice, together with corruption in the state churches, that most fueled animosity against Christianity. Deists rejected Christian revelation, assuming a Creator, but one not meaningfully involved with mankind once the universe was created. They believed reason, not divine revelation, is the way to understand everything. Another group called the philosophes—many of whom were deists—stressed reason alone as the way to understand the world. In the view of these thinkers, religion can be boiled down to morality, and everything else should be discarded: sacred writings, ceremonies, clergy, and most if not all that is considered supernatural. They viewed traditional Christianity as both false and unnecessary.

Renaissance thinkers borrowed the scriptural metaphor of "light" vs. "darkness" to argue that they were "enlightened" by ancient documents—including pagan writings. Importantly, while maintaining that there was "light" to be found outside Scripture and the teachings of the church, most Renaissance scholars remained Christians.

Adopting the practice of Renaissance scholars, eighteenth-century thinkers opposed to Christianity adopted the scriptural metaphor of light and darkness in labeling their own movement "the Enlightenment." They also labeled the Middle Ages "the Dark Ages" because of their contempt for Christian culture. These terms for periods of Western history thus had their origin in anti-Christian bias.

Charles Sanders Peirce did not accept historic Christianity and wasn't interested in the religious arguments of medieval scholars. Nevertheless, he admired the precision and comprehensiveness with which Christian scholars of the Middle Ages did their studies. He believed that the manner in which they did their work was consistent with the way scientific investigation should be conducted.[9] This was not a naive judgment. Peirce was deeply familiar with the philosophies of the ancient world and the Middle Ages, reading their writings in the Greek and Latin in which they were originally written. He was also an accomplished scientist and philosopher.

Many scholars have not shared Peirce's views, however. Bias against religion in general and Christianity in particular prevented Enlightenment thinkers from recognizing any value in medieval thought. In 1784, the German philosopher Immanuel Kant published an article "What Is Enlightenment?" to define the movement. He wrote that people should think for themselves rather than simply accepting what they are told by some authority. To support this, he argued that governments should allow freedom of thought in religion as well as in other matters.[10] So far, so good; Americans avoided some of the problems of Europe by refusing to establish a national church in the United States. Thus, no taxes were raised for the support of an American church by the federal government, and the federal government did not impose religious beliefs on the people. Americans were free to

---

9. Peirce, "Lessons," in *Collected Papers*, 1:13–14.

10. Kant, "An Answer to the Question: What Is Enlightenment?," in *Kant: Political Writings*, 55.

believe as they chose and to support the religious institutions they chose—a freedom guaranteed by the Bill of Rights. Although some states retained official churches in the earliest years of the nation, by the mid-nineteenth century no state had a tax-supported church.

However, Kant's position wasn't just that government should not impose Christianity on its citizens. Kant maintained that people would only enter intellectual maturity when they rejected traditional doctrines and reasoned out their beliefs for themselves—including those of traditional Judaism and traditional Christianity. He singled out Christian doctrine as the biggest impediment to the advancement of the human race.[11] This view became prevalent among scholars in the nineteenth century.

The philosopher/educator John Dewey (1859–1952), who strongly influenced the educational systems of many countries including the United States, fully embraced this view. He viewed religion with complete contempt, believing it to be a waste of time and effort that was better done away with.[12] Fully committed to Darwinism, Dewey viewed human beings as biological organisms that must constantly adapt to new circumstances to survive.[13] Therefore, from his perspective, tradition is always to be viewed as harmful—past adaptations have nothing to do with future conditions.

Due to the influence of Kent, Dewey, and others, it has become common to educate students that all tradition is destructive. Certainly some traditions are harmful—and that needs to be recognized. However, this is only part of the story. The Scriptures hold a view of tradition that is more in line with reality: some traditions are destructive, but some traditions are not only helpful, they are essential to our welfare. Throwing something overboard just because it isn't new ignores the fact that some traditions were begun with good reason by intelligent people for the benefit of others.

For those who want to argue that Christians should accept the Bible and not tradition, it is important to understand that the sixty-six books of the Protestant Bible are each authoritative individually and in their own right; but the choice of which specific books to include in the Bible comes to us as a tradition. In the early centuries of Christianity, copies of documents were only held by certain churches. Care was needed to ensure that certain documents were truly inspired. There were documents under consideration for inclusion that were rejected from both Testaments. Eventually, a

---

11. Kant, "An Answer to the Question: What Is Enlightenment?," in *Kant: Political Writings*, 59.

12. Dewey, *Common Faith*, 27, 28, 33.

13. Copleston, *History of Philosophy*, 8:353–57.

consensus was reached as to which documents were truly inspired of God and should be treated as sacred text.

Melito, bishop of Sardis, listed the recognized books of the Old Testament in AD 170.[14] The first list of all twenty-seven books of the New Testament comes to us from Athanasius, bishop of Alexandria (ca. 296–373), who listed them in his Easter letter in AD 367.[15] All sixty-six books became the Christian canon, or rule of faith. Some books from the period after Malachi was written but before the birth of Christ that are not included in the Protestant canon are included in the Roman Catholic and eastern Orthodox Bibles. However, there is no dispute in the wider Christian community concerning the sixty-six books included in the Protestant Bible. The choice of books in the Protestant Bible comes to us as a canonical tradition, one that is worth respecting and preserving.

A Practical View of Tradition

A tradition is something that is passed on from one person to another, generally across generations. An unbiased, objective view of tradition recognizes that traditions cannot be ruled helpful or harmful as a group; each tradition must be evaluated individually. This is the scriptural view of tradition: some traditions are harmful while others are beneficial.

The traditions that were of concern to the writers of Scripture are, of course, those that involve spiritual beliefs and practices. There is a recognition that God spoke to his people across many times and cultures, yet in doing so, he presented information and principles to be passed down from one generation to another. This is recognized, for example, in Deuteronomy 6:1–7 and Psalm 78:1–4, where teaching one's children about the Law is a sacred duty for ancient Israel. The uncritical acceptance of tradition in the time of Christ, however, became a significant problem.

About four hundred fifty years before the birth of Christ, Jews returned to Palestine from the Babylonian captivity. There was a renewed emphasis upon conformity to the Mosaic law and temple worship. There were those in the Jewish community who were devoted to the Lord and sincerely sought to live according the to the Law. Unfortunately, outward compliance without faithfulness to God became the norm for many. Arrogant, hard-hearted, self-centered people made a show of living by the Law to exalt themselves rather than to glorify the Lord. Rich and powerful Jews interpreted the Law in a manner that distorted its true meaning and violated its spirit (Matt

---

14. Bruce, *The Books and the Parchments*, 100.
15. Bruce, *The Books and the Parchments*, 112.

23:13–37; Luke 16:19–31). They used twisted arguments to justify their evil behavior (Luke 16:14–15).

It is unfortunate that the New Testament writings against the distortions of the Law are interpreted by so many as a blanket condemnation of the Mosaic law itself. Jesus lived his entire earthly life under the Law of Moses, and did not sin (Gal 4:4–5; John 8:46; Heb 4:15). The conflict between Jesus and the Jews was not about the Mosaic law itself, but with serious distortions of the Mosaic law (Matt 5:17–20; 23:16–28). The problem of traditions continued to be a problem in the Jewish community long after New Testament times. The replacement of the Mosaic law by the New Covenant promised in Jeremiah 31 and realized in the gospel of Christ is a separate issue.

In view of the distortion of the Law in New Testament times, the Scriptures of the New Testament delineate a sharp difference between the traditions created by people and the commandments of God; between cold adherence to a set of arbitrary rules and a warmhearted determination to please the Lord. Those corrupting the Law, of course, portrayed themselves as defending "the customs which Moses handed down to us" (Gk. *ta ethē ha paredōken hēmin Mōüsēs*, Acts 6:14). However, what they were defending were their self-serving interpretations of the Law. From the divine perspective they were "the tradition of the elders" (Gk. *tēn paradosin tōn presbyterōn*, Matt 15:2–3, 6; Mark 7:3, 5) and "the tradition of men" (Gk. *tēn paradosin tōn anthrōpōn*, Mark 7:8; Col 2:8; cf. Col 2:22). Referring to his Jewish heritage, Paul spoke of them as "my ancestral traditions" (Gk. *tōn patrikōn mou paradoseōn*, Gal 1:14).

If some of the distortions of the Law were new in Jesus' time, self-serving interpretation of the Law was not. Jesus referred to Isaiah 29:13 to highlight that the outward worship of his adversaries was not matched by an inward devotion to God. It was their failure to truly honor and know the Lord during the time of Isaiah as well as in the time of Christ that led people to twist the Law, creating traditions that incorporated this corruption into their culture. The distortion of what God delivered to the people was also the subject of Stephen's defense. Stephen noted that on Mount Sinai Moses "received living oracles to pass on to you" (*hos edexato logia zōnta dounai hēmin*, Acts 7:38).[16] These were good traditions that were to be passed on to successive generations of the Hebrew people (cf. Matt 5:17–20).

Likewise, those teachings of Jesus and the apostles he chose to found his church are good traditions to be preserved and handed down. We see this in the Apostle Paul when he relates how he received the account of

---

16. Some ancient manuscripts read "to us."

Jesus' Last Supper, and the accounts of Jesus' death and resurrection (1 Cor 11:23; 15:1–11). In both cases, Paul received a tradition that he passed on to others.

Traditions were an important part of Paul's teaching. Paul congratulated the Corinthians for preserving the traditions (Gk. *tas paradoseis*) he had given them (1 Cor 11:2). He encouraged the Thessalonians to preserve and to live by the traditions he delivered to them (Gk. *tas paradoseis*, 2 Thess 2:15; Gk. *tēn paradosin*, 2 Thess 3:6). Paul charged Timothy with both holding and protecting "the treasure"—literally, "the good deposit" (Gk. *tēn kalēn parathēkēn*) that had been entrusted to him (2 Tim 1:14). From the context we know that this was the "standard of sound words" that Timothy heard from Paul (2 Tim 1:13; cf. 1 Tim 6:20). Nor was it the Apostle Paul alone who gave importance to tradition. Jude wrote with a sense of urgency to exhort his readers to "contend earnestly for the faith which was once for all handed down (Gk. *tēi hapax paradotheisēi*) to the saints" (Jude 3).

The Christian faith is built upon traditions which have been faithfully handed down to us by those who witnessed sacred history and who heard God speak to them (2 Pet 1:16–21). Therefore, we cannot lay aside all traditions as harmful. Good traditions are those which have come directly from the Lord or are in harmony with what we have been taught by the Lord. In other words, traditions that either come directly from Scripture or are not contradictory to Scripture are traditions that should be accepted and preserved. They were given not just for people who first witnessed and received them, but for people who came after and wanted to draw near to God. The source of these traditions is the Lord himself—especially the life, ministry, and teachings of Jesus of Nazareth.

4

BUILDING ON THE CORNERSTONE

> In the beginning was the Word, and the Word was with God,
> and the Word was God. . . .
> And the Word became flesh, and dwelt among us, and we saw His glory,
> glory as of the only begotten from the Father, full of grace and truth. . . .
> No one has seen God at any time; the only begotten God who is in
> the bosom of the Father,
> He has explained *Him*.
>
> JOHN 1:1, 14, 18

> God, after He spoke long ago to the fathers in the prophets in many portions
> and in many ways, in these last days has spoken to us in His Son, whom He
> appointed heir of all things, through whom also He made the world.
>
> HEBREWS 1:1-2

> The stone which the builders rejected has become the chief corner *stone*.
> This is the Lord's doing; it is marvelous in our eyes.
>
> PSALM 118:22-23

Jesus the Cornerstone

JESUS of Nazareth taught, and the writers of the New Testament affirmed, that Jesus is the cornerstone of the Christian faith (Luke 20:17; Eph 2:20; 1 Pet 2:4-7; Ps 118:22-23). The cornerstone of any building is that stone around and upon which the rest of a building is constructed; in this case, the Christian faith represented in his followers—the church of Jesus Christ. Using a slightly different metaphor, though perhaps with this in mind, the

Apostle Paul wrote that there can be no foundation for the gospel other than Jesus (1 Cor 3:11). Many modern scholars have not been quite so sure.

Thinkers in the Enlightenment stopped speaking of Christianity in favor of discussing religion in general. They then stripped religion of almost everything supernatural, reducing religion to morality. The philosopher Immanuel Kant (1724-1804) wrote that all religions are essentially equal except, perhaps, for morality.[1] Kant argued that all traditional religions would pass away at some future time when reason alone would cause everyone to act morally.[2]

There was no place in this new type of thinking for Jesus of Nazareth. Some Bible critics have argued that Jesus of Nazareth may never have lived. Most other scholars have not wanted to deny the existence of Jesus, but insist that his importance is largely limited to the distant past. The Harvard philosopher Josiah Royce (1855-1916), voicing an opinion common in modern times, argued that Christianity could be meaningful to future generations only if Jesus of Nazareth was no longer the center of the faith.[3]

While this opposition to Jesus is generally framed as necessary due to the increase in knowledge since ancient times, the truth is that this is simply old-style unbelief marching under a new banner. The expectation that some will accept and some will reject the gospel is seen throughout the New Testament. Jesus was clear that people would be divided in response to his message (John 3:16-21; 15:18-25; Matt 10:16-22, 32-36; 24:9; Luke 21:12-17). In the parable of the sower and the soils, Jesus spoke of four different responses to his teaching; three of the four a rejection of him and his teaching (Mark 4:3-20).

When Paul preached to the philosophers of Athens on Mars Hill, the philosophers prevented him from continuing after Paul spoke of the resurrection of Jesus from the dead (Acts 17:32). When Paul spoke to the Sanhedrin—the ruling council of the Jews in Jerusalem (the same council that condemned Jesus and handed him over to the Romans to be put to death)—disagreement over resurrection caused an uproar because one party, the Sadducees, did not believe in an afterlife (Acts 23:6-10). When Paul spoke before the Roman governor Porcius Festus, Festus stopped Paul when Paul spoke of Jesus' resurrection. "Festus said in a loud voice, 'Paul, you are out of your mind (Gk. *mainē*)! *Your* great learning is driving you mad (Gk. *manian*)'" (Acts 26: 24). The English word "maniac" is derived from the Greek word used in Acts that is translated "mad" here. Festus was accusing Paul

---

1. Kant, *Religion within the Limits of Reason Alone*, 164.
2. Kant, *Religion within the Limits of Reason Alone*, 112-13.
3. Royce, *Problem of Christianity*, vol. 1, lecture 1.5, and vol. 2, lecture 16.14.

of being raving mad. Paul replied to Festus: "I am not out of my mind (Gk. *ou mainomai*), most excellent Festus, but I utter words of sober truth (Gk. *alētheias kai sōphrosynēs rhēmata apophthengomai*)" (Acts 26:25). Madness or sober truth? That is the issue in all three of these situations. In each case, it did not require modern science for some in New Testament times to decide that Jesus wasn't what he and his followers proclaimed him to be. The choice to believe or to disbelieve is the same as it has ever been. There is no less reason to believe in Jesus today than before.

For Jesus, his identity as the cornerstone promised in Psalm 118:22-23 also meant that he would surely face rejection by some who should have known better, for it indicated that the Jewish religious leadership would reject him. At the same time, it meant that he, as the cornerstone, would provide the most important basis for God's work in the world. Psalm 118:22-23 was also the basis for Paul's statement to the Corinthians that Jesus was a "stumbling block" to the Jews and "foolishness" to the Gentiles; but to those who follow Jesus: "Christ the power of God and the wisdom of God" (1 Cor 1:23-24). There is no Christianity worthy of the name without Jesus of Nazareth.

Son of David, Son of God

Matthew's account of the birth of Jesus tells how magi traveled to Jerusalem looking for the birth of a Hebrew king worthy of worship. Evidently, these magi were students of various signs in the heavens and also reverenced Jewish tradition. They were not familiar enough with the Hebrew Scriptures to know where this new king would be born, so they went to Herod the Great in Jerusalem to ask where to go. King Herod summoned the top religious scholars and leaders of the Jews, who informed him that according to a prophecy given by the prophet Micah, this king would be born in Bethlehem, the city of King David. It was Bethlehem's association with David that made these religious leaders certain that this verse, Micah 5:2, speaks of a son of David who would become the greatest king of the Jews.[4] The quote in Matthew gives the sense of the text of the original Hebrew in Micah, but is not an exact quote. Matthew evidently combines the sense of Micah 5:2 with text from 2 Samuel 5:2 or 1 Chronicles 11:2. In this manner, Matthew emphasized that this new king would be a son of David and that the promises to David would be fulfilled in him.[5]

---

4. Micah 5:1 in Hebrew Bibles.
5. Turner, *Matthew*, 84.

In his account of Jesus' conception, Matthew also referred to Isaiah 7:14, explaining that the birth of Jesus would be the fulfillment of Isaiah's prophecy that the child to be born would be: "God with us" (Gk. *Meth' hēmōn ho theos*), in Hebrew, *ʿimmānûēl* or in English, Immanuel (Matt 1:19–23). Isaiah lived in a time when the kingdoms of Israel and Judah were about to undergo judgment from God. This judgment followed the stubborn refusal of most of the people to honor God and to live by his ways. The northern kingdom of Israel would be conquered and eliminated by the Assyrians; the southern kingdom of Judah would be invaded by the Assyrians, but would survive. God told Isaiah a son would be born who would be called Immanuel—"God with us"—as an assurance that God would not abandon those who were truly his people. This assurance was given to sustain those faithful to *Yahweh* even though judgment would be brought against their land. The birth of Immanuel took place in Isaiah's lifetime not long after his birth was foretold. However, the text gives reason to understand that its complete fulfillment would not be made at that time.

Isaiah 7:14 states, "A virgin (Hebr. *hāʿalmâ*) will be with child and bear a son." Some scholars in modern times prefer the translation "young woman" for "virgin." However, the Greek translation widely used in the time of Jesus, the Septuagint, translates the Hebrew word *ʿalmâ* by the Greek word *parthenos*, virgin. This, together with Matthew's choice of *parthenos* in Matthew 1:23, strongly supports the translation "virgin." Matthew reinforces this by emphasizing that Joseph "kept her [Mary] a virgin until after she gave birth to a Son" (Matt 1:25). The concept of a virgin having a baby that would have not only the name, but the identity "Immanuel" was not completely fulfilled in Isaiah's time. The birth of this boy represented the presence of God with his people, but this child did not *embody* the presence of God. Thus, Matthew refers to this prophecy by Isaiah and points to its complete fulfillment in the birth of Jesus of Nazareth—a birth that followed a conception of human life brought about by the Spirit of God in the virgin Mary.[6]

The identification of Isaiah 7:14 with the birth of Jesus long afterward may seem out of place except for the other verses that follow in Isaiah's writings. Isaiah 9:6–7 foretells the birth of a child (Hebr. *yeled*), a son (Hebr. *bēn*), who will sit on the kingly throne of his father David. Surprisingly, this human son will carry the names: "Mighty God" (Hebr. *'ēl gibbôr*) and "Eternal Father" (Hebr. *'ăbî-ʿad*). Some scholars have suggested that these are not references to deity; however, the context argues against this. Isaiah

---

6. Partial fulfillment in the time of Isaiah and complete fulfillment in the conception of Jesus of Nazareth is the only interpretation that does justice to the text. See the discussion by Oswalt in *Isaiah: Chapters 1–39*, 202–14 and by Blomberg in *CNTUOT*, 3–5.

says that this son will sit on the throne of David in a reign that will have no end (Hebr. 'ên-qēṣ), extending from "now" (his ascension to the throne) "to eternity" (Hebr. mēʿattâ wᵉʿad-ʿôlām). Further, such language would only have been written if Isaiah was convinced it came from *Yahweh*; otherwise, Isaiah's high view of God would have precluded his use of these names to refer to a child. No author of Old Testament Scripture had a higher view of God than Isaiah.

In Isaiah 6:1-7, Isaiah had a vision in which he came into the presence of God in Solomon's temple in Jerusalem. Isaiah saw God sitting on his throne, "lofty and exalted." Spiritual beings called out: "Holy, Holy, Holy, is the Lord of hosts, the whole earth is full of His glory" as God's glory filled the temple. The temple shook as it filled with clouds of God's presence. So terrified was Isaiah at being in the presence of such a holy, righteous God that Isaiah cried out in anguish, expecting to be struck dead for his sins. Instead, God forgave and cleansed Isaiah. Such a high view of God does not mix easily with a prediction that a human child would also carry names that identify the child as God; but that is exactly what is written in Isaiah 9:6-7.

Peter wrote that the prophets of the Old Testament were curious about the fulfillment of what they foretold. The prophets were told by "the Spirit of Christ within them" that what they were writing was for the benefit of those who came after them (1 Pet 1:10-12). Jesus referred to these prophesies when he explained his life and mission to his followers (e.g., Luke 24:13-27). It was Paul's custom to use Old Testament Scriptures to argue that Jesus is the fulfillment of prophecy (Acts 17:1-3).

Matthew and Luke make clear in their gospels that the conception and birth of Jesus was unique in history. It would have been more acceptable generally to both Jews and Gentiles for them to have left this out of their Gospels. They deliberately included the virgin birth because it was essential to show that Jesus was the Son of God before his conception, and remained so. The temple in Jerusalem was understood to be the place where God manifested his presence in a unique way. Matthew notes that Jesus taught concerning himself: "something greater than the temple is here" (Matt 12:6). John, Paul, and the author of Hebrews all state clearly this same truth that Jesus is the Son of God, has always been, and always will be, even after taking human flesh (John 1:1-18; Phil 2:5-11; Heb 1:1-14).

Jesus confirmed his preexistence. In one instance, he baffled Jewish religious leaders when he asked them to explain the text of Psalm 110:1, "The Lord says to my Lord: 'Sit at My right hand until I make Your enemies a footstool for Your feet'" (Matt 22:41-46; cf. Mark 12:35-37; Luke 20:41-44). The first "Lord" is God the Father, the second, the Christ (cf. Acts 2:34-35; Heb 1:1-4, 13). David refers to the Christ as "my Lord." Jesus asked how the

Christ could be the son of David if David called Christ "Lord." In another instance, Jesus angered those who opposed him by saying, "Truly, truly, I say to you, before Abraham was born, I am," thus indicating his preexistence (John 8:58).

The Son Honors the Father

Traveling home from celebrating the Passover in Jerusalem, Joseph and Mary discovered that the twelve-year-old Jesus was nowhere in their group of relatives and acquaintances. After a day's journey back to Jerusalem and another three days searching the crowded city, they found Jesus in the temple asking questions of some of Judaism's senior religious teachers. Those present were impressed by the insight and understanding Jesus exhibited; these distinguished rabbis were evidently enjoying their discussion with this precocious, well-mannered young man. Jesus' parents, however, were rattled and tired after their four-day search. Mary asked Jesus why he had not been more considerate of his parents. Jesus, at the same time, was surprised that his parents didn't know where he was (Luke 2:41–50).

There are two schools of thought as to how Jesus' response to his parents should be translated. Many scholars believe the best translation is: "Did you not know that I must be in my Father's house?" Other, equally competent scholars favor some variation of: "Did you not know that I must be in those things that concern my Father?" While acknowledging good reason for the first, I favor the second translation because the words "temple" or "house" do not appear in the Greek text of Luke 2:49 and are singular, and the Greek word *tois* is plural and would generally be translated "the things" or "the matters."[7]

My preference aside, there are good arguments for both translations. Whichever is correct, several things are clear. First, Jesus had an advanced understanding of Old Testament Scripture even at the age of twelve. Young men of his age would have been expected to have a basic knowledge of Scripture and to be prepared to discuss their interpretation with others. However, Jesus' pursuit of those discussing Scripture at the most sophisticated level together with his ability to gain the respect of the senior rabbis would have been unique.

Second, in his answer to his parents, Jesus was speaking of his heavenly Father: God. Joseph and Mary were apparently confused by Jesus' answer because they thought the father Jesus spoke of was Joseph. Third, the Greek word *dei* means "must," "duty," "obligation." The use of *dei* in this passage

---

7. Alford, *Alford's Greek Testament*, 1:466.

indicates that Jesus felt deeply obligated to serve his heavenly Father. This motivated Jesus to be involved in serving God in a deeper way than his family; they were satisfied with a traditional Passover observance, he went beyond. He expected his parents to understand this.[8] Service to the Father would become a hallmark of Jesus' life and ministry.

Jesus always honored his Father (John 8:49). He came in the name of the Father—meaning more than that he associated himself with the Father's name—meaning that he came in a manner completely consistent with the Father's holy character (John 5:43). Jesus taught that he always sought the will of God the Father (John 5:30). He called doing the will of the Father "food to eat"—that which sustained his life (John 4:32–34). There is certainly an echo here of Deuteronomy 8:3: "Man does not live by bread alone, but man lives by everything that proceeds out of the mouth of the Lord"— words that Jesus quoted when tempted by Satan (Matt 4:3–4; Luke 4:3–4). Jesus explained: "I have come down from heaven, not to do My own will, but the will of Him who sent Me. . . . And He who sent Me is with Me; He has not left Me alone, for I always do the things that are pleasing to Him" (John 6:38; 8:29; cf. John 7:28–29). Jesus said the words that he spoke were given to him by the Father; the things that he did were things the Father showed him to do (John 5:19; 7:16; 8:28).

The Son Reveals the Father

Jesus also taught that he has a unique relationship with God the Father. He said that he is the only one who really knows the Father and is able to reveal God to others (Matt 11:27). In John 1:18, John used an interesting and telling Greek word to describe what Jesus did by his coming—though it is a word that requires some explanation. This word is *exēgēsato* from the verb *exēgeomai*. John used this word to indicate that Jesus interprets the purely spiritual to those who are part of a physical universe.

John might have used the Greek verb *hermēneuō* had he wanted to compare what Jesus did simply to translating or explaining from a foreign language. John could have used the Greek verb *phaneroō* had he only wanted to say that Jesus showed the Father. He could have used the Greek verb *apokalyptō* had he wanted to stress that Jesus revealed that which was hidden regarding the nature of God. Andreas Köstenberger suggests that John could also have used "the more common term for 'to make known,' *gnōrizō*."[9] It seems John used *exēgeomai* because it includes all of these

---

8. Green, *Luke*, 155–57.
9. Köstenberger, *John*, 50.

concepts, and was often used for the explanation of sacred things; in the pagan world, for the interpretation of dreams, omens, and oracles—here, of course, for the explanation of God's character and will.[10] Ceslas Spicq wrote of John 1:18: "This verse means that the Son, by his person and his teaching, presented, expressed, and gave a human translation to the divine mystery."[11]

The unique relationship Jesus has with the Father goes farther than being *like* the Father. In responding to Philip, Jesus asked, "Do you not believe that I am in the Father, and the Father is in Me?" (John 14:10). This special relationship has to do with an identity that Jesus shared with the Father. In the first verse of John's Gospel, John identifies Jesus as "the Word" (Gk. *ho logos*). John writes not only that "the Word was with God" (Gk. *ho logos ēn pros ton theon*) but that "the Word was God" (Gk. *theos ēn ho logos*).[12] Like God the Father, Jesus—the Son of God—is divine. At one point, Jesus told his critics: "You are from below, I am from above (Gk. *egō ek tōn anō eimi*); you are of this world, I am not of this world" (John 8:23).

Any doubt as to whether Jesus actually claimed to be deity is erased by the events of his ministry. At one point, those who opposed Jesus were seeking to kill him because Jesus called God his Father, and so made himself equal (Gk. *ison*) with God (John 5:18). They considered his statement to be blasphemy. The sin of blasphemy was punished by stoning to death in the Law of Moses (Lev 24:10–16). Later, Jesus said plainly: "I and the Father are one" (Gk. *egō kai ho patēr hen esmen*, John 10:30). The crowd prepared to stone Jesus, saying: "You, being a man, make yourself out *to be* God" (Gk. *su anthrōpos ōn poieis seauton theon*, John 10:33). The reaction of his critics makes clear that Jesus taught that he is deity.

In his prayer recorded in John 17, Jesus said that the time had come for him to be glorified with the same glory he had before he took human flesh (John 17:5). In Philippians 2:5–11, Paul describes how Jesus came to earth, served God fully, and therefore is due great glory. Philippians 2:10 foretells that all people will someday acknowledge that Jesus is Lord of all—bending to his will even if they don't want to do so. In Isaiah 45:20–25 God reserves the right of worship to himself alone; applying this to Jesus shows that he is deity. Paul, a highly educated Jew, saw no problem declaring both the Father and the Son to be God.

---

10. Spicq, "*exēgeomai*," in *TLNT*, 2:21–23.

11. Spicq, "*exēgeomai*," in *TLNT*, 2:23.

12. In the phrase "the Word was God" the word "God" (Gk. *theos*) is a predicate nominative, indicating that both God and the Word are equal. This is not saying "the Word was divine," as if Jesus only had a nature *like* God, but that Jesus is as much God as God the Father. In addition, placing the word "God" (Gk. *theos*) first in this phrase indicates in Greek that there is an emphasis on the Word (Gk. *ho logos*) being God.

There is only one true God, sovereign over the universe. But, God is both Father and Son; the same substance and character, yet also different. That may not fit easily into our thinking. But God is unique, and without his uniqueness, the creation would not have the potential for all of the good things within it: person-to-person relationships, love, and self-giving. Nor would there likely be a way for creatures to have a personal relationship with their Creator.

John is saying that Jesus reveals God to us in terms that human beings can understand. This is more than just teaching. John is telling us that Jesus brings God to us in a way that human beings can observe and relate to in a manner similar to the way we observe and relate to other people. Jesus has brought deity, the sacred, into the everyday world of human beings. We learn from his life as well as from his words. When John says "no one has seen God at any time," John is saying that no one has seen God the Father visually, even though they may have seen a vision—a representation—of God; but the Son shows the Father to us in the sense that he is fully God as foretold in Isaiah 9:6; Jesus' character is the same as the Father's.

In the night in which Jesus was betrayed, when Philip asked Jesus to show the disciples God the Father, Jesus replied, "Have I been so long with you, and *yet* you have not come to know Me, Phillip? He who has seen Me has seen the Father" (John 14:9). This Scripture refers back to what John wrote in John 1:18. In a similar vein, Paul wrote that Jesus "is the image of the invisible God" (Col 1:15). Similarly, the author of Hebrews wrote that Jesus "is the radiance of His [God the Father's] glory and the exact representation of His nature" (Heb 1:3). Throughout his time on earth, Jesus showed us God the Father in our midst.

We learn about God the Father as we read through the Gospel accounts of Jesus' life and ministry. We see Jesus constantly seeking to draw people to himself. When someone seeks him out, he responds in love, meeting their needs if it is possible to do so without compromising with sin. This often involves teaching or healing. Jesus is constantly in command. He teaches and heals with authority. When necessary, he confronts those who have sinned. Even on the cross, when he is restricted from movement and filled with pain and fatigue, he ministers to those around him. He asks forgiveness for his enemies, not because he is weak, but because the strength of his character and being enables him to be compassionate. His life is characterized by redemptive love. He yields his life to the Father when his work is accomplished.

Born to Touch Lives

In Jesus, God has come near to human beings in a new way; Jesus is truly "God with us," reaching out to people in love, beckoning all people into God's fellowship (John 1:1–13). However, it is the reaction of people to him that determines the outcome of an encounter with the divine. To those who recognize their need of God and draw close to him, there is mercy and blessing; but to those who resist God, there is fear, isolation, and judgment. This was seen in Isaiah's time as God used Assyria to punish those who turned against him, yet sustained those who loved him. It was seen in the magi drawing close to worship the newborn Jesus and departing with joy, in contrast to King Herod slaughtering children born in Bethlehem in a vain attempt to eliminate his fear of Jesus. It is seen in the words of Paul, who said that the fragrance of Jesus would be the aroma of life to those who love him, but the aroma of death to those who hate him (2 Cor 2:14–16).

5

Following Jesus

You know of Jesus of Nazareth, how God anointed Him with the Holy Spirit and with power, and *how* He went about doing good and healing all who were oppressed by the devil, for God was with Him. We are witnesses of all the things He did both in the land of the Jews and in Jerusalem. They also put Him to death by hanging Him on a cross. God raised Him up on the third day and granted that He become visible, not to all the people, but to witnesses who were chosen beforehand by God, *that is*, to us who ate and drank with Him after He arose from the dead.

ACTS 10:38–41

Therefore let all the house of Israel know for certain that God has made Him both Lord and Christ—this Jesus whom you crucified.

ACTS 2:36

Jesus of Nazareth

JESUS is far better known today than other religious teachers of his time. The morality he taught, however, did not distinguish him fully from contemporary Jewish religious teachers such as Gamaliel, whom Luke called "a teacher of the Law, respected by all the people" (Acts 5:34). This is seen in Luke 10:28, where a lawyer agrees with Jesus concerning which two commandments of the Law of Moses were the most important. It is also seen in Acts 5:27–39, where Gamaliel counsels caution because those who oppose the preaching of the gospel might be shown to be opposing God; advice he would not have given had Gamaliel believed that Jesus' teachings were false by Old Testament standards. What made Jesus' teaching unique was his teaching concerning himself and what this meant for the entire world.

The Witness of John

All four Gospels tell of the ministry of Jesus' cousin: John the Baptist. John warned that the wrath of God was coming upon all who sinned. He called Jews to confess and repent of their sins to receive forgiveness and to escape the wrath of God. John baptized in the Jordan River those who committed themselves to live according to the righteousness demanded in the Mosaic law. Large numbers of people went to John from many walks in life, showing that many people had a real thirst for God. Among these were tax collectors and soldiers—those considered among the least likely to honor God. John gave specific instructions how to live their life in a manner pleasing to God.

John's call to repentance was based firmly on the moral standards of the Law of Moses, including the Ten Commandments. This is important for the entire gospel because both Luke and John tell us that those who were chosen to be witnesses to Jesus' life and teachings were with John the Baptist when Jesus was baptized; in other words, they had already devoted themselves to high standards (Acts 1:21–22; John 15:26–27). John's Gospel tells of two disciples of John the Baptist who became followers of Jesus, specifically naming Andrew (John 1:15–40). As apostles, such men were not given to false witness in their testimony to the life of Christ. They would not have misrepresented the message Jesus gave them to preach.

John's ministry was not simply to get people to reform; it was also to testify to the coming of someone far greater than he. All four Gospels record John's witness that someone would follow who preexisted John and who was mightier than John. Whereas John baptized with water, this one would baptize with the Holy Spirit (Matt 3:11; Mark 1:8; Luke 3:16; John 1:33). When God sent John to minister, God told John: "He upon whom you see the Spirit descending and remaining upon Him, this is the One who baptizes in the Holy Spirit" (John 1:33). It is worth noting that John the Baptist said this person preexisted him. Had John referred to an individual who was conceived before John, that would not have been Jesus, for Luke is very clear that John the Baptist was conceived before his cousin Jesus (Luke 1:5–38). The person John the Baptist was speaking of was Jesus—as all the Gospels make clear.

The Anointing of the Christ

When Jesus went to John the Baptist to be baptized, John did something he never did with anyone else: he tried to talk Jesus out of it (Matt 3:13–15). John argued that it was John who needed to be baptized by Jesus, not the other way around. Jesus insisted that it was necessary to fulfill righteousness, however, and so John baptized Jesus. It was then that God confirmed Jesus' choice.

When Jesus came up from the water and prayed after his baptism, John saw the Holy Spirit descend upon Jesus and remain like a dove. The heavens then opened and a voice came out of heaven saying: "This is My beloved Son, in whom I am well-pleased" (Matt 3:17; Mark 1:11; Luke 3:22). This was the divine indication that Jesus was the exalted baptizer whose coming John foretold. This was also the anointing by which Jesus became "the Christ."

Before Jesus' baptism, he was the Son of God, but he was not "the Christ." The English word "Christ" comes from the Greek *Christos*, meaning "Anointed One." *Christos* is the Greek translation of the Hebrew *māšiaḥ*—in English "Messiah." To say "Jesus Christ" is to say "Jesus (the) Anointed One." To understand what this means, we must understand his anointing.

In the Old Testament, certain servants of God were anointed with oil. To be anointed at the direction of *Yahweh* meant *Yahweh* would enable that person in an office or task. It also meant that this person would be held accountable to *Yahweh* for doing that task faithfully. The concept of anointing for a specific task is important. Any anointing at the direction of *Yahweh* is for a specific role or roles that *Yahweh* has chosen for that individual.

Christians interpret anointing oil as representative of the Holy Spirit. This is true even though it was possible for those in the Old Testament to be empowered by the Holy Spirit without going through an anointing ceremony. For example, the craftsmen who were charged with making the tabernacle as well as all of the accessories and garb of those who served the tabernacle had no such ceremony (Exod 31:1–11; 35:30—36:3). Nor did Joshua when Joshua inherited Moses' place as the leader of Israel (Num 27:18–23). The leaders of Israel during the time of the judges were not anointed with oil. These individuals were empowered to deliver the Israelites from a specific danger even if they, themselves, did not walk fully in the ways of the Lord (Judg 3:9–11; 6:33–35; 11:29–33; 14:5–9, 19). God worked through these judges to preserve Israel so that he could fulfill his plan. They were, nevertheless, anointed with the Holy Spirit for their service.

Anointing with oil indicated a more formal divine-commissioning, though still with a specific office in mind. The Law of Moses required priests to be anointed with oil as part of the consecration to their office—especially the high priest (Exod 28:40–41). The oil used for their anointing was a special oil with a unique mixture of ingredients that was not to be used on anyone else or for any other purpose (Exod 30:22–33). The high priest is referred to as "the anointed (Hebr. *māšiaḥ*) priest" in Leviticus 4:3, 5, and 16.

Kings were to be servants of *Yahweh*, and so were anointed. Saul was anointed the first king of Israel by the prophet Samuel at the direction of *Yahweh* (1 Sam 9:15—10:1). This anointing was done in a private meeting of Samuel with Saul. The anointing emphasized that while there was a king in Israel because the people asked for a king, the choice of the king was *Yahweh's*; therefore, Saul was responsible first and foremost to *Yahweh* rather than to the people. Saul did not want this office. His attempt to avoid it failed because God laid that responsibility upon him (1 Sam 10:14–25). God's choice was emphasized by David when twice in 1 Samuel 24:6 he called Saul "*Yahweh's* anointed" (Hebr. *mᵉšiaḥ Yahweh*).

The role of Jesus as God's anointed King was emphasized in the Revelation to John. There, Jesus is identified as "the ruler of the kings of the earth" (Gk. *ho archōn tōn basileōn tēs gēs*) and twice as "King of Kings, and Lord of Lords" (Gk. *basileus basileōn kai kurios kuriōv*, Rev 1:5; 17:14; 19:16). Revelation 11:15 emphasizes this point as well; a verse that, like Revelation 19:16, plays an important role in Handel's *Messiah*. The most famous part of the *Messiah*, "the Hallelujah Chorus," celebrates the triumphant proclamation of this Scripture: "The kingdom of the world has become *the kingdom* of our Lord and of His Christ; and He will reign forever and ever" (Rev 11:15). Notice carefully: "*our* Lord" (Gk. *tou kyriou hēmōn*) but "*His* Christ" (Gk. *tou christou autou*). Jesus is not the Christ because he has been chosen by the world; he is God's Christ, God's "Anointed One." And he is also chosen to be *our* Lord.

In the Old Testament, the anointing of God's servants was specific to their mission and not a blanket approval of everything they might choose to do. This is made clear by the ways these servants were blessed and, at times, the way they were judged. For example, early in the reign of Israel's first king, Saul was told to wait for seven days at Gilgal for the prophet Samuel to arrive. Samuel was coming to offer sacrifices and to give direction before the Israelites went into battle against the Philistines (1 Sam 10:8). Saul became impatient when the seven days passed and Samuel didn't appear; so Saul began offering the sacrifices himself (1 Sam 13:8–9).

Samuel arrived in the midst of Saul offering sacrifices, upon which Samuel reprimanded Saul for taking the role of a priest (1 Sam 13:10–14). In other cultures of the ancient Near East, the king was also a priest. In Israel, the Law of Moses made the government and the priesthood separate so that the king could not use his power to corrupt religious teachings and practice. Saul crossed this line when he acted as priest in violation of the Mosaic law. As if this were not enough, Saul's actions were fully contrary to Samuel's instructions. As a result, Saul would lose his place, and another king would be chosen for Israel.

Saul had an impressive personal appearance, looking every bit a king; but he did not serve faithfully in the role he was chosen to fulfill. The next man appointed by *Yahweh* to be king, David the son of Jesse from the town of Bethlehem, would serve the Lord with all his heart (1 Sam 13:14; 16:1–13). We learn that when Samuel anointed David to be king of Israel, "the Spirit of the Lord came mightily upon David from that day forward" (1 Sam 16:13). Like Saul, David and those who followed David as king are referred to as "the anointed one" (e.g., 2 Sam 19:21; 22:51; 2 Chr 6:42; Ps 2:2; 18:50; 132:17). Some of these references look ahead to the ruler spoken of in Isaiah 9:6–7—a son of David whose rule would never end. This is the fulfillment of Yahweh's covenant promise to David that Yahweh would raise up someone to sit upon the throne of David forever (2 Sam 7:8–17; 1 Chr 17:11–15; 2 Chr 6:16). The hope of the Hebrews for a blessed, righteous ruler is reflected in Psalms 2; 8:46–50; 21; 72; 110; and 132; as well as in 1 Samuel 2:10; Isaiah 11:1–10; Jeremiah 23:5–6; Ezekiel 37:24–25; and Hosea 3:5.

The coming of this eternal King coincided with the establishment of the kingdom of God. This was a central part of the message of both John the Baptist and Jesus, as shown especially in Matthew, Mark, and Luke. The essence of this message is captured well in the Lord's Prayer: "Your kingdom come (Gk. *elthetō hē basileia sou*), your will be done (Gk. *genēthētō to thelēma sou*), on earth as it is in heaven" (Matt 6:10). The verbs come first in each Greek phrase, emphasizing the importance of the coming of the kingdom and the doing of God's will. In heaven, as shown in Revelation 4 and 5, God's will is the norm of behavior; it is always done. God's kingdom on earth means that his people seek to do what is pleasing to him. The rule of Jesus in individual lives brings people into practical, day-to-day fellowship with those in heaven who seek to please God, establishing the personal rule of Jesus in their hearts and lives.

The Mission of Jesus Christ

The anointing of Jesus, while it had a foundation in the Old Testament, was also different from earlier anointings in some ways. This is because Jesus' mission, while it shared aspects with earlier servants of God, was unique, and had a unique timetable for its completion. Jesus used the following words from Isaiah 61 to explain his mission to those in his hometown:

> The Spirit of the Lord is upon Me,
> Because He anointed Me to preach the gospel to the poor,
> He has sent Me to proclaim release to the captives,
> And recovery of sight to the blind,

To set free those who are oppressed,

To proclaim the favorable year of the Lord. (Luke 4:18-19; Isa 61:1-2)

These words speak of a mission of proclamation and redemption. Importantly, Jesus stopped short of declaring "the day of vengeance of our God" (Isa 61:2).

Proclaiming a message from the Lord is the mission of his prophets. The prophet might foretell the future, but more often spoke of the time in which he lived, calling on people to be faithful to God. The Old Testament speaks of a prophet being anointed with oil only once: the anointing of Elisha to be the successor of Elijah (1 Kgs 19:9-16). Otherwise, the choice of a prophet was made by *Yahweh* by giving a commission and giving his words for the prophet to speak. The anointing was most often, therefore, by the Spirit of God coming upon a chosen individual for a specific message, just as with Jesus.

The second part of Jesus' mission involved release from sin and the consequences of sin, which is the work of a priest. Unlike the priests of the Old Testament, however, whose priesthood under the Law of Moses was restricted to Moses' brother Aaron and his descendants, Jesus' priesthood is an eternal one based upon the order of Melchizedek. This order, limited to Jesus, was foretold in Psalm 110:4. Fulfillment required Jesus to be the sacrifice as well as the person offering the sacrifice. To make himself the sacrifice, Jesus had to identify with sinners even though he, himself, had no sin. This Jesus did when he submitted to be baptized by John as if he, Jesus, needed to repent of sin. God the Father's love and approval was confirmed after Jesus' baptism, as shown in the words from heaven.

The kingship of Jesus would follow the successful completion of Jesus' work as prophet and priest. This is why Jesus did not read "the day of vengeance of our God" in Isaiah 61:2. As the full text of Isaiah 61:1-2 made clear, first would come Jesus' work as prophet, then Jesus' work as priest, and finally his reign as King. This was the unique, multifaceted mission for which he was anointed by the Holy Spirit.

In addition to this sequence of roles, there was also a sequence in Jesus' role as King of kings and Lord of lords. As the Son of God, Jesus already deserved reverence from all creatures in the universe. In his role as the Christ, however, his reign as King of kings and Lord of lords would begin after he completed his work at the cross. His reign would begin first in his church—in the hearts, minds, and lives of those who are his followers. Later, in the Day of Vengeance promised in Isaiah 61:2, Jesus would rid the universe of all who opposed the rightful rule of God (Matt 25:31-46).

Jesus was made the Christ by God the Father because of Jesus' self-conscious acceptance of this mission at his baptism. Jesus taught his disciples that the greatest person is the greatest servant, "For even the Son of Man did not come to be served, but to serve, and to give His life a ransom for many" (Mark 10:45; cf. Matt 20:28). Before the Last Supper, Jesus washed the feet of his disciples (John 13:1–17). John makes clear that Jesus knew he was the Son of God when he took the task of the lowest servant. Not long after, Jesus would go to the cross in the service of both God and people. In Philippians 2:5–11, Paul recounts Jesus' self-conscious decision as the Son of God to take the role of a servant even though it meant crucifixion. Jesus selfless service led to his resurrection from the dead and to his glorification as Lord of all.

Jesus as the Focus of Christian Faith

It seems difficult to overemphasize the significance of Jesus as the Christ of God. Jesus becomes the center of the faith because it is through him that we meet and know God (1 Tim 2:5; Eph 2:11–22). This is the unique role for which he alone has been chosen. He is: "the Alpha and the Omega, the first and the last, the beginning and the end" (Rev 22:13). He is the center of the faith, that which brings all parts together into a whole (Heb 12:2). The end of history is when all of his people come into fellowship with him in such a way that God is fully revealed (1 John 3:2; 1 Cor 13:9–10, 12).

We learn from the book of Acts that early Christians called their faith "the Way" (Gk. *ho hodos*) before they referred to themselves as Christians (Acts 9:2; 11:26; 19:9, 23; 22:4; 24:14, 22). However, no one Scripture explains why early Christians adopted "the Way" to identify followers of Jesus. Jesus spoke of the narrow way that "leads to life" (Matt 7:14). Acts speaks of "the way of the Lord" (Acts 18:25). Matthew and Acts speak of "the way of God" (Matt 22:16; Acts 18:26). Peter refers to "the way of the truth," "the right way," and "the way of righteousness" (2 Pet 2:2, 15, 21). Zacharias speaks of "the way of peace" (Luke 1:79). Hebrews speaks of "the way into the holy place" that has been opened up by Jesus, which fits nicely with Paul's teaching that Jesus has opened the way for us to have full fellowship with God (Heb 9:8–15; 10:19–20; Rom 5:1–2; Eph 2:18; 3:11–12). Just once, in John's Gospel, Jesus identifies himself as "the way, and the truth, and the life" (John 14:6). While many and perhaps all of these were in view when Jesus' followers called their movement "the Way," the prominence of Jesus as the Christ certainly showed itself in the designation of the followers of Jesus as "Christians"; a term common enough to be used by King Agrippa after Paul challenged him to become a follower of Jesus (Gk. *Christianon*, Acts 26:28).

Christian Discipleship

A significant aspect of Jesus' anointed ministry involved the seeking out of individuals to be his disciples. This was unusual in a time when students commonly chose teachers to instruct them rather than vice versa. Some of those Jesus sought out would later be sent out as apostles to establish his church. However, there was no distinction between the apostles and all of the others Jesus called to himself in at least one respect: all were called to become his disciples. John the Baptist said that his mission was to herald the coming of Jesus; Jesus of Nazareth called people to himself. In a passage known as the Great Commission, Jesus told his apostles to "go therefore and make disciples of all the nations . . ." (Matt 28:19; cf. Acts 14:21).

Discipleship requires more than an interest in Jesus, his teachings, and his ministry. Many sought him who did not become disciples or who, like Nicodemus, became disciples later on. Discipleship requires commitment. Failing to become a disciple does not in any way preclude someone from being a seeker—examining Jesus and his teachings to decide what the correct relationship to Jesus might be. From those who are seekers, Jesus deserves at the very least a hearing with an open mind, because so many have found him and his teachings to inspire the most worthy thoughts and deeds human beings are capable of. Once convinced there is merit in Jesus as the Christ, the next step is discipleship.

Those wishing to be Jesus' disciples commit themselves to Jesus in a definite manner. The Greek word for "disciple" in the New Testament is *mathētēs*, which indicates a pupil, a learner. A disciple of Jesus observes and meditates on Jesus' acts and teachings as well as the other teachings of the Scriptures to learn how to live. Paul wrote that in Jesus "are hidden all the treasures of wisdom and knowledge" (Col 2:3). Peter said that God has given us "everything pertaining to life and godliness" (Gk. *zōēn kai eusebeian*, 2 Pet 1:3).

It takes time to learn and apply all that it means to be a faithful disciple of Jesus. Even the Twelve did not understand many of Jesus' teachings at the time he taught them; they understood them later. The New Testament shows, for example, how Peter grew throughout his life. After Peter's commitment to follow Jesus, we see him both doing well and acting foolishly. Peter changed after Jesus' crucifixion and resurrection. He changed again at Pentecost. He then had to learn that Gentiles were to be equal partners in the gospel with Jews (Acts 10). After this, Peter needed to be confronted for failing to live out this teaching (Gal 2:11–14). Even when Jesus' teachings are understood, only time and experience enable us to know how to apply them (Heb 5:14). Discipleship is a lifelong process.

Discipleship of this kind requires the highest level of respect for Jesus as Christ and Lord. John the Baptist told those who came to him that the one who would follow was no mere preacher, he was so exalted that John wasn't even worthy to untie the thong of his sandals (Matt 3:11; Mark 1:7; Luke 3:16; John 1:27). The context here is the same as in Jesus' later washing of the disciples' feet (John 13:1–17).

Traveling in sandals over dirty, dusty roads in a warm climate, where roads often contained dung from animals used for transportation, made feet both sweaty and dirty. This made the handling of sandals and feet extremely distasteful. For this reason, removing sandals or washing feet was considered a task for only the lowliest servants. John placed himself even below these servants in relation to the exalted nature of the Christ. This recognition of Jesus' exaltedness was and is appropriate. The washing of the disciple's feet in no way lowered Jesus, it indicated the nature of his kingdom. In sending out his apostles to make disciples, Jesus said, "All authority has been given to Me in heaven and on earth" (Matt 28:18). We are not following a memory, a figure of the past, a mere memory or idea, but a living Lord who is Lord of all now—even if, at this point in time, all people do not give him the respect he is due.

Discipleship in the New Testament sense also requires association: being with Jesus. Although not present in bodily form since his ascension into heaven, he is present in his Spirit. Jesus said, "I will never desert you, nor will I ever forsake you" (Heb 13:5). Jesus promised, "Lo, I am with you always, even to the end of the age" (Matt 28:20). We must ask Jesus, through his Spirit, to open our minds to his teaching and its relationship to our lives (Jas 1:5). To spend time with Jesus is also to regularly read and meditate upon his teachings, and to spend time with him in prayer. This gives the Holy Spirit both the knowledge and the time to influence our thinking and our lives.

Discipleship requires the application of Jesus' teachings to daily life. Jesus told his apostles that in making disciples they were to teach his followers to "observe all that I commanded you" (Matt 28:20). He said that those who are truly his disciples keep his word (John 8:31). This may sound burdensome, but Jesus had an important teaching in this respect.

Jesus said that his followers would find the "yoke" of his teachings easy and light (Matt 11:30). "The yoke" was a common way to refer to the obligations of the Mosaic law as, for example, in Lamentations 3:27. Jesus was saying that for those who learned from him, the yoke of his teachings was light in comparison to burden of the Mosaic law. In fact, he said those who learned from him would "find rest for your souls" (Matt 11:28–30). This is not because there are no obligations in terms of conduct—the obligation to live a moral life did not disappear with the gospel. Rather, taking on the yoke of Christ removes unnecessary burdens of the Mosaic law, enables his followers to avoid the burdensome consequences of unrighteous behavior, and provides life, strength, and peace through the inner presence of the Holy Spirit.

In addition to following his teachings, we can learn by imitating Jesus, the founder of the faith and the one who has most perfectly lived it (Heb 12:2). We may also learn from others who have made a commitment to follow Christ. Paul, for example, invited the Christians in Corinth to follow him in following Jesus (1 Cor 11:1). Reading about the lives of outstanding Christians is a helpful way to learn from those who exemplified Christlikeness. Since Jesus spent his life serving others; imitation means finding ways to serve the Lord with our time and resources, finding ways to reach out to touch the lives of others, and seeking to bless them just as Jesus blesses us (Phil 2:5–11; Acts 10:38).

In imitating Jesus there are, of course, ways we can do so and ways we cannot. When Jesus interacted with people, he had discernment that is beyond our ability, and he had the ability to do things that we cannot possibly do. We can, nevertheless, follow him in his devotion to God the Father, in his determination to live by Scripture, and in his enabling by the Holy Spirit to overcome the challenges of the world. The example of Jesus and other disciples in overcoming the problems of the world gives us the confidence that we, too, can prevail in our discipleship. Because he suffered and overcame, we can face suffering and overcome. We can also have the confidence that God will use these challenges to help us grow more like Jesus (Jas 1:2–4; Rom 5:1–5; Heb 12:1–13; 1 Pet 1:3–9).

The Decision We Cannot Avoid

Not everyone is ready to make the commitment to become a disciple of Jesus. It is understandable that some people may want to learn more about Jesus before they make that commitment. Serious seeking requires a firm commitment to learn about Jesus, his works, and his teachings, and a determination to let the facts speak for themselves.

Some people try to resolve all questions about what the Bible teaches before placing faith in Jesus. The problem with this approach is the risk of getting bogged down in comparatively minor issues while missing the clear, overall teaching of the Scriptures. It is an issue of priorities. The most important point to settle is who Jesus is and what that means to each of us, and there are plenty of Scriptures in both Testaments clear enough to settle that question. There is also plenty of time to study the more obscure portions of Scripture later on. The important thing is to settle who we are in relation to Jesus and what kind of commitment that requires.

Scripture is clear that everyone stands or falls in their relationship to Jesus because he has been chosen to be the Christ of God. Moses foretold that God would raise up a prophet like Moses, and everyone would be required to listen to this prophet (Deut 18:15, 18–19). Jesus fulfilled this prophecy (Acts 3:22–23; 7:37). Other Scriptures describe how people would be blessed or condemned by their reaction to this prophet (Isa 28:16; Luke 2:25–35; 1 Pet 2:4–10; cf. Ps 118:22–23; Isa 8:14). Therefore, it is important for everyone to settle the issue of their relationship to Jesus Christ. It is a pursuit that should be engaged in honestly and prayerfully.

The commission of Jesus as the Christ, and his successful fulfillment of that role, means that God is reaching out to us in love no matter who we are and what we may have done (1 Tim 1:15–16). Jesus was chosen to be the Christ for our benefit. He has done his part; we need to do ours. Those who give Jesus the full respect he deserves and enter into his fellowship become his disciples.

In any case, seeker or disciple, learning from Jesus means considering both his manner of life and what his teachings mean for our lives.

6

Receiving the Witness

> The testimony which I have is greater than *the testimony of* John; for the works which the Father has given Me to accomplish—the very works that I do—testify about Me, that the Father has sent Me.... You search the Scriptures because you think that in them you have eternal life; it is these that testify about Me... if you believed Moses, you would believe Me, for he wrote about Me.
>
> JOHN 5:36, 39, 46

> How shall we escape if we neglect so great a salvation? After it was at the first spoken through the Lord, it was confirmed to us by those who heard, God also testifying with them, both by signs and wonders and by various miracles and by gifts of the Holy Spirit according to His own will.
>
> HEBREWS 2:3-4

JUST as the Holy Spirit helped earlier servants of God, Jesus' anointing with the Holy Spirit remained with him, helping him to accomplish his unique service to the Father.

The gospels tell us that after Jesus' baptism, the Holy Spirit led him into the wilderness to be tested. The Israelites were led into the wilderness by Moses when they journeyed to Mount Sinai and camped before the mountain. Later, they traveled through the wilderness as they moved toward the land *Yahweh* promised to give them. Supported by the providence of God that gave them water, manna, and quail, and with the presence of God in their midst, many of the Israelites nevertheless failed to be faithful to God. Jesus would go into the wilderness with far less and prove his faithfulness as a human being by depending on the guidance of Scripture and the presence of God's Spirit.

Throughout Jesus' ministry, as he did the will of the Father, the Holy Spirit testified to Jesus' identity through the works Jesus did. The author of Hebrews tells us that the Holy Spirit enabled Jesus to go to the cross—that Jesus "through the eternal Spirit offered Himself without blemish to God" (Heb 9:14). Later, the Holy Spirit would confirm Jesus as the Son of God through resurrection and confirm the preaching of those who first testified that Jesus is Lord and Christ.

The Testimony of Works

All four Gospels testify that the witness of John the Baptist helped prepare the way for the ministry of Jesus. It was through John's witness that Jesus' disciples first came to know him and trust him. However, Jesus insisted that there was a greater witness than John—a witness that only God could give (John 5:36). John's witness could be considered an opinion and was shaken by John's imprisonment; the works that Jesus did were a greater (Gk. *meizō*) witness because they were inseparable from Jesus, often public, and generally impossible to fake. Jesus said that if his hearers couldn't believe his words, they should believe because of his works (John 10:37-38). Indeed, when John the Baptist's faith faltered because of his imprisonment, Jesus referred to his works to assure John that John's faith in Jesus was justified (Matt 11:4-5; Luke 7:22).

An incident in Jesus' ministry shows the importance of the public nature of Jesus' works (Matt 9:1-8; Mark 2:1-12; Luke 5:17-26). At one point, four men carried a paralyzed man on a pallet to Jesus for healing. Jesus was teaching inside a house. The men saw that it was impossible to move the paralyzed man through the crowd, so they climbed to the roof of the house, removed part of the roof, and lowered the paralytic on his pallet through the opening down to Jesus. As you may have guessed, this was not a modern roof—but one more easily broken through and later repaired!

Jesus recognized the faith of those who brought this man for healing, and felt compassion for the crippled man. He told the paralytic that his sins were forgiven. The scribes and Pharisees in the house concluded that Jesus had committed blasphemy because only God can forgive sin. On this point they were correct, only God can forgive sin; but they were not considering the evidence to Jesus' identity. Jesus then challenged his critics to answer which was easier: forgiving sin or healing paralysis. Jesus was pointing out that to say the man's sins were forgiven took only words, whereas healing could not be feigned. Then Jesus told the paralytic to get up and walk to demonstrate that "the Son of Man has authority on earth to forgive sins"

(Mark 2:10). The paralytic was healed immediately and walked out of the house on his own.

Biblical Miracles

The ministry of Jesus Christ was accompanied by miracles. A miracle occurs when the Creator does something in the universe that does not occur by natural means.

Nature has been given the ability to cause things to happen without God's intervention. Perhaps the best example of this is the ability of creatures to bring about new life. We often call birth a miracle because the birth of human beings and certain animals is wonderful. But, technically, birth is not a miracle; it is a natural occurrence. A miracle occurred when Abraham and Sarah gave birth to Isaac past the age Sarah would naturally have been able to bear children. Likewise when John and Elizabeth gave birth to John the Baptist. Even more so, the birth of Jesus by Mary. These births required the intervention of God the Creator.

There are lesser examples of the power of choice in nature, of course. Even when instinct controls behavior, there is some measure of choice in the behavior of animal life. For example, beavers that build a dam to create a safe habitat for their home change the environment for fish and other animals in that area. Bees prosper plants and trees near where they choose to nest, which can have an influence on other animal life in the area. Birds that eat seeds carry those seeds to areas where the wind would never have taken them, changing not only the flora, but also the landscape if erosion is prevented by the plants that grow from the seeds that pass through the birds. The powerful, causative abilities of chemistry and physics are seen throughout the universe. Certain things that result—such as tornadoes, volcanoes, hurricanes, rainbows, and waterfalls—may be extraordinary, but they are in no way miraculous. They follow natural laws.

Some define a miracle as the breaking of a natural law. While this isn't wrong as far as it goes, it is incomplete at best. A miracle—at least a biblical miracle—cannot be defined without reference to a purposeful act of God. This understanding of miracles is important to understanding the fallacy of some arguments against the occurrence of miracles.

As Creator, God is able to work miracles at any time. God's hand is seen in much of the sacred history recorded in Scripture. Historically, however, there have been four periods of time in which most biblical miracles took place: the exodus under Moses, the ministries of the prophets Elijah and Elisha during Israel's kingdom period, the ministry of Jesus, and the foundation of the Christian church. It seems that for vast periods of time in biblical history, miracles, if they occurred, were infrequent.

The author of Hebrews wrote of "signs" (Gk. *sēmeiois*), "wonders" (Gk. *terasin*), and "various miracles"—literally "diverse works of power" (Gk. *poikilais dunamesin*) that accompanied the ministries of those who first preached the gospel of Jesus Christ (Heb 2:4). These should not be considered different types of miracles, but descriptive of all biblical miracles. They are wondrous works, sometimes bringing great blessing, at other times terrifying judgments. They are powerful works—works far beyond what any human being is capable of. And importantly, they are all signs: each points to God as real and able to do works that can only be performed by the Creator. God's ability to do such works is never diminished. He can break into the affairs of earth to do miraculous works whenever he decides it is desirable or necessary to do so. Miracles clustered in a certain period of time indicate that God is moving forward his unique plan of redemption in a significant way.

Miracles in the Ministry of Jesus

Jesus performed many miracles in the course of his ministry, often with crowds present to observe. The events of the final week of Jesus' life—both good and bad—were set in motion when Jesus raised Lazarus from the dead. Mary, Martha, and Lazarus of the town of Bethany were close friends of Jesus. When word came to Jesus that Lazarus was gravely ill, Jesus waited until some time after Lazarus died to go to Bethany (John 11:6, 14).

Jesus had raised others from the dead in the course of his ministry. When Jesus learned that a man carried out of a city for burial was the only son of a widow, he stopped the funeral procession and brought the dead man back to life (Luke 7:12–17). When a little girl Jesus promised to heal passed away before Jesus arrived at her home, Jesus continued to the house and brought the young girl back to life (Luke 8:41–42, 49–56). However, in both cases Jesus intervened in passing, and the deceased had not been dead long.

There seems to be evidence that there was a belief among the Jews that a dead person's spirit left the body after three days. If this is true, it may explain why Jesus delayed his arrival at Bethany for four days.[1] In any case, it would have been obvious to anyone present that Lazarus was past any possible medical attention. Mary and Martha seemed resigned to Lazarus' death when Jesus appeared. Disappointed that Jesus had not come to

---

1. Köstenberger, *John*, 333.

heal their brother, there seemed to be no thought that life could be restored (John 11:39–40). Bodies decompose quickly in Palestine, and no embalming would have been done, causing Martha to object that it would not be a good idea to roll the stone away from the entrance to Lazarus' tomb.

When Jesus raised Lazarus from the dead, it became obvious that Jesus had purposely allowed Lazarus to die and be buried so that Lazarus could be restored to life publicly (John 11:4). This not only highlighted God's sovereignty over life and death, it demonstrated that Jesus was who he claimed to be. Word of what happened spread quickly to nearby Jerusalem, which was within easy walking distance of Bethany.

Reaction to bringing Lazarus back from the dead was mixed. Some of those who came out to praise and welcome Jesus on the first Palm Sunday did so because of the raising of Lazarus (John 12:9–18). On the other hand, when the Jewish religious authorities heard of this, they decided to find a way to put Jesus and Lazarus to death (John 11:38–57; 12:10–11, 19). Interestingly, the religious authorities did not deny that Jesus restored Lazarus to life; they were worried that Jesus' following would grow, and as a result, their influence with the people would diminish. Think about that for a moment!

Jesus' disciples maintained no such skepticism of the ultimate success of Jesus' mission even if they, like Mary and Martha, didn't understand the full consequences of Jesus being "the resurrection and the life" (John 11:25–26). They were present when Jesus did so many other miraculous things. Reminiscent of how God provided manna, quail, and water to the Israelites traveling through the wilderness with Moses, Jesus was able to feed multitudes of people by blessing just a few fish and loaves of bread. They had witnessed Jesus walk on water. Even more dramatically, they had seen Jesus rebuke a severe storm, and the wind and waves became calm. "What kind of a man is this," they asked, "that even the winds and the sea obey Him!" (Matt 8:27). While that miracle was unique, healing miracles were commonplace in Jesus' ministry.

As in the healing of the paralytic discussed above, crowds came to Jesus for healing. The Gospels contain accounts of the healing of specific ailments, including the cleansing of leprosy and the restoration of damaged eyes and limbs. People came for healing in large numbers. In many cases, people were healed of every kind of affliction (Matt 4:23; 8:16–17; 9:35; 12:15; Mark 1:33–34; Luke 6:17–19; cf. Isa 53:4). Imagine what it would be like today if someone went to a hospital and healed everyone no matter the ailment—all hospital beds emptied. This is what it was like when Jesus ministered to the people.

It seems common for critics to claim that the writers of the Gospels believed all diseases were caused by demons. However, the Gospels differentiate between those who were ill due to disease or injury, and those who were afflicted with unclean spirits. In Luke 4:40, for example, Luke tells of the healing of those sick with various afflictions (Gk. *asthenountas nosois poikilais*). In the very next verse, Luke notes that unclean spirits came out of many, but not all, who were healed. There are many examples of healing without the verbal communication that took place when unclean spirits were cast out.

The differentiation between the healing of injuries and disease, and the healing of those afflicted with unclean spirits, is significant. It shows the mastery of Jesus over two different realms: the physical and the spiritual. Collectively, these miracles show Jesus' mastery over all of creation, and testify to Jesus as the Creator, the only one who could have such control over creation. They also reveal the character of Jesus, and thus of God.

Jesus' miracles were not a sideshow or a splashy display. The raising of Lazarus is the only miracle where Jesus waited for spectators to gather. Those miracles that did not relieve suffering or remove immediate peril—such as walking on water and twice telling Peter where to find a bountiful catch of fish—advanced Jesus' ministry. They fit perfectly with Jesus' teaching and preaching ministry. They also foreshadowed Jesus' resurrection from the dead, without which all of the other miracles would have been robbed of any abiding value.

Witnesses to Jesus Christ

In Jesus' time, Jewish students chose a rabbi to teach them about their faith; Jesus, however, chose his twelve disciples—those who would bear witness to his life and teachings after his death and resurrection (with the exception of Judas, the one who would betray him, John 15:16). After Jesus' ascension, the remaining disciples chose someone to take Judas' place. The requirement to be one of the Twelve was to be present with Jesus from the time Jesus was with John the Baptist until the time Jesus ascended into heaven after his resurrection (John 15:26–27; Acts 1:21–26; cf. John 1:35–37). The Holy Spirit would work through these and others to witness to Jesus and his message (John 14:25–26; 16:13–14).

Arguments against the Miraculous

C. S. Lewis observed that Christianity is unique among the religions of the world in that if there are no miracles—especially Jesus' bodily resurrection from the dead—Christianity could not exist.² In this, Lewis was embracing the view of the Apostle Paul (cf. 1 Cor 15:12–20).

In his defense before King Agrippa and Governor Festus, Paul insisted that when he spoke of the resurrection of Jesus from the dead, the words he spoke were true (Gk. *alētheias*) and sound-minded (Gk. *sōphrosynēs*; Acts 26:25). Festus and Agrippa remained unconvinced, even though the events of Jesus life had, as Paul said, "not been done in a corner" (Acts 26:26). Skeptical responses notwithstanding, from the earliest days of the Christian church, the testimony of miracles has been a major part of the Christian argument that Jesus is the Christ. For this reason, miracles have come under attack by those determined to oppose the Christian faith.

One of the more prominent attacks upon the reality of miracles came from the eighteenth-century philosopher David Hume.³ Hume's argument against miracles is considered to be a masterpiece of reasoning by many who oppose Christianity. A careful reading from a Christian perspective, however, finds his arguments unpersuasive.

One of the first observations we can make is that Hume makes strong statements without supporting them. For example, Hume states that there could never be sufficient witnesses to verify that a miracle has taken place. In other words, Hume argues that all witnesses to miracles should be dismissed without even the slightest consideration. Certainly Hume has given some thought to this subject before rendering his position, but he seems to demand that his readers affirm his conclusion without further thought. It is bad enough when something like this is done by a salesman trying to sell us a used car; it is completely unacceptable with something as important as whether God performs miracles.

Second, Hume's logic would seem to hold against a report of anything new, not just miracles. Following this logic, people would have been justified in refusing to consider the reports of those who first saw the Grand Canyon, the reports of the first explorers in Antarctica, or the reports of the first deep-sea divers. Hume doesn't tell us why his argument doesn't apply in those conditions. Certainly Hume is correct to argue against gullibility; there must be a standard by which we filter truth from falsehood. Rumors can come with what seems like good authority, but upon examination are often just somebody's "say-so" rather than fact. We can agree with Hume that we need to be careful when we are told something new and unique.

---

2. Lewis, "Grand Miracle," 80–81.

3. Hume, "Of Miracles," 492–99. First published in *Philosophical Essays concerning Human Understanding* (1748), later published and known today as *An Enquiry concerning Human Understanding*.

However, it is possible to be careful and at the same time not exclude reports of things that are true but outside our experience.

Third, Hume fails to distinguish Christian witnesses to miracles from those of other religions. This seems to be akin to saying that, since there have been many fraudulent claims to cure certain diseases, all who claim to cure these diseases are deceivers or deceived. Lumping snake-oil salesmen and primitive medicine men together with medical researchers and medical doctors ignores the fact that medical science has found cures for some diseases that the others could not cure. Christianity is the only major religion that is based upon historical events (cf. 1 Cor 15:3–11; 1 John 1:1–3; 2 Pet 1:16–18; Luke 1:1–4; 2 Cor 2:17; 4:1–2). We learn of historical events through those who lived during the time they took place.

When given a report of something that is unique, the issue is the integrity of the witness or witnesses. Assuming someone is not telling us something in jest: Do we know this person well enough to trust that he or she is trustworthy? Do we know this person well enough to know their motives? If the witness has integrity, does the witness have the ability to make a good judgment as to whether what he or she reports is true or not? Some people are well motivated, but not good judges of what they experience. Finally, did circumstances give the witness the opportunity to really know whether what he or she reports is true? Or was the experience so fleeting or so remote that the witness didn't have time to be sure of what he or she thought was seen or heard?

Honesty and good judgment are qualities necessary for any good researcher. As to the possibility of myth or fraud, Paul said these events were "not done in a corner" (Acts 26:26). Peter wrote that they did not follow clever myths, but "were eyewitnesses" (Gk. *epoptai genēthentes*) of the "majesty" of Christ (2 Pet 1:16–18). John wrote that they saw, heard, and handled the risen Christ (1 John 1:1–3). These people knew what constituted a good witness, and demonstrated they met those criteria.

The accounts of the miracles performed by Jesus were confirmed by the Twelve (John 15:26–27; Acts 1:1–3, 15–26). We know these men had moral integrity because they had been baptized by John the Baptist; which means they were seeking to be pure before God, the same God who said: "You shall not bear false witness." Another indication that the Gospel accounts are trustworthy is that they show the shortcomings of the disciples. Further, they demonstrated they believed what they said when they put their lives in danger to preach the gospel message and build the church of Jesus Christ.

Regarding the ability to know what they saw, it did not take an expert to tell when people were lame, sick, blind, leprous, infested with evil spirits, or dead, so we know they were also capable of knowing when these people were healed. Finally, the disciples were with Jesus from the time of Jesus' baptism by John until the time of Jesus' ascension into heaven; they had plenty of time to observe Jesus close up. The origins of Christianity are the best documented events of the ancient world.

Fourth, Hume seems to make a major mistake lumping Christian miracles with recurring natural events. Many types of events in the natural world repeat themselves. Even Immanuel Kant, apparently following Hume, fell into the fallacious thinking that unless miracles could be observed frequently, like natural phenomena, there can no evidence that miracles take place.[4] But miracles, by definition, are not at all like natural phenomena.

Tornadoes may not happen every day, but they happen frequently enough to show themselves as real. Meteors don't fall from the sky at rigidly predictable times in precise places; but some meteors fall from the sky in generally predictable intervals and there are similarities in the way they all behave when they enter the atmosphere. Other events, like Galileo's experiments with gravity, may be reproduced at will by controlled experiments. Miracles, on the other hand, are by their very character unique and occasional. They are performed by an intelligent deity to accomplish something unique for one or a relatively small number of individuals at specific points in time. The intention of God is that they not be a normal part of human experience in this age; so they may never be treated the same as recurring natural events. Hence, they are miracles!

Having said that, it is nevertheless also true that the miracles of the New Testament fall into the category of that which is observable and measurable. When the blind see, the lame walk, lepers are cleansed, and the dead live again, the evidence is as clear as any natural event because they occur in the natural world. The diseases Jesus cured were serious afflictions that caused unmistakable harm, so when a cure was affected, the result was also unmistakable. Unlike the patients of modern healers, *every* person who came to Jesus was healed. It is hard to fake a large number of miracles to people who have known and lived with those sick and injured for many years. However, nothing in Scripture leads us to the conclusion that such events should be commonplace.

C. S. Lewis believed that Hume was wrong to think of the probability of miracles as the same as the statistical probability of natural events.[5] Lewis nevertheless saw a different relationship between many biblical miracles and natural events. He observed that the God who performs such miracles

---

4. Kant, *Religion Within the Limits of Reason Alone*, 83–84n**.
5. Lewis, "Grand Miracle," 81.

is the same God who stands behind the universal processes of nature.[6] For example, when Jesus turned water into wine, it was unique because it was instantaneous and without means; whereas, grapevines turn water into grapes, and thus wine, over time on a smaller scale on a regular basis. Again, the conception of Jesus occurred without a human father; whereas, apart from this instance, God uses human fathers to accomplish procreation. These natural processes would not have occurred had God not provided the means. Lewis argues that this does not make miracles less miraculous, but that both miracles and processes in the natural world, despite their important differences, point to the same divine Creator.

Last, Hume fails to recognize that the nature of the miracles performed by Jesus Christ and the early apostles fits with the character of God revealed in both Testaments. When Peter described the ministry of Jesus, he said: "God anointed Him with the Holy Spirit and with power, and . . . He went about doing good and healing all who were oppressed by the devil, for God was with Him" (Acts 10:38). There is no account of Jesus using his power to harm anyone. Nor are there any instances in which Jesus performed a miracle simply as a stunt. Jesus waited until there was an audience before raising Lazarus, but that was because Jesus was offering himself to the Jews as their Messiah (John 12:12–18; Luke 19:28–44).

There were instances in the early Christian church when there were acts of divine judgment. Ananias and Sapphira died because they lied to the leaders of the church. Elymas the magician, a Jewish false prophet, was struck blind for a time for opposing the ministry of Paul and Barnabas (Acts 13:4–12). Paul told the Corinthians that some of their number were sick, weak, or had passed away because they had observed the Lord's Supper without sufficient reverence for Jesus (1 Cor 11:27–30). Such actions were necessary for early Christians to know the gravity of dealing with the living God—that God is still the God revealed in Deuteronomy: a God who rewards righteousness and punishes wickedness (cf. Heb 12:25–29). Those who received these punishments were examples to those who followed. Without these, it would be much easier to mistake the nature of the New Covenant brought through the ministry of Jesus as a license to sin. Nevertheless, almost all of the miracles of the New Testament were miracles of healing rather than punishment. They are all redemptive in the sense that each one is intended to lead us to the Redeemer—our Creator.

C. S. Lewis observed that whether people accept accounts of miracles or not is very much a matter of how they view the world. No one will accept the existence of miracles unless he or she believes both in the consistency

---

6. Lewis, "Miracles," 29–32.

of nature and the existence of a reality beyond nature.[7] People who were present when Jesus performed his miracles had already been prepared by the God of Abraham, Isaac, and Jacob to know that the Creator of all things is involved in the world and sovereign over what he created. Many of the Gentiles who came to faith in Christ in those early days were "God-fearers" like Cornelius. The God-fearers worshipped *Yahweh* at the synagogues and followed the morality taught in the Law, but were not fully obedient to the entire law of Moses. These Gentiles already believed in the sovereignty of *Yahweh* (Acts 10:1–3, 22, 31; cf. Luke 7:1–10). At the same time, the circumstances of Jesus' ministry and the nature of Jesus' teachings presented major obstacles to his acceptance by believing Jews just on the basis of his teachings.

Consider the following:

- The ministry of Jesus Christ lasted only three years at most. This is far less time than other major religious and philosophical teachers who have gained a large following.
- The moral teachings of Jesus were essentially the same as other rabbis of his time, so it was not his moral teachings that made him unique.
- Jesus was put to death on a cross. His followers prepared his body and laid it in a tomb. Yet, afterward, they proclaimed that Jesus is "the resurrection and the life."
- Jesus was arrested and ridiculed by the ruling council of the Jews: the Sanhedrin; by the secular ruler of Palestine: Herod; and by the Roman authorities under Pontius Pilate; following which Jesus was put to death by the ruling authorities in a manner reserved only for those considered to be at the lowest level at society. Yet, his followers proclaimed that Jesus is "King of kings and Lord of lords."
- Worst of all for the Jews, who were devoted to the Law of Moses and fiercely devoted to the one, true God: Jesus was put to death in a manner in which the Law of Moses declared a person was under the curse of God (Deut 21:22–23; cf. Gal 3:13). Yet, Jesus' earliest followers—primarily Jews—maintained that Jesus is the Anointed One of God: the Christ, and nothing less than the divine Son of God, Second Person of the Trinity, equal to God the Father.

Given these circumstances, it is hard to see how Christianity could ever have become established without the strong testimony of miracles—especially without Jesus' bodily resurrection from the dead.

7. Lewis, "Miracles," 27.

The Apostle Paul, as a young man named Saul, knew the leaders of the religious Jewish community personally. They surely would have told Paul all that they knew about Jesus' life and death. If there were strong evidence that Jesus was a charlatan, or that his resurrection was a fake, the Apostle Paul would never have become a disciple of Jesus, let alone an apostle and an evangelist. The evidence that extraordinary things happened in the life and ministry of Jesus confirmed his identity and ministry then as it does today.

7

Receiving the Teaching

When the Helper comes, whom I will send to you from the Father, *that is* the Spirit of truth who proceeds from the Father, He will testify about Me, and you *will* testify also, because you have been with Me from the beginning.... But when He, the Spirit of truth, comes, He will guide you into all the truth ... He will glorify Me, for He will take of Mine and will disclose *it* to you.

JOHN 15:26–27; 16:13–14

For this reason we also constantly thank God that when you received the word of God which you heard from us, you accepted *it* not *as* the word of men, but *for* what it really is, the word of God, which also performs its work in you who believe.

1 THESSALONIANS 2:13

He who has ears to hear, let him hear.

JESUS, LUKE 8:8

At the conclusion of his Sermon on the Mount, Jesus told his listeners that they had a choice: to build their lives upon his teachings and survive, or to ignore his teachings and perish. Just as the Christian faith centers upon Jesus of Nazareth, so, too, the teachings of the Christian faith are based on his teachings.

The Teachings of Jesus as a Trust

The Gospels tell us that many people heard Jesus teach throughout the towns and cities of Palestine, and on some occasions in the temple in Jerusalem. Often, a number of Jesus' followers accompanied him in his travels in addition to the twelve disciples we usually associate with him. We read, for instance, of seventy of his followers that he chose to go ahead of him and minister before he visited a place. Jesus had such confidence in these disciples that he said any acceptance or rejection of their preaching was to be taken as a response to Jesus himself and to God the Father (Luke 10:16). The Scriptures indicate that there were often many more than these with Jesus. For example, Paul wrote that at one point more then five hundred brethren were present with the resurrected Christ. These "brethren" (Gk. *adelphois*, a term that includes both men and women) were devoted followers of Jesus or they would not have been with the resurrected Christ (1 Cor 15:6). They likely had a thorough knowledge of Jesus' teachings. Nevertheless, Jesus' teachings were too important for their preservation to be left to a large, diverse group. Jesus prayerfully chose a small group of individuals to preserve, communicate, and pass down his message.

God generally uses means to achieve his work in this age. When God works directly we say that God works "immediately"—in other words, "without means." God worked immediately when he created the universe from nothing. When a miracle is performed, God works immediately. The healing of the man with a withered hand, for example was granted immediately by Jesus; no doctor, medication, or treatment was involved (Mark 3:1–5). When *Yahweh* first gave the Ten Commandments, he gave them to the Israelites immediately, speaking directly from Mount Sinai to the people gathered below (Exod 19:16—20:20). Later, Moses would be the means by which *Yahweh* would communicate to the people. When Jesus was raised from the dead after his crucifixion, his resurrection was an immediate act of God.

God chooses prophets to whom he often communicates knowledge immediately. Thus Peter talks about prophets being borne along by the Holy Spirit (2 Pet 1:20–21) and Paul can call the Scriptures "God-breathed" (Gk. *theopneustas*, 2 Tim 3:16). God can communicate directly with anyone at any time. No doubt, God still communicates information directly to individuals when there is an urgent need to do so. However, no one should expect God to communicate immediate knowledge frequently or on demand.

The burden of being a prophet of God is a heavy one—requiring great care. What seems like the Lord speaking could be an unholy spirit or our imagination. In Deuteronomy, God cautions the people that they may be tested: if a prophet does a marvelous thing but advises contrary to what God has said, the people are to reject that prophet (Deut 13:1-4). This requires a prophet's message to be consistent with moral and spiritual teachings that are clearly from God. It also requires his listeners to evaluate the message carefully. This is true in the New Testament as well as in the Old (1 Cor 14:32).

God warns that there will be prophets that he did not send (Deut 18:20-22). Some will pretend they represent God, but are serving themselves or Satan (2 Cor 11:13-15). Both Jesus and Paul warn us to observe the lives of those who call themselves prophets to know whether they truly speak for God (Matt 7:15-20; 2 Cor 11:15). These cautions also apply to those who believe God is speaking to them today about their lives or the lives of others. John warned: "Beloved, do not believe every spirit, but test the spirits to see whether they are from God, because many false prophets have gone out into the world" (1 John 4:1). Especially in our time, when the culture encourages people to think that truth is felt, it is essential for Christians to understand that while God may speak directly to us today, it takes more than that something "feels right" to know that one has received direct communication or insight from God (1 Thess 5:19-22).

A little attention to terminology is helpful here. "Revelation" refers to information or insight that is communicated directly from God (e.g., 1 Pet 1:12). "Inspiration" refers to the process whereby God enables his prophets to speak or to write the Scriptures and to reveal exactly what God wants to communicate (2 Tim 3:16; 2 Pet 1:20-21). While the prophets are inspired, it is the product of inspiration, the preaching or the written Scriptures, that provides revelation to others. It is, therefore, the product—the message or the written document, not the person—that has the authority of God vested in it. When God enables those who receive revelation to understand what God has revealed through preaching or the Scriptures, we refer to this as "illumination" or "enlightenment" (Eph 1:15-19; Heb 6:4). All three—revelation, inspiration, and illumination—involve the direct, immediate work of the Holy Spirit; but revelation meant for all people at all times comes only through God's chosen prophets.

Jesus was a prophet, receiving revelation from God and passing it to others (Deut 18:15-19; Acts 3:22-23; 7:37, 51-53; cf. Heb 12:25). This was part of his mission as an apostle of God the Father (Heb 2:3; 3:1). It is important to observe that Jesus taught his disciples in much the same manner as any other teacher. They learned by observing Jesus, listening to his teachings, and asking questions. A prophet, in this case Jesus, is the means whereby God reveals what he wants people to know.

The means by which Jesus would found his church and lay down the sacred tradition for each generation of Christians was the twelve apostles. Jesus spent a night in prayer before deciding who should be in this group (Luke 6:12–16; cf. Mark 3:13–19). He called them "apostles" to indicate the special mission he had for them (Luke 6:13). These were the men he kept closest to himself (John 15:26–27). When it was necessary to select a replacement for Judas, Peter indicated that the replacement must have been with Jesus from the time of Jesus' baptism by John the Baptist until Jesus ascended into heaven after his resurrection (Acts 1:15–26).

An apostle is someone who is sent with a mission. There are different kinds of missions, and thus different kinds of apostles. We need to be careful to understand the specific mission of each one called an apostle. The requirement to be one of the Twelve shows that they were apostles in a unique sense. The ministry of the Holy Spirit to this group was also unique. It was to the Twelve, not to all followers of Jesus, that Jesus promised the Holy Spirit "will guide you into all the truth" (John 16:13). Notice Peter's words in Acts 10:38–42, where he indicates that Jesus carefully chose the primary witnesses to Jesus' life and message.

The presence of the Twelve with Jesus from the time of John the Baptist is important because the coming of Jesus to be baptized by John, and the importance of it, was not published beforehand. That means these men traveled to John to declare their devotion to God, to repent of their sins, and to be baptized by John before they knew of Jesus. These were highly motivated men. They were not just any witnesses, but those who had first committed themselves to God, his commandments, and the Truth. They would not have thought it excusable to misrepresent the life and teachings of Jesus. They provided firsthand, eyewitness experience in the real world (1 John 1:1–5; 2 Pet 1:16–18). The Holy Spirit ensured their recollections and reasoning were accurate (John 16:13).

Paul received both the testimony of Christians and the direct teaching of the Holy Spirit (Gal 1:11–12; 2 Cor 12:1–6). Nevertheless, Paul recognized the importance of the Twelve and the traditions about Jesus that came from them. In his First Letter to the Corinthians, Paul recognized the primacy of the Twelve, placing them before him and distinguishing his calling as an apostle from theirs (1 Cor 15:1–10). He told the Galatians that while the gospel he preached was not deficient with respect to the preaching of the Twelve, yet, he traveled to Jerusalem twice, once specifically to make sure he was preaching the gospel accurately (Gal 1:15–19; 2:1–10). The importance of the Twelve is indicated in the Revelation to John in that the twelve foundation stones upon which the Holy City rests carry "the twelve names of the twelve apostles of the Lamb" (Rev 21:14). It is also indicated in the plan God has for the Twelve in the age to come (Matt 19:28).

The testimony of the Twelve is at the very foundation of the entire New Testament. Though most of the books of the New Testament were written by other than the Twelve, all teachings either derived from their basic testimony or were consistent with their teaching. After the books of the New Testament were written, there were a number of documents written by another generation of Christian leaders known as the Apostolic Fathers. These writers quote from the writings in our New Testament, further guaranteeing the early date and authenticity of our New Testament works. Additional confirmation comes from Eusebius's *Ecclesiastical History*, which was written in the early fourth century and includes quotes from the New Testament.

Other works outside the New Testament that were not referred to by the Apostolic Fathers or Eusebius were written later, and contain teachings thoroughly at odds with those documents that were known to be credible. The Nag Hammadi texts so popular with opponents of traditional Christianity today, for example, were written well after the writings of the New Testament, and promote gnostic beliefs clearly rejected by the early Christian church.[1] There is simply nothing about these other writings that recommends them in place of the writings of the New Testament.

A reliance on the New Testament is a reliance on the teachings of Jesus. Jesus himself is the source of our faith. Importantly, this affects our understanding of the Old Testament as well. While certain teachings of the Old Testament point to Jesus as the Christ, it is because Jesus held the Old Testament as authoritative that Christians do also. It is Jesus and the authoritative Christian tradition of his teachings that provide confidence in the moral and spiritual teachings of both Testaments. And, following this, confidence that God speaks to us authoritatively through these books.

What God Intended Us to Understand

A correct understanding of scriptural teaching begins with the conviction that God intended to make certain things known to us through these writings. If God intentionally molded Scripture to communicate specific things, then our task is to seek what God intended to say to us, not to twist it to some other meaning. Quick judgments are sometimes deceiving. Our first impression of what a Scripture teaches may feel comfortable and right—and still be badly mistaken. Unfortunately, not all people seem to understand

---

1. For a good treatment of this subject, see Green, *Books the Church Suppressed*.

that their impression of what Scripture teaches may not be what God intended to communicate.

Not far from where I live, there are a number of hills that, viewed from a distance, resemble an enormous man sleeping on his back. A portion of this area has been set aside as Sleeping Giant State Park. It seems that Native Americans who settled this area believed that a good spirit cast a spell on an evil spirit to make the evil spirit stay asleep. This sleeping spirit was thought to be the "sleeping giant" underneath the earth, rocks, trees, and shrubs of the hills. Of course, there is no giant underneath even though there may appear to be; the "giant" was only ever present in people's imaginations. It appears to be something, but it is something else. Most of us have looked at clouds or other natural objects and seen a pattern that resembled something else—a psychological phenomenon called pareidolia. Similarly, some people read a portion of Scripture and imagine what it means to them. If it seems right, and feels right, they believe they know what God is saying through that text. However, in too many cases, it is not what God intended to communicate to us—it is a simply a product of their imagination.

Peter spoke of two types of people who twist the Scriptures in a destructive manner: the unstable and the ignorant (2 Pet 3:16). There is a cost of devotion that the unstable (Gk. *astēriktoi*) are unwilling to pay. Their lack of commitment to the Lord and to the truth leave them open to evil influences that can lead them to live outside the will of God (2 Pet 1:9; 2:18–22; 3:16; cf. Jas 1:6–8). The faithful have a deep appreciation for God's saving grace and live accordingly (2 Pet 1:1–8, 10–15; 3:1–13). Nevertheless, they, too, are prone to go astray if they don't take the time to truly understand what they read (2 Pet 3:14–18).

The effect of misinterpreting Scripture is often negative, and sometimes strongly so, whether a person is well-motivated or not. Of course, a great deal of Scripture is understandable to most people if they read carefully and take the plain meaning. Yet, as Peter also points out in his second letter, there are "some things" in the Scriptures that are "hard to understand" (Gk. *en hais estin dysnoēta tina*, 2 Pet 3:14–16). The best approach is to be humble and to search carefully for what God is communicating to us. The things God seeks to communicate are important; so to misunderstand can have serious consequences.

One person who did not follow a careful approach was Søren Kierkegaard. Kierkegaard was a bright, devout Christian who lived in Denmark in the early 1800s. He became obsessed with the story of Abraham and Isaac on Mount Moriah, devoting a book entitled *Fear and Trembling* to this subject.[2]

---

2. Kierkegaard's *Fear and Trembling* was first published in 1843 under the

Kierkegaard should have paid more attention to the fact that an angel stopped Abraham from sacrificing Isaac. It is obvious from the text of Genesis that God had no intention of allowing Abraham to sacrifice his son. Further, Abraham had God's promise of posterity through Isaac; so Abraham complied with God's command convinced that God would somehow fulfill his promise. The author of Hebrews tells us that Abraham was so confident of God's promise that he believed God would even raise Isaac from the dead if necessary (Heb 11:17-19). It was a test, a test that only God can rightly give, and a test that was unique to Abraham as the father of a great nation.

Because Abraham would become not only the father of all the faithful who were his blood descendants but also the spiritual father of all who have true faith in God, there is and never has been any other individual to whom God has given the same test (Gal 3:6-9; Rom 4:1-25). The story of Abraham is thus part of a larger narrative in Scripture: a narrative that first emphasizes God's plan as it is worked out through the people Moses led out of Egypt, and second emphasizes God's saving plan for all the people of the world through Jesus Christ. Unfortunately, Kierkegaard failed to recognize this.

Kierkegaard focused only on the command to Abraham to sacrifice Isaac, and was offended that God would ever ask such a thing of anyone. Kierkegaard came to the erroneous conclusions that God is irrational and that God makes himself difficult to find for all but those completely devoted to seeking him.

As Creator, God should be expected to reveal himself when and where he chooses, and to reveal only as much as he chooses. This would be intimidating were it not that God is a God of love who continually reaches out to show kindness and blessing. He is a deliverer and savior, not just the Creator.

A loving God may control how and when we can know him, but he does not hide himself. The Scriptures plainly show us a God who wants to be found, and thus a God who wants us to understand what he says to us. The Old Testament relates stories of judgment upon the wicked—but more importantly, it tells of God's restraint. God did not kill Adam and Eve when they sinned. He saved Noah's family from the flood. He continued to guide Abraham even after Abraham sinned by fathering Ishmael. He did not allow Lot and his daughters to die when bringing judgment on Sodom and Gomorrah. He continued to work out his plan through the Hebrews in spite of their many, many lapses into sin. He even spared the people of Assyria after Jonah preached to them and they repented. If God were not a

---

pseudonym Johannes de Silentio.

God who delays punishment so people have a chance to experience mercy, there would be no Old Testament, no coming of Jesus, no New Testament (2 Pet 3:3–9). We wouldn't be here to read about these things or have the opportunity to be present in the age to come—a future in which God wants to bless us throughout eternity (Eph 2:1–7; cf. Rom 5:6–11). This mercy includes communication.

The expressions "inerrancy" and "infallibility," applied to Scripture, are based on the idea of intentionality: because God is good, intelligent, caring, strong, and wise, God gives us the Scriptures with the intention of communicating certain things to us. When we understand what God intends to communicate, we will find that it is completely worthy of our trust. Therefore, what God communicates is without error (inerrant), and the guidance it gives is always reliable (infallible). Much of this is declarative truth: things God tells us directly. But Scripture also presents material meant to help us learn by example from the experiences of those who lived before (Rom 15:4; 1 Cor 10:1–6).

Ancient Meaning Governs Ongoing Application

A successful approach to Scripture seeks to understand what God intended to communicate to the original readers before drawing conclusions for today. In other words, before we can understand what God is saying to us, we must understand what God was saying to them. To be sure, the Bible is a universal book. The Scriptures were given to be useful to all people through all of the years the writings are in existence. They reveal universal lessons and truths applicable to all times. However, each book or letter also had an original audience, and because God doesn't change, what he communicated to the original audience must form the basis of our understanding of what is revealed to all later readers.

The opposite of this is to open the Bible and immediately take the words as applying to us in our situation today. Some people believe they can receive divine guidance by throwing open the Bible and reading where the Bible opens, or by sticking their finger into the Bible while their eyes are closed. The verses found this way are often so irrelevant to the guidance sought it is comical; but it is all too often misleading and harmful as well. It is also harmful when the culture and circumstances of the original writing are not taken into consideration in interpreting Scripture. It takes more effort to read the Scriptures as they were first written and then draw conclusions to life in our own times, but it is far more helpful. For example: who was the Law of Moses given to and for what purposes? These are questions we must ask if we are to understand its meaning for today.

Further, every Scripture reading must be understood in the context of the entire Bible. For example, the question of the proper place of the Law of Moses in the life of a Christian cannot be decided by reading the Law of Moses alone. The writings of the New Testament help us to understand the purpose of the Law after the resurrection of Christ. In addition, other parts of Scripture, both Old and New Testaments, show us the moral character of God. From this we can conclude that while the civil and ceremonial laws of the Law of Moses applied only to the Hebrews, the moral and spiritual teachings of the Law are still in effect. We do not, for example, offer sacrifices for our sins at a temple, or eat only the foods allowed by the Law of Moses, or need to observe the feasts defined there. However, as set forth in the Ten Commandments, it is still immoral to worship idols, lie, steal, commit adultery, or take someone's life without sufficient justification (such as self defense). Similarly, the prohibitions of the Old Testament against idolatry, against involvement in occult practices, and against false religions have not passed away. There are often general lessons even if we do not obey specific laws. For example, when we learn that many of the dietary and civil requirements of the Law of Moses protected the health of the Hebrews, we learn that God wants us to take care of our bodies. We should eat wisely and follow the best medical advice.

With regard to justice, culpability and penalties were no longer to be governed solely by emotion once the Law came into effect. The Law of Moses set standards for witnesses, set uniform penalties for offenses, and stopped blood feuds by placing justice in the hands of the community rather than individuals. Following Jesus, Paul recognized the ongoing application of certain parts of the Mosaic law for church discipline (Matt 18:16; 1 Tim 5:19; Deut 17:6; 19:15; cf. Num 35:30). This has continuing application to justice generally as well, forming a basis for criminal justice in the Western world.

The Old Testament, then, must not be discarded. Not only does the Old Testament provide important groundwork for understanding God and his ways, without it the New Testament cannot be properly understood. An understanding of the Old Testament aids greatly in helping readers to understand the last book of the Bible, the Revelation to John, which has more references and allusions to the Old Testament than any other book in the New Testament. At the same time, it is only as we look at the writings of the Old Testament from the perspective of the New Testament that we can understand the proper place of the earlier writings in our lives. The Revelation to John shows the ultimate fulfillment of biblical teaching. All of this follows from understanding the writings as they were originally given.

From this it also follows that God did not reveal what he wanted us to know all at once, but continued to add to his message over time. The theological term for this is "progressive revelation." By reading each part as it was meant to be understood, seeing each book of the Bible as part of a whole, and observing the development of teaching, it is possible to understand each part of the Bible in its place. There will still be some parts of Scripture that we do not understand. We should be honest to differentiate what we know for certain, what we believe to be true, and what we don't know. Fortunately, there is much we can know, and what we are able to know is sufficient for our spiritual needs—if not always to satisfy our curiosity.

Returning to Kierkegaard, although a reverent, sincere Christian, he did not keep these concepts in mind. By reading the story of Abraham on Mount Moriah as an isolated text, Kierkegaard missed that while God did not require Abraham to go through with sacrificing his son, God the Father did require his Son, Jesus Christ, to die on a cross. This contrast is even more striking given that Mount Moriah was the site of the temple in Jerusalem, and Jesus was crucified not far from the temple. Humanly speaking, Jesus traced his lineage back to Abraham. It was necessary for Abraham, as father of the nation from which the Christ would come, to understand something of the high cost that was necessary for humanity to find salvation. It was not wrong for Kierkegaard to understand the emotional strain upon Abraham as Abraham went to do something that would be horrible for anyone to contemplate—especially someone who had waited so long for a son. But it was wrong for Kierkegaard to brood over this and to isolate this account from the full teaching of Scripture. We are no less susceptible than Kierkegaard to mistaking the true meaning of Scripture. If we are wise we will learn from his mistakes.

Serving God with Our Minds

Scripture teaches us that it is not enough just to love God with our emotions; we must love God with our minds. It is also true that even though some truths are more important than others, as John Calvin—following Augustine—recognized: all truth is God's truth.[3] Therefore, we should not allow ourselves to be limited unnecessarily in our efforts to think correctly before God. We cannot divorce how we think from the way we live our lives.

There is a misunderstanding because of the different way we use the word "heart" in our time from the way it is used in the Bible. Today we often use "heart" as a metaphor for emotions separate from reasoning. That

---

3. Calvin, *Institutes of the Christian Religion*, 1.2.1 and 2.2.15–16; cf. Augustine's *Confessions*, 5:6 and 7:9–10.

leaves the impression that every time the Scripture refers to the heart, it is speaking solely of human emotions. In reality, both the Hebrew words for "heart" in the Old Testament, *lēb, lēbāb*, and the Greek word for "heart" in the New Testament, *kardia*, refer to the heart as the seat of the entire, inner life of the mind. This includes emotions to be sure, but also includes beliefs, attitudes, understandings, and thinking processes. Writing of the Old Testament, Andrew Bolling observed,

> In its abstract meanings, "heart" became the richest biblical term for the totality of man's inner or immaterial nature. . . . The whole spectrum of emotion is attributed to the heart. . . . Thought functions may be attributed to the heart. . . . Wisdom and understanding are seated in the heart. . . . The heart is the seat of the will[4]

Similarly, Johannes Behm writes of the New Testament

> that the heart is the centre of the inner life of man and the source or seat of all the forces and functions of soul and spirit is attested in many different ways in the NT. . . . In the heart dwell feelings and emotions, desires and passions. . . . The heart is the seat of understanding, the source of thought and reflection. . . . The heart is the seat of the will, the source of resolves.[5]

A large portion of Jesus' Sermon on the Mount is devoted to stressing the inward nature of righteousness and sin (Matt 5:21—6:18). This was a strong rebuke of Jewish culture during the life of Christ. Today, many interpret this to mean they should never have an inappropriate thought come into their heads or they should never experience negative emotions. However, these are unavoidable. Human emotions are physiological; we can control them to some extent with the Lord's help by our general attitude toward what happens all around us, but we cannot eliminate them. There is no state of grace in this age where we will not be subject to trials and temptation. What matters is what we do with negative thoughts and emotions. If we discard inappropriate thoughts quickly and redirect the energy of negative emotions in a positive direction, we do no sin. However, if we entertain and nurse negative thoughts and emotions, we will, as James taught, inevitably fall into sin (Jas 1:13–15). In the Sermon on the Mount, Jesus discusses those who hold on to negative thoughts and emotions as if the inner thought life doesn't matter.

---

4. Bolling, "*lēb, lēbāb*," in *TWOT*, 1:466–67.
5. Behm, "*kardia*," in *TDNT*, 1:611–12.

The Apostle Paul was distressed that his fellow Jews had a zeal for God that was "not according to knowledge" (Gk. *ou kat' epignōsin*, Rom 10:2). Confronting Jews who exhibited this problem, Jesus said, "Do not judge according to appearance (Gk. *kat' opsin*), but judge with righteous judgment (Gk. *tēn dikaian krisin krinete*, John 7:14–24)." Since we all have a tendency to live by our own standards, we must all learn to look at things as God would have us see them (Isa 53:6; cf. Prov 12:15; Deut 12:8; Judg 17:6; 21:25).

Often when the Scriptures speak of knowledge in relation to God, they speak of "knowing" in the same sense that we "know" our friends and relatives (e.g., John 17:3; Phil 3:8). This kind of knowing is the very foundation of a Christian life. At other times, the stress is not on personal relationship, but what is learned from instruction or experience, leading to discernment. The Apostle Paul told the Ephesians that love is more important than knowledge (Eph 3:19; cf. 1 Cor 13:8, 13). Nevertheless, later he exhorted them not to be foolish (Gk. *aphrones*), but to understand (Gk. *suniete*) "the will of the Lord" (Eph 5:17).

Paul's prayer for the Philippians was that they would continue to increase in love. As they did so, there would be an increase "in real knowledge and all discernment" (Gk. *en epignōsei kai pasēi aisthēsei*, Phil 1:9). This increase would come, at least in part, from the instruction Paul was about to give in his letter, involving both theological truth and practical instruction—all of which was directed toward the way the Philippians lived (Phil 1:9–11; 1:27—2:15).[6] Similarly, in Colossians, Paul writes, "We have not ceased to pray for you and to ask that you may be filled with the knowledge of His will (Gk. *tēn epignōsin tou thelēmatos autou*) in all spiritual wisdom and understanding (Gk. *en pasēi sophiai kai sunesei pneumatikēi*), so that you will walk in a manner worthy of the Lord, to please *Him* in all respects, bearing fruit in every good work and increasing in the knowledge (Gk. *auxanomenoi tēi epignōsei*) of God" (Col 1:9-10). The author of Hebrews also envisioned a growth in discerning good from evil as Christians live out their faith (Gk. *tēn hexin ta aisthētēria gegymnasmena echontōn pros diakrisin kalou te kai kakou*, Heb 5:14). This requires a lifelong process of the Lord opening our minds in response to prayer coupled with the discipline of meditating upon God's Word.

The early Pietist movement, initiated by Philipp Jakob Spener (1635–1705), came to promote what many came to refer to as "heart religion not head religion." Spener was concerned because so many Christians held to correct doctrines but did not have the warm devotion to Christ

---

6. Alford, *Alford's Greek Testament*, 3:155–56.

characteristic of Martin Luther. Pietists sought warmhearted devotion to the Lord rather than a cold, intellectual faith. That Spener wasn't interested in emotions alone is shown in that he promoted the practice of the *collegia pietatis*, the "fellowship of the pious"—weekly group Bible study to promote an informed faith. Though few know it by this terminology today, group Bible study remains a common practice in many evangelical Christian churches. In any case, Scripture requires a devotion of the mind, not just emotion. Nevertheless, the true goal should be "heart and head religion," not just one or the other. Paul said, "I will pray with the spirit and I will pray with the mind also (Gk. *kai tōi noi*); I will sing with the spirit and I will sing with the mind also (Gk. *kai tōi noi*)" (1 Cor 14:15).

A correct interpretation of a portion of Scripture will also take into consideration the traditional interpretation of that Scripture. While archaeology and the study of ancient languages has led to new insights about life in ancient times, the central teachings and morality of Christianity have long been established in ways that do not lend themselves to change. It is important to stress that we are talking about major Christian doctrines and morality here.

The Methodist theologian Thomas Oden refers to the canon of St. Vincent of Lérins (died ca. 450). St. Vincent taught that what should be believed by Christians is what "has been believed everywhere, always, and by all"; in the original Latin: *quod ubique, quod semper, quod ab omnibus creditum est*.[7] John Wesley referred to this rule in determining Christian belief and practice.[8] According to this canon, Oden explains, "any new scholarship claiming fidelity to the apostolic tradition must be tested by the texts of the written Word and by the historical memory of the meaning of the written Word."[9] This defines what is referred to as "orthodox Christianity" (notice, small "o").

---

7. Oden, *Rebirth of Orthodoxy*, 156–86.

8. Wesley, "A Roman Catechism, Faithfully Drawn Out of the Allowed Writings of the Church of Rome," in *Works*, 10:128.

9. Oden, *Rebirth of Orthodoxy*, 167.

8

Understanding God

Do you not know? Have you not heard?
The Everlasting God, the Lord, the Creator of the ends of the earth
Does not become weary or tired.
His understanding is inscrutable. . . .
Thus says God the Lord,
Who created the heavens and stretched them out,
Who spread out the earth and its offspring,
Who gives breath to the people on it and spirit to those who walk in it,
"I am the Lord, I have called you in righteousness. . . .
I am the Lord, that is My name;
I will not give My glory to another,
Nor My praise to graven images."

ISAIAH 40:28; 42:5–6, 8

Thus says the Lord, "Let not a wise man boast of his wisdom, and let not the mighty man boast of his might, let not a rich man boast of his riches; but let him who boasts boast of this, that he understands and knows Me, that I am the Lord who exercises lovingkindness, justice and righteousness on earth; for I delight in these things," declares the Lord.

JEREMIAH 9:23–24

People travel great distances to see the natural wonders of the world. Crowds gather to see those who are stronger, faster, more athletic, smarter, wealthier, larger, and especially, it seems, more beautiful than others. By this measure, there should be no shortage of people who seek God.

UNDERSTANDING GOD

The Christian theologian Anselm (1033–1109) described God as "a being than which none greater can be conceived."[1] Indeed, God far exceeds anything in creation in every way. King David expressed the wish to "dwell in the house of the Lord all the days of my life, to behold the beauty of the Lord" (Ps 27:4). Great crowds sought to see and to be with Jesus when he walked the earth. Paul wrote that when Jesus returns at the end of this age, he will be "marveled at among all who have believed"; in other words, even those who knew him and looked for his return will find him more wonderful than they ever expected (2 Thess 1:10). Truly, this will be the fulfillment of the David's words: "In your presence is fullness of joy; in your right hand there are pleasures forever" (Ps 16:11; cf. 1 Cor 2:9; Isa 64:4).

Further, understanding what God has revealed about himself and what that means for us is important in knowing how to respond to him. To misunderstand God is to be as foolish as someone who tries to play chess by the rules of checkers. God is known only as he reveals himself to us; but we are fortunate because God has made himself known in many ways, and, of course, supremely in Jesus Christ. A proper understanding of God also helps us to better understand ourselves.

God Revealed through His Creation

Most thinkers and philosophers throughout history have recognized that there is something greater than the physical universe that explains its existence. Most have concluded that a deity is responsible. However, many in our time seem to congratulate themselves for discovering the wonders of the universe without truly pondering how such wonders could have come about. The scientist and philosopher Charles Sanders Peirce (1839–1914) published a paper late in his life in which he argued that no one who truly contemplates the origin of the beauty and sophistication of our natural universe could doubt the reality of a divine Creator.[2] Scripture tells us that the universe elicited faith from Abraham, Job, Isaiah, and the psalmists.

Peirce also thought that the ability to understand the universe should not be taken for granted. He was impressed with the ability of human beings to theorize about the universe in a manner that corresponds with reality. In a letter written just a few years before his death, Peirce affirmed his belief that this ability comes from our Creator.[3] In this, Peirce agreed with John Calvin,

---

1. Thompson, "Ontological Arguments," 59.

2. Peirce, "Neglected Argument for the Reality of God," in *Essential Peirce*, 2:434–50. First published in 1908.

3. Peirce to Mr Kehler, 22 June 1911 (L231), in *New Elements of Mathematics*, vol. 3.1, 206. Peirce called theorizing "retroduction." The appeal of theorizing, for Peirce, is

who taught that understanding and progress in all disciplines of knowledge comes from the Lord.[4] Along the same lines, C. S. Lewis argued that the ability to understand the universe could not likely come from evolution, for evolution is only affected by what promotes survival, not accuracy of understanding.[5]

Similarly, the ability to understand God requires explanation. Certainly there are lots of creatures on our planet that do just fine without a single thought about their Creator. From an evolutionary standpoint, it would seem that the ability to cope with any situation or threat would be faster without taking time to think about deity, religion, and morality. Yet, human beings have a hunger for spiritual knowledge and spiritual fulfillment. As St. Augustine (354–430) observed, the human heart is not at peace until there is peace with God.[6]

Paul told the Romans there are two things that, though invisible, should be crystal clear about God from creation: his divinity (*theiotēs*) and his eternal power (*aidios autou dynamis*, Rom 1:20). In other words, there should be no doubt that the universe is the creation of a divine being. Modern science has increased our knowledge of both the intricacies and the enormous size of our universe. Only a vastly intelligent and powerful being could bring all of this into existence.

At the same time, while we can know some things about God from the universe, the universe is not God, nor is it a part of God; it is *other* than God. Therefore, while it is reasonable to conclude that we can learn some things about the Creator from the nature of the universe, it is not reasonable to assume that we can take everything about the universe and reason back to the nature of its Creator. Beyond divine power, intelligence, and creativity, what we know of God can only come as he reveals himself by his actions and his words.

The Nature and Character of God

It should come as no surprise to anyone that God is unlike any other being that exists. What we know about God from creation prompts us to consider those characteristics that God has revealed about himself.

---

that he considered it to be the only kind of reasoning that can produce new knowledge.

4. Calvin, *Institutes of the Christian Religion*, 2.2.15–16.
5. Lindsley, "C.S. Lewis on Miracles."
6. Augustine, *Confessions*, 1:1.

God Is Holy

The prayer Jesus used to teach us how to pray begins with the petition: "Hallowed be your name," or more literally, "Let your name be sanctified" (Gk. *hagiasthētō to onoma sou*, Matt 6:9, Luke 11:2). It is an appeal for the holiness of God to be recognized on earth and for people to respond with appropriate reverence. Sometimes used solely to describe just one aspect of God's character, the word "holy" is often used for the character and nature of God viewed as a whole. In the exalted, throne-room visions of God, for example, we are told of creatures who continually remind all present that God is holy (Isa 6:1–7; Rev 4:1–11).

The meaning of "holiness" is always dependent upon the deity this concept is applied to. A temple, for example, is holy to the deity or deities worshipped at that temple. So, what was holy to the Baals—the false gods worshipped in Palestine in Old Testament times—differed from what was "holy" to the God of the Hebrews. The activities at a temple to Baal differed from the activities at a temple to the Egyptian god Amon-Re, both differed from the Greek temple of Apollo at Delphi, and all differed from what the Law of Moses required at the Hebrew tabernacle described in Exodus. This is true even though there were similarities: all had temple buildings, all had priests, all had altars, all had sacrifices, all prayed to a deity, and so forth.

"Holy" in relation to a deity reflects back on the nature of that deity. Paul wrote to the Corinthians that people worship many different deities that are called "lord," but there is only one true God (1 Cor 8:5–6). Therefore, God the Creator of all, the only true God, has his own holiness, and this sets the standard for what may legitimately be considered holy in his creatures (1 Pet 1:14–16; Lev 11:44–45; 19:2; 20:7).

The concept of holiness includes completeness: there is nothing lacking in God. It also includes proportion; each part of his nature and character are in perfect balance with every other part. Thus, while accurate to discuss certain aspects of God' nature and character, it can lead to problems when God is treated as less than a whole, or when one of his attributes is pitted against another. Love and justice in God's character, for example, are in perfect harmony with one another.

The Old Testament teaches that the only true God is holy in terms of his steadfast love, purity, wisdom, righteousness, justice, power, and perfections. These teachings were so contrary to the cultures of the ancient world that it was essential to establish them fully before giving more detail. Throughout the Scriptures there is an emphasis upon the uniqueness, purity, perfections, and wholeness of God's holy character. Everything following that is said about God's character and nature is part of his unique holiness.

God Is Self-Existent

Our existence as creatures is dependent upon our ability to have many things: air, water, food, clothing, a moderate temperature, shelter from severe weather, and so forth. Our Creator does not need anything apart from himself to exist. Rather, he is the source of everything else that exists. It has been a topic of serious consideration among some reverent Christian philosophers whether God is constrained by anything outside himself. The answer is that there is absolutely nothing that exists that does not have its origin in God, nothing apart from God that he did not create; therefore, God is not constrained by anything outside himself—even ideas and concepts. God is only constrained by his own character and nature. That is often difficult for creatures like ourselves to comprehend, but it is the clear teaching of Scripture, nonetheless.

Paul wrote to the Corinthians, "For us there is *but* one God, the Father, from whom are all things (Gk. *ta panta*), and we *exist* for Him; and one Lord, Jesus Christ, by whom are all things (Gk. *ta panta*), and we *exist* through Him" (1 Cor 8:6). Paul wrote of Jesus that "all things have been created through Him and for Him . . . and in Him all things hold together (Gk. *synestēken*)" (Col 1:16–17). John wrote that all things were created through God the Son, and without him nothing came in to being that became (John 1:3). In the Revelation, God is called the one "who was and who is and who is to come"—the one who is eternal—the one who always has been and who always will be (Rev 4:8; cf. 1:4).

Most religions conceive of the universe existing in cycles of time. Just as there is winter, spring, summer, fall, and then winter again—a cycle of death to life to death that repeats countless times—they conceive the universe and everything in it as existing in a series of cycles—some relatively brief, some requiring aeons. Pagan gods are considered to be part of nature. Only the god considered to be the "primal stuff" of the universe is generally thought to be ongoing, the god that represents all of nature. The God of the Bible is thus wholly different. He exists separately from the material of the universe, which depends on him, not vice versa. He not only has life, he is life itself.

There is nothing that can ever harm, destroy, or diminish God. The theological term for God's self-existence is *aseity*. Put in simpler terms: God is immortal, eternal, indestructible. God alone has immortality (Gk. *ho monos echōn athanasian*, 1 Tim 6:16). This is the absolute basis for everything else about God. It is an important reason to trust God both now and in the future.

Jesus taught that because God is life, God is able to give life to others (John 5:26; cf. 1 Tim 6:13). Paul called God *aphthartō*, which means imperishable, incorruptible (1 Tim 1:17). He wrote that part of the good news is that God is able to communicate life (*zōēn*) and incorruptibility (Gk. *aphtharsian*) to human beings (2 Tim 1:10; cf. 1 Cor 15:52–55).

Earlier we discussed how God's revelation of his self-existence to Moses at the burning bush served as a guarantee that God would always be present to fulfill his promises to the Israelites. That same assurance is at the heart of Jesus' promise, "I am with you always," for Jesus, too, can say of himself: "I am" (Gk. *egō eimi*), and so he will always *be* (Matt 28:20; John 8:58).

God Is Spirit

Jesus taught, "God is spirit" (*pneuma ho theos*, John 4:24). The word "spirit" does not mean that God is unreal or just an idea. God preexisted the physical creation that is our universe; therefore, he is necessarily of different substance than creation. He has created other beings that are purely spiritual in nature, such as cherubim and angels. These purely spiritual creatures existed before the physical universe we know (Job 38:4–7). That does not mean that God is shut out of the universe of which we are part. God's presence and the spiritual beings that he has created are able to function in and interact with creation as God wills. The physical world that we are part of is sustained by his will, without which neither the physical universe nor we would exist (Col 1:16–17; Heb 1:3).

God and other spiritual beings do not have gender. God is generally referred to in Scripture with male pronouns and roles; however, God also portrays himself in terms of motherhood when appropriate (Isa 66:13; Luke 13:34). An emphasis upon the feminine would have presented a greater potential for misunderstanding the one, true God given how feminine deities were perceived in other religions of the ancient Near East.

Human roles attributed to God are analogies, and as such there are important differences as well as a similarities. God is certainly not guilty of the abuses of those roles by human beings. Accusations to the contrary are clearly refuted by his words and actions (Isa 5:1–6; 48:1–22; 58:1–11; Jer 9:24; Ezek 18:1–32; Hos 11:1–4; 13:4–5).

The association of God with human roles is important, but only in helping us understand the Lord's role in our lives. The predominant use of male pronouns and roles is a warmer way to refer to God because it emphasizes that God is personal, a living being, not an inanimate object. Speaking of a "Father-Son" relationship within the Trinity is especially meaningful.

It means no more to speak of God in this way than to attribute a face, eyes, ears, mouth, arms, or hands to God; to distort *any* of these anthropomorphic ways of speaking of God is to forget who God is. This does nothing to value men or women more than the other, nor does it diminish the biblical teaching of the full image of God in both men and women (Gen 1:26–27). Therefore, the scriptural precedent should be followed. John Oswalt observes, "All that is personally and spiritually true of mothers and fathers is true of God. But he is not of the same essence as we, and to begin to blur the distinction is to lose our grip on reality and be plunged into an abyss."[7]

It is because God is other than the physical universe that we cannot see him (John 1:18). Paul writes that God "dwells in unapproachable light" (Gk. *phōs oikōn aprositon*, 1 Tim 6:16). This is partly because sin has formed a separation between human beings and God's presence; but to a greater degree, because he is a purely spiritual being (apart from the incarnate Christ). We cannot see him unless he chooses to manifest his presence to us.

We are able to understand many things about God. Nevertheless, God, in his totality as a spiritual being, is incomprehensible. His greatness in many areas is far beyond anything that our finite brains can fully imagine. Even though we are spiritual beings as well as physical beings, the world our senses generally make most real to us at this point in time is the physical world. From the garden of Eden on, the source of doubt and disobedience is focusing on the immediate physical realities of creation while forgetting the more permanent, underlying reality of the spiritual realm. Read through the Bible with this in mind, and notice how again and again the sin is looking at what is physical and nearby, and forgetting God. Moses, for example, acted as if his rod had the power to bring water from rock when, instead of following the Lord's command to simply speak to a rock, he hit the rock with his rod (Num 20:8–12). It seems like such a small thing here because Moses had been told to use the rod before; but placing faith in God rather than physical items is at the very foundation of the Old Testament versus the magic and idolatry of the pagans. Paul wrote of those who are in fellowship with God, "We look not at the things which are seen, but at the things which are not seen; for the things which are seen are temporal, but the things which are not seen are eternal" (2 Cor 4:18).

The power of the spiritual realm often surprises and overwhelms those who experience it. The list of those who were surprised or terrified by God's presence includes: the Israelites who heard God speak at Mount Sinai; those who saw the shining face of Moses after Moses had been in the presence of God; Elijah's servant at the revelation of horses and chariots of fire; Isaiah

---

7. Oswalt, *Isaiah: Chapters 40–66*, 679.

after coming into the presence of God; Ezekiel at his vision of the Lord; Daniel after receiving revelations that made him exhausted and sick; Zacharias when the angel announced that Zacharias and Elizabeth would have a son who would become John the Baptist; the shepherds who heard the angelic announcement of Jesus' birth; the disciples when they saw Jesus walk on water; Peter, John, and James at the transfiguration; the disciples when the resurrected Christ appeared to them; Saul on the road to Damascus; Cornelius at the vision of an angel, and John at his vision of Christ (Exod 20:18–20; 34:29–35; 2 Kgs 6:15–17; Isa 6:1–7; Ezek 1:26–28; Dan 7:28; 8:27; 10:4–9; Matt 14:22–27; 17:1–8; Luke 1:8–17; 2:8–14; 9:28–36; Luke 24:36–43; Acts 9:1–9; 10:1–4; 26:12–15; Rev 1:12–17). However, for God's people, the spiritual realm will one day be comforting rather than intimidating.

Scripture teaches that at a future time of God's own choosing, the spiritual will engulf and transform the physical creation. This will not eliminate the physical world; but it will transform it, bringing the spiritual and the physical into harmony, and eliminating all the shortcomings of the current creation.

God Is Sovereign

God is sovereign because there is nothing else like him, nothing else more powerful than he is. Everything else that exists has been created by him, and so is subject to him. God is thus transcendent—far above everything he has created. He is therefore called the Almighty, the All-Powerful, the Omnipotent (Gk. *ho pantokratōr*). He cannot be forced to do anything that is against his will. The only limits upon God are those imposed by his own nature.

At the same time, sovereignty means God is not limited by his transcendence; he is immanent in his creation. God's immanence means nothing that is within creation is outside his reach or his awareness. He is thus all-knowing, omniscient, as well. Jesus said that God knows when every sparrow falls and that God knows the number of hairs on each person's head—detailed knowledge indeed (Matt 10:29–30).

God's nature limiting his behavior means that he will not do what is illogical or destructive. God's actions, informed by his knowledge of creation and that which is the utmost good, are always wisest. Thus, the Lord's Prayer asks that God's will always be done (Matt 6:10). That doesn't mean that we will always understand God's action or inaction. Because God knows so much more than we know, and is able to reason far better than we are able to reason, his actions may puzzle us at times (Isa 55:8–9). He also sees the effects of action and inaction in the long run, whereas we are often short-sighted (Isa 42:9; 48:3, 6; cf. Isa 41:21–23).

Even if we do not understand how, we are always blessed when we choose to be part of his plan rather than to try to force him to be part of ours (Isa 55:9–11). Consider that our pets live with us all the time. They see and hear most everything we do—at least at home. However, their minds are not equipped to understand a good portion of our lives. They may hear us discuss work, wages, taxes, and paying for goods and services, but all of these acts are outside their comprehension. In a similar manner, God is able to comprehend what is incomprehensible to us. We can understand a great deal about him and about creation, but we can never approach the depth and breadth of the knowledge God has. We must content ourselves with knowing about his characteristics and take comfort from his immeasurable strengths. Gaining that trust follows both from focusing upon the ways God has revealed himself, especially in Jesus Christ, and from asking him for the gift of faith. Expressing gratitude to God and rejoicing in him also promotes faith.

However, there should be no mistake that God's sovereignty means that he reserves to himself decisions about who is entitled to his fellowship and the eternal destiny of each soul. The Lord told Moses, "I will be gracious to whom I will be gracious, and will show compassion on whom I will show compassion" (Exod 33:19). Here, as elsewhere, no one is able to resist him.

God Is Changeless

In his letter, James reminded his readers that God can be trusted not only because we can rely upon his existence, but also because his abilities do not diminish and his value judgments do not change (Jas 1:16–17). This characteristic is referred to theologically as God's *immutability*. God's changelessness must be carefully understood, however.

Some philosophers and theologians imagine God never changes in any way. They conceive of a God that exists in the straightjacket of his own nature—a God who cannot change in the same way the ancient philosopher Parmenides thought any change in the universe is illusion. In contrast, some contemporary theologians suggest that God learns from experience in the same way that human beings learn from experience, changing his plan for history as history develops. In truth, God is changeless in some ways, and not in others.

God is changeless in those characteristics which are his essential nature: his being and character. He will never be less than what he is. He will never do what is ultimately illogical. He will never do what is ultimately harmful. He may accommodate human beings at times so as not to overburden them and to lead them toward a better understanding of morality, but his moral judgments do not change. Paul referred to God as: "God, who cannot lie" (*ho apseudēs theos*), an expression that may be translated "does not lie" as well as "cannot lie," but either way points to the fact that God's nature does not permit him to lie (Titus 1:2). The promises of God are not only wonderful because of what is promised, but because the God who promises them can be trusted never to go back on his word.

On the other hand, to assume God is completely changeless in all ways is to envision him as incapable of anything akin to our thought, planning, and interaction with his creation. The key witness against this interpretation of God is the incarnation of the Son of God, and Jesus' earthly life, death, resurrection, and glorification. Surely this sequence of events brought something new that the Second Person of the Trinity, and thus God, never experienced before. The Bible also gives many examples of God changing his response to people based on their behavior or in response to intercession. However, given God's intelligence and wisdom, it isn't reasonable to assume that God needs to revise his plans or how he responds to certain behavior as a result of new experiences.

When the author of Hebrews says that Jesus learned obedience and was perfected, he was referring to Jesus' experience of what it meant to be obedient as a human being, which was an entirely new experience for the Son of God (Heb 5:8-9). However, that does not mean that God changed how he responds to people based upon Jesus' experience. This does not in any way diminish what the author of Hebrews celebrates: "Jesus Christ *is* the same yesterday and today and forever" (Heb 13:8). This Jesus is the one who has experienced life as a human being and who is able to intercede on our behalf to meet our needs (Heb 2:17-18; 4:14-16). What this means is that God does not change by whimsey. His actions are ruled by an inner nature and personal capability that never waiver. God's steadfastness is another reason we can fully trust in God.

This leads to the question why there was a change in the way God related to people in biblical times; not only the difference between the Old and New Covenants, but changes within the Old Testament. Part of the answer is that God accommodates people in their different cultures and historical situations. If he did not do so, many more people would be in trouble; he is interested in the greatest mercy without compromise. Another part of the answer is that God is demonstrating to all that his final plan, the New Covenant, is the only way to accomplish his purposes fully, that nothing else would work. His earlier covenants provided a sufficient measure of grace, and also laid the groundwork for the New Covenant (cf. Rom 4:1-17; Gal 2:19; 3:6-9, 17-24). The New Covenant was established well before the

God Is Benevolent

God's character is marked by an attitude of goodwill that flows from his inner being. The Scriptures use "light" as a metaphor for goodness and "darkness" as a metaphor for destructiveness and evil. Using these terms, John assures us that "God is Light, and in Him there is no darkness at all" (1 John 1:5). God's nature defines righteousness. God not only will never do evil, he cannot look upon evil with favor or approve evil (Hab 1:13). His preferred method of overcoming evil is with good (Lam 3:32–33; cf. Rom 12:19-21).

God's inherent goodness leads to benevolence to others. John put it briefly: "God is love" (*ho theos agapē estin*, 1 John 4:8). This is far from just an emotion or an inclination; it is active, self-giving love that seeks to enrich the one loved. This love flows from the relationship of the members of the Trinity for one another (John 3:35; 17:23, 26; Rom 5:5). In his creation, God expands the object of his love—especially to people. "Every good thing given and every perfect gift" has its source in God, either as the direct source or through the creation he brought about (Jas 1:17). The Greek word *agapē* has become well known for describing this love. However, other words and expressions throughout the Scriptures also emphasize this aspect of God, as does the entire teaching of the Bible.

One of the most important words in the Old Testament is the Hebrew word *ḥesed*. The meaning of this word is not easy to capture in a single English word or phrase. In contrast to the common Hebrew word for love, *ʾahab*, *ḥesed* is translated at various times as "kindness," "mercy," or "loyalty." In an attempt to capture the broader meaning, it is also sometimes translated "covenant love," "steadfast love," or "lovingkindness." Mercy, of course, is kindness to someone in need. The Lord's loyalty is seen in faithfulness to his covenant agreements even when people are not faithful to their part. All of these terms refer to God's actions toward his creatures. A form of this word is used repeatedly in Psalm 136 to emphasize that the Lord's "lovingkindness is everlasting."

God is gracious in that he gives willingly and freely to the benefit of others. Thus grace (Gk. *charis*) is often used to describe God's acts toward his creatures. God is faithful; he can always be depended upon to fulfill his promises (1 Cor 1:9; 10:13; 2 Cor 1:18; 1 Thess 5:24; 1 John 1:9).

In recognition of the harmony that results from God's presence, faithfulness, and actions, he is called "the God of peace" (Gk. *ho theos tēs eirēnēs*, Rom 15:33; 16:20; Phil 4:9; 1 Thess 5:23; Heb 13:20). In one place, he is called "the God of love and peace" (Gk. *ho theos tēs agapēs kai eirēnēs*, 2 Cor 13:11). The peace he brings reflects the inner peacefulness of his own nature.

God Is Just

God is righteous in his nature, and thus in all of his relationships (Lam 3:33). As Creator, he administers the universe, making certain that the actions and relationships of his creatures reflect his benevolent nature (Jer 9:23-24; Lam 3:34-36).

Those who do business with God can always rely on his integrity. Although he expects his creatures to do all they are capable of doing and demands that they do so, he does not expect more than can be reasonably expected. "For He Himself knows our frame," David celebrated, "He is mindful that we are *but* dust" (Ps 103:14; cf. Ps 145:8-9). Isaiah wrote of the coming Christ: "With righteousness He will judge the poor, and decide with fairness for the afflicted of the earth. . . . A bruised reed He will not break and a dimly burning wick He will not extinguish" (Isa 11:4; 42:3). Speaking to Jonah, God explains that he withheld judgment upon a repentant Nineveh not only for the sake of the people, but also out of consideration for the domestic animals (Hebr. *b^{e}hēmâ*, cattle or sheep, Jonah 4:11).

Outside Scripture, God is often portrayed as cruel for venting his wrath against sinners; but he should not be seen this way for at least three reasons. First, God's wrath is generally delayed—often for a very long time. From Adam and Eve to those in modern times, God holds off final judgment to give people time to repent. Second, God's wrath against sin is a strong indication of the changelessness of his moral character. If God can overlook sin and sinners forever, then God might forget his benevolence and his promises of mercy and blessing to his people as well. In other words, to be worthy of trust, God's moral nature must remain uncompromised. Third, because of God's wrath, the wicked cannot continue to claim victims indefinitely. His justice may not be as swift as some may like, but it will be complete. The wicked will be brought to justice for the torment they have caused others, while those who have suffered will be recompensed. God's compassion for those who suffer is often seen even when he delays judgment upon the stubbornly wicked.

A major event of the Old Testament, and a defining moment in sacred history, was the delivery of the Israelites from slavery in Egypt. The Israelites were told that if they abused the disadvantaged, they would answer to the judgment of God (Exod 22:21-24; Lev 19:17-18, 33-34; Deut 23:15-16; 24:7, 10-15, 17-22; 27:18-19). The concern of God on behalf of the oppressed is a recurring theme in the Psalms and in the prophetic literature of the Old Testament. David wrote, "The Lord performs righteous deeds and judgments for all who are oppressed" (Ps 103:6; cf. Ps 9:7–9; 146:5–10). The prophet Zechariah declared: "Thus has the Lord of hosts said, 'Dispense true justice and practice kindness and compassion each to his brother; and do not oppress the widow or the orphan, the stranger or the poor; and do not devise evil in your hearts against one another'" (Zech 7:9–10). Through Isaiah, God reprimanded the people for valuing religious rituals over righteous lives. Rather than fasting from food, God told the people to fast from doing wickedness. "Is this not the fast which I choose, to loosen the bonds of wickedness, to undo the bands of the yoke, and to let the oppressed go free and break every yoke?" (Isa 58:6). God promised judgment upon those who did not repent of oppression (Jer 21:12; Amos 4:1–3; 5:12; 8:4–10; Mic 2:1–4; Mal 3:1–5).

In the time of the New Testament, the people in Palestine were mostly poor, in part because of the heavy taxes levied by the Romans occupying their land. In addition, they suffered oppression from the way the Romans governed them, oppression from the self-serving schemes of Herod the Great and those rulers who followed him, and oppression by a corrupt Jewish religious establishment. The birth narrative in Matthew, and especially Luke, should be read with this in mind. The poetic words of Mary and Zechariah in the early chapters of Luke are especially revealing of the longing of pious Jews for God to release them from their oppressors.

The greatest oppression, of course, is that which is brought by the presence of sin—encouraged and promoted by Satan (Eph 6:12; cf. John 8:44). This is the oppression Jesus came to free people from as a first step toward the restoration of righteousness throughout creation. God will end all oppression and bring justice to all at the end of this present age. The ministry of Christ gives a foretaste of the eventual healing of all those who have suffered in this age. Peter said that Jesus "went about doing good and healing all who were oppressed (Gk. *katadunasteuomenous*) by the devil, for God was with Him" (Acts 10:38).

God Is Triune

As we noted earlier, God is Triune: consisting of God the Father, God the Son, and God the Holy Spirit; not three Gods, but one God of one substance and one character. While some have preferred a more easily understandable concept of God, it should not seem outrageous or unreasonable that a God who can create the universe we live in is more complex than we, as human beings, might first expect. The biblical teaching on this subject is clear, but it took several centuries for Christian theologians to formulate this teaching in a way that truly reflects the teachings of Scripture.

There is significant teaching on the Trinity in the writings of Irenaeus (ca. 130–ca. 200), who recognized that the Trinity is not simply the way God manifested himself in sacred history, but is inherent in the nature of God. Tertullian (ca. 155–ca. 220) contributed the terminology of three "Persons." The Cappadocian fathers—Basil the Great (ca. 330–379), Gregory of Nazianzus (ca. 329–ca. 389), and Gregory of Nyssa (ca. 335–ca. 394)—developed the most comprehensive understanding of the Trinity: three, equally divine Persons of one substance. They were also able to describe the relationship between the humanity and the deity of Jesus Christ in a manner that most fully reflects the teaching of Scripture. These teachings became orthodox for Christians.

Some have noted that the deity of Christ and the deity of the Holy Spirit were accepted early on by the Christian community. This is seen not only in the writings of the New Testament, but in the writings of other early Christian writers known as the church fathers. Certainly, this is because, as Jesus noted by his reference to Psalm 110, there are certain portions of the Old Testament that cannot be understood unless God is Trinity. References to the "angel of the Lord" is another case in point (e.g., Gen 22:11; Exod 3:2; cf. Exod 14:19; 23:20–22).

Perhaps the most significant aspect of the Trinity is relationship. God is not an impersonal power or force. What is commonly referred to as Jesus' "High Priestly Prayer" of John 17 shows that Jesus wanted the same relationship of love between God and human beings, and among the followers of Christ, that is enjoyed by members of the Trinity with one another. The relationship of Father, Son, and Holy Spirit with one another is the kind of love that brings harmony, orderliness, and peace—the kind of love that cannot be broken, ever.

This aspect of God's nature means that God may be known not just intellectually, but in a personal relationship as well. The love between members of the Trinity is not just a model for fellowship between God and people, but between people. It is the basis for social holiness: the basis for peace, orderliness, and harmony in all human relationships.

The Practical Consequences of God's Reality and Character

God is of central importance to all people because God has determined the universe in which we live our lives. By "universe" I mean more than the physical universe that we inhabit as creatures; the entire context in which we have our existence has been determined by God. Without him we have nothing. We cannot determine our own reality or our own future. The choices we have are those he has given us, and those choices are to accept his benevolence or to reject him completely.

Those who complain that God and his nature are not to their liking are missing an important point: ultimately, it doesn't matter. If the only existence we have is the one given us by God, then we don't have a good option to reject him. God offers life.

If the objection is that the life God offers is too confining, the truth is that all life is confined by constraints. If an oak tree could make a choice, it might like to be planted anywhere it wants, even high in the atmosphere or totally under water. But, all things are not possible. The only life that an oak tree can have and prosper is when it has the right kind of soil and the right amount of sunlight, rain, and warmth. The life God offers is the only one that truly enables human beings to fully experience their human potential. Jesus promised "abundant life" to his people, not a life that stifles; but having that life requires living in conformity with how our Creator means for us to live (John 10:10). This is not to say that living for God in a world where evil is so prevalent is easy; but it is to say that we can only truly overcome and escape the evil of the world by embracing the highest power and the highest good—and only in God can we realize that goal.

Some are critical of God because there is evil in the world. They argue that God must either be too weak to overcome evil or not good enough to want to do so. That argument also misses the point. Even if it were true that God is one or the other—and it isn't—that wouldn't change the circumstance that, as creatures, we are fully dependent upon God. Being angry at God does not change the universe we live in, it doesn't make him less in charge of all creation, nor does it change the fact that only in God is there a future with a hope of something better. God affirms that there is evil in the world, but he promises that evil's days are numbered. He promises that those who live in fellowship with him will outlive the evils of this age, and there is persuasive evidence in Jesus Christ that God's promises will be fulfilled. Meanwhile, the hardships of the present age are here to remind us of our mortality and our need for the deliverance that only God can offer.

God the Father, God the Son, and God the Holy Spirit have a relationship of mutual love and service with one another. It is to share this love that God seeks creatures to bless. Scripture teaches that God wants "a people for his own possession" so he can give them a fulfilling, joyful life (Titus 2:14; 1 Pet 2:10; Ps 16:11). This is seen in the scriptures where God promises, "You shall be My people and I will be your God" and expresses his desire to dwell in the midst of his people (Jer 30:22; Exod 29:45; Lev 26:12; Jer 31:1; Ezek 37:27; 2 Cor 6:16; Rev 21:3). In Ephesians, Paul writes that it is God's intention that "in the ages to come He might show the surpassing riches of His grace in kindness toward us in Christ Jesus" (Eph 2:7). Such words highlight the source of Christian confidence for the future.

The existence, nature, and character of the one true God are the greatest truths of our world. In a very real sense, it is God who is the gospel—the "good news" of the Scriptures, for everything else that is worth having flows from him. His desire to share good things with others, and especially to share himself, is the reason he created human beings. To know him is to experience life (cf. Ps 133:3).

9

Seeing the Need

> Then God said, "Let Us make man in Our image, according to our likeness."
> ... God created man in His own image, in the image of God He created him; male and female He created them. God blessed them; and God said to them, "Be fruitful and multiply, and fill the earth, and subdue it; and rule over ... every living thing that moves on the earth." ... God saw all that He had made, and behold, it was very good.
>
> GENESIS 1:26–28, 31

> Through one man sin entered into the world, and death through sin, and so death spread to all men because all sinned.... Death reigned from Adam until Moses, even over those who had not sinned in the likeness of the offense of Adam.
>
> ROMANS 5:12, 14

> For all that is in the world, the lust of the flesh and the lust of the eyes and the boastful pride of life, is not from the Father, but is from the world.
>
> 1 JOHN 2:16

WHAT is the purpose of creation? This question crosses the mind of most people at one time or another. For many, the purpose of creation seems a great enigma incapable of solution—so much so that in a number of works of fiction, promising to reveal "the purpose of life" is seen as laughable at best and a hoax at worst.

The Bible has no such difficulty, and no embarrassment about providing an answer. The purpose of creation, and of life, is revealed clearly and consistently across the Testaments. In doing so, Scripture reveals not only the purpose of creation, but the goal of redemption. It is one of the great unifying themes of the Bible.

God's Plan for Creation

We mentioned earlier that the first purpose of the book of Genesis was to provide background for the Israelites who left Egypt to know who they were, how they became slaves in Egypt, and that God promised their deliverance to Abraham (Gen 15:13–14). At the same time, what is contained in Genesis is not simply important to the Hebrew people, it is important for everyone. Genesis forms the historical and theological basis for everything else taught in Scripture. Thus, when it comes to understanding God's purpose in creating the universe, we must start in Genesis and then move on to consider later Scripture.

The first chapter of Genesis tells us that human beings are the pinnacle of God's creation. The second chapter provides more detail. It is clear that Adam (the name of the first human being and also the Hebrew word for "man") is unlike any other creature in at least three highly significant ways. First, human beings were created in the "image," the "likeness," of God. Second, human beings were created to have a level of fellowship with God greater than any other creature. And third, human beings were created to rule over the earth; all creation was placed under their care.

Genesis 1:26 tells us that God made people in his "image" (Hebr. ṣelem) and "likeness" (Hebr. $d^e mût$). The following verse tells us that this image applies to both men and women equally. Since "image" is used without "likeness" in Genesis 1:27, "likeness" clarifies the meaning of "image" rather than indicating a separate quality. The use of "likeness" underscores that human beings are like God in some ways without diminishing the uniqueness of God their Creator.[1]

Genesis chapters 1 through 3 show what it means for people to be made in the image of God. Because God uses language to communicate with Adam and Eve, we see that they have an intelligence markedly higher than the animals. Because Adam and Eve are given instructions which they have the ability to disobey, we know that they have the ability to make moral decisions—also something that sets them higher than the animals. Because they did not forfeit their earthly lives the day they disobeyed God, we know that Adam and Eve were created spiritual as well as biological beings. God warned Adam that he would die the very day he ate from one particular tree

---

1. Hamilton, "$d^e mût$," in *TWOT*, 1:191–92.

in the garden of Eden (Gen 2:16–17). Mortality was part of the punishment for their sin, but physical death would come much later (Gen 3:19; 5:5). The death Adam and Eve died the very day they disobeyed, therefore, was a spiritual one (cf. Eph 2:1–3; Col 2:13).

It is the image of God that enables human beings to have a fellowship with God that is deeper and fuller than any other created beings. Genesis 2:15–23 shows God interacting with Adam, and Genesis 3:8 tells us that God walked in the garden of Eden seeking fellowship with Adam and Eve, a fellowship that was broken when they disobeyed God.

It is the image of God that also enables human beings to rule over the earth. God charged Adam and Eve and their progeny to tend the garden he gave them, to subdue the earth, and to rule over the animals. The charge to "be fruitful and multiply, and fill the earth" shows that God's plan was always to create a people who live in harmony with God and with one another—a people richly blessed by life on the planet he provided for them (Gen 1:28). These are the people that, like the nation of Israel, God said he forms (Hebr. *yēṣer*) for himself (Isa 43:21). They inherit the promise: "You will be My people, and I will be your God" (Ezek 36:28; cf. Jer 7:23; 11:4; 30:22; Ezek 34:30; Zech 8:8; Rev 21:3). They will later be known as "the called-out ones": in Greek *hē ekklēsia*, and in English "the church."

Although we must speculate based on the material in later Scripture, it seems that the plan was always for people to be granted eternal life after a time of testing. However, when the disobedience of Adam and Eve intervened, God was not unprepared for such an occurrence, and this plan was delayed, not defeated.

God chose Abraham to be the person through whom he would advance his plan to create a people for himself (Gen 15:1–21; 17:1–8). This would be fulfilled through Abraham's son Isaac, and Isaac's son Jacob (Gen 17:15–22; 26:1–4; 28:10–17). When you read through the Scriptures relating to Abraham, Isaac, and Jacob (later named Israel), take note of the promises from God to make them fruitful, relating this promise to God's plan for Adam and Eve that human beings be fruitful and fill the earth. It was the descendants of Abraham, Isaac, and Jacob who grew in number in Egypt until they became a people, not just a family or a tribe. It was this people God delivered from slavery in Egypt in the exodus. If this seems too remote, consider that God promised that through Abraham "all the families (Hebr. *mišpᵉḥōt*) of the earth will be blessed," which includes your ancestors, you, and your offspring (Gen 12:3). As would be expected, among the earliest inheritors of this promise were the Israelites who took part in the exodus from Egypt. However, as Apostles Peter and Paul noted, it is a living promise (Acts 3:25; Gal 3:8).

God promised Moses that he would take the Israelites to be his people and that he would be their God (Exod 6:7). This promise was reinforced to Moses when the Israelites first arrived at Mt. Sinai and multiple times in Deuteronomy, and was later recognized in a psalm (Exod 19:3–6; Lev 26:12; Deut 4:20; 7:6; 14:2; 26:18; Ps 135:4). Even when the promise was repeated with somewhat different language, the thought was present that God is in the business of creating a people with whom he would have a unique fellowship.

It should be carefully noted that this promise is not restricted to blood descendants of Abraham. The promise is to all those who, like Abraham, are "friends of God," regardless of their race or ancestry (Gal 3:6–8; Rom 4:16–17; cf. Exod 12:47–48; Num 9:14). Thus both Peter and Paul spoke of the faithful to God as a people for God's "possession" (1 Pet 2:9; Titus 2:14; cf. Heb 12:22–24). The purpose of the New Testament writers is clearly to show that those who follow Christ are part of this people. The ultimate fulfillment of God's plan is recognized in Revelation 21:3: "Behold, the tabernacle of God is among men, and He will dwell among them, and they shall be His people, and God Himself will be among them."

The vocabulary here is helpful. The people who are God's possession are said to be a "holy people" (Hebr. *'am qādôsh*, Deut 7:6; Gk. *ethnos hagion*, 1 Pet 2:9). In this case, because of the emphasis on possession, the foremost meaning of the word "holy" is "separate": separate *from* the world and separate *to* God. Such people are also certainly holy in the sense that they reflect *Yahweh's* character. Their lives center on him and he dwells among them. The Hebrew word translated "possession" in the Old Testament is often *sᵉgūlâ*, which indicates not just a possession, but a treasured possession (Exod 19:5; Deut 7:6; 14:2; 26:18; Ps 135:4; Mal 3:17).[2] Peter and Paul use the Greek word *peripoiēsis*, and Paul uses the Greek word *periousios*, to refer the people of God as God's personal possession (1 Pet 2:9; Eph 1:14; Titus 2:14).

The concept of being God's *possession* might be unnerving were it not for the nature of God. God is the giver of life. He does not give it to his people to take it away from them, but for them to experience all the fulfillment and joy he planned for them before creation. Jesus said that he came that people "may have life, and have *it* abundantly" (Gk. *zōēn echōsin kai perisson echōsin*, John 10:10). Everything that sustains life and makes it worthwhile comes only from God. However, creatures do not always remember this; they try to take his place, thinking they can provide life for themselves. This, unfortunately, is the affliction of the human race.

---

2. Patterson, "*sᵉgūlâ*," in *TWOT*, 2:617.

The Fall and God's Response

Adam and Eve were created in a world that was already filled with plants and animals. Biological life was far from the only created life forms they would interact with, however. Purely spiritual beings were created even before the earth was formed. Genesis focuses on Adam and Eve and their descendants, the ancestors of those in the exodus from Egypt; but there are indications of these spiritual beings in the serpent and the cherub.

Even if we leave out the ability to walk, it is an understatement to say that the serpent in Genesis 3 is different from the serpents we know of today. The serpents we are familiar with certainly do not have the ability to talk! It appears that the serpent's ability to speak was given to it by Satan, the adversary of God.

While some may want to think of Satan as just a mythical being, Jesus left no doubt as to the existence of the devil. Jesus taught that Satan is "a liar and the father of lies" and has been "a murderer from the beginning" (John 8:44). The word "murderer" here is literally "man-killer" (Gk. *anthrōpoktonos*). The Greek phrase "from the beginning" (Gk. *ap archēs*) here is synonymous with "in the beginning" (Gk. *en archēi*) that begins the Gospel of John as well as the Greek translation of Genesis widely used in New Testament times. This is not by accident. John, reflecting Jesus' teaching, wants us to recognize that Satan has been active in human affairs from the earliest days of the human race.

The speech process is complex. Animals, including serpents, have neither the brains, nor the musculature, nor the other organs required for speech. The only similar incident in Scripture is recorded in Numbers 22, where Balaam insisted on going to pronounce a curse on the Israelites, and the angel of the Lord stood in Balaam's path to block him. Three times the donkey Balaam was riding turned aside from walking into the angel of the Lord, and each time Balaam hit the donkey with a stick to show his displeasure. After the third time, the angel of the Lord enabled the donkey to speak and to complain that the punishment was undeserved. Balaam's eyes were then opened to see the angel of the Lord standing in the path. Here the donkey became a tool of God to communicate with Balaam; in a similar manner, the serpent in Genesis 3 became a tool of Satan to tempt the first couple to reject God. In both cases, speech was generated by spiritual beings, not the animals involved.

Satan is known as "the tempter" (Gk. *ho peirazōn*, Matt 4:3; 1 Thess 3:5), a role he certainly plays in Genesis 3.[3] This is a role Satan would later play with Jesus (Matt 4; Mark 1:13; Luke 4:1–2; cf. Heb 2:18; 4:15).

---

3. Dalman, *Is the Bible Really True?*, 18–19.

Scripture outside Genesis indicates that Satan was created a powerful spiritual being, but became filled with pride and led other spiritual beings in an attempt to subvert God. In Isaiah 14 and Ezekiel 28, human kings are spoken of in terms more fully applicable to Satan, giving us a glimpse into the spiritual prehistory and early history of earth. In the book of Daniel we learn that there is spiritual warfare in this age; but we learn from the book of Job, from Zechariah chapter 3, and from 2 Thessalonians 2:7 that the ability of Satan and Satan's servants is restricted by the will and power of God. There is no dualism—no equal power of good and evil as the ancient Persians believed. Nor are good and evil equal parts of the universe as is thought to be the case in the *yin-yang* of eastern mysticism. God is entirely sovereign.

Satan is defeated first by God's sovereign control of all creation, then by God's saving work through the cross of Jesus Christ, and finally by being cast from creation (Gen 3:14–15; Col 2:8–15). The forces of evil must submit to God in this age, and will be completely eliminated from creation in the next. This is the outworking of the victory Jesus won on the cross, where Jesus triumphed over evil and gained supreme authority over all the spiritual forces of evil (Eph 1:18–23; 6:12; Col 2:13–15; Heb 2:8–15).

In the meantime, it serves God's purposes to allow Satan and his spiritual servants to participate in creation for the perfection of God's people. Malevolent spiritual forces attempt to turn people against God. If this seems an insufferable burden for the human race, it is important to remember that Jesus entered this world, lived in it as a human being, overcame temptation, and suffered on the cross. God not only did not abandon us to evil, he confronted it head-on, suffered from it, and overcame it in the person of Jesus of Nazareth. This perspective should always be kept in mind when considering the evil that is in the world.

All of this was in the future when Adam and Eve were tempted, of course. The serpent convinced first Eve, and through Eve, Adam, that they should trust him and not God. Although Eve may appear to have sole responsibility for succumbing to the wiles of the serpent, Adam should have intervened and corrected his wife before they transgressed. Adam allowed the serpent to deceive them both. Trusting a created being (the serpent) rather than their Creator, they closed themselves off from both the fellowship they had with God and the life God wanted to give them. Their choice essentially restricted them and their offspring to what creation alone could offer. This was the beginning of the pagan idolatry Paul described in Romans 1:21–23. The all-important relationship between Creator and creature was broken. Although they still had biological life, they forfeited the spiritual life that is sustained by fellowship with God. They were still spiritual beings, but their spirit was dead to God. This is where their greed, pride, and self-centeredness brought them.

It is important to recognize that God did not bring a final judgment upon Adam and Eve, as he well could have. Instead, he multiplied pain in childbirth and the toil required for food. These punishments were designed to help Adam and Eve understand the reality of their situation, that as creatures they were dependent on God for their lives. The consequence of physical death would reinforce the dependence of human beings on God, reminding human beings that sin leads from, not to, life and blessing (Rom 5:12–14). God's punishment on the serpent was more than a change in how the serpent propelled itself across the ground; it included a promise that Satan, who was working through the serpent, would one day be overcome at the cross in what is known as the proto-gospel or Adamic covenant: Genesis 3:15.

It is also important to recognize that although God allowed Satan to be the tempter, God did not *cause* Adam and Eve to fall. In his epistle, James affirms that people fall into sin because of their own corrupt desires, not because God causes them to sin (Jas 1:13–15). There was no necessity for them to eat the one and only fruit God forbade them to eat (Gen 2:16–17). Nor was there any magic in the fruit. It was the choice to disobey God that broke their fellowship with God; the act, not the fruit itself. The fruit did not change or corrupt them; they corrupted themselves. They simply demonstrated this by eating the fruit.

Adam and Eve's choice was more than naivete—more than just a poor choice. They had just one rule to follow, and they had been clearly warned of the consequences of breaking that rule. This is often referred to as the "covenant of works" because they were required to do something to maintain their relationship with God. The "covenant of grace" then refers to all covenants of the Bible beginning with the Adamic covenant (Gen 3:15), because each new covenant, culminating in the New Covenant, is a step forward in the saving grace of God.

The Immediate Consequences of the Fall

Why did Adam and Eve disobey God? Creatures, including pure spiritual beings and human beings, are limited in their ability to comprehend their surroundings. If a creature has the ability to choose where to focus attention and thought, there is the ability to become absorbed in some things and to ignore others, and thus the ability to focus on the wrong things. Temptation always has the affect of narrowing attention from the careful consideration of all factors to impulsive carelessness of consequences, and thus from the eternal perspective to the here and now.

Creatures experience the universe as part of it and as if they are the center of it. The physical universe is always present. Creatures constantly sense it through sight, hearing, smell, taste, and touch. The spiritual, on the other hand, requires attention to the "unseen" as what is most real (2 Cor 4:18; Heb 11:1). It is easy for the careless to focus on physical things and to forget spiritual things. Both in sacred history and in the world around us, we constantly see people prefer created things they experience to God, who is generally not seen or felt. This is what Paul describes in Romans 1:20–25. It is manifested in idolatry in all its many forms.

God granted free will to his creatures because love is not something that can be forced. In the Trinity, love is freely and joyfully given. God wants his people to choose to love him, not to be forced into a relationship. Those who prefer creation over their Creator will never be able to enter into the relationship God created them for. However, that is *their* choice, not God's. God gave Adam and Eve an opportunity to show their love for him. They failed, choosing to please themselves rather than God.

Satan, acting through the serpent, presented himself as an "angel of light," to use Paul's thought in 2 Corinthians 11:3 and 14. Adam and Eve's fall into sin began with their choice to believe the serpent rather than God regarding the consequences of eating the fruit. They treated God as if he were below their level and below the level of the snake—which was pure arrogance. Choosing to eat the fruit showed total disregard for God's knowledge, wisdom, authority, and feelings. Clearly, they were honoring the serpent and treating God with contempt.

In terms of the Ten Commandments, Adam and Eve violated the first three by setting the authority and dignity of creatures over that of God. Certainly, one factor that led to their sin was the decision to accept the serpent's accusation that God lied about the benefits of the fruit. This was a serious accusation against God that was accepted all too easily. There was also ingratitude involved, since God had given them so very much. This is the kind of ingratitude Paul describes so well in Romans 1:21. Further, in terms of the tenth commandment, they coveted what wasn't theirs, but God's. Eve found the forbidden fruit appealing, thought eating it would taste good and feel good, and wanted knowledge beyond what she had. Once these became the sole objects of her focus, nothing else mattered. As James wrote in James 1:14–15, once a wrongful desire arises, if not resisted, it leads to sin.

The Greek word used for "covet" in the New Testament is *epithumia*, as in Romans 7:7 and 13:9. Its meaning, however, is determined by context. Often, *epithumia* simply refers to human desires. As creatures, we have been created to desire many legitimate things. Eve's desire to see beautiful things, to eat good food, and to be wiser than she was were all perfectly legitimate desires. The problem often comes not when we want to do what is wicked and destructive at the outset, but when we seek to satisfy legitimate desires in unhealthy ways—unhealthy because ultimately destructive. That is what happened to Adam and Eve. In the terms of John's first letter, they succumbed to "the lust of the flesh (Gk. *hē epithumia tēs sarkos*; the fruit was thought to be a delicacy) and the lust of the eyes (Gk. *hē epithumia tōn ophthalmōn*; the fruit was pleasant to look at) and the boastful pride of life (Gk. *hē alazoneia tou biou*; the food was thought to provide wisdom)" (1 John 2:16). This was the temptation; the sin itself was a rejection of the wisdom, goodness, and sovereignty of the Creator who had given them nothing but blessings.

The consequences of giving in to temptation were calamitous. There was an immediate break in fellowship with God, as demonstrated by them hiding when they heard God approach. There was also an immediate break in human relationships, as shown by their refusal to take blame for their sinful behavior. Both Adam and Eve tried to put the blame for their actions on someone else. Eve blamed the serpent for deceiving her. However, while the serpent was the agent by which they were tempted, he did not compel them to disobey God; that was their choice. Adam did far worse, putting the blame on Eve when he should have corrected her rather than joined her, then blaming God for giving him Eve to be his wife.

The Universality of Sin and Its Effects

The entry of sin into human existence corrupted Adam and Eve to the extent that even their offspring were affected. While Genesis records examples of faithfulness and genuine devotion to the Lord on the part of some, it is also a record of the breakdown of human behavior and social relationships. The first person to be born, Cain, killed his younger brother, Abel. Cain's murderous behavior grew not only from his resentment of Abel's success, but also from Cain's insistence that he, not God, had the right to choose what constitutes acceptable worship. The remainder of Genesis is an often sad story of deplorable behavior, not only of people toward God, but of people toward one another. The world became afflicted with violence (Gen 6:11). Not only were certain people overcome by their evil nature, even the best people like Noah and Lot were caught up in unrighteous and degrading behavior. The Scriptures of the Bible are unique among writings of the ancient world in showing the faults of those who are the heroes of the faith. This all highlights the ominous nature of sin.

In his letters to the Romans and Galatians, Paul is clear that all human beings (except Jesus Christ) have been tainted by sin (Rom 3:23; Gal 3:22). In Romans 3:10–18, Paul quotes from the Psalms to show that human nature has been so corrupted that people, left on their own, have no interest in God, and their behavior is self-centered and destructive. In Romans 5:12–21, Paul declares that sin, the pollution of sin, and the divine condemnation due to sin came upon the entire human race through the sin of Adam. All of these consequences of sin were transmitted to the human race because of Adam's one act of disobedience to God. John the Baptist could talk not just about sins as individual acts, but also as sin—singular—being an affliction of the entire human race (Gk. *tēn hamartian tou kosmou*, John 1:29).

Every person, as a descendant of Adam, has inherited an inward tendency to rebel against God. This inward tendency to sin is called "original sin." Original sin affects everyone, but manifests itself in different ways in different people. As people were created in the image of God, some of that image remains in human intelligence, in the ability to enter into social relationships, in the potential for moral behavior, and in the potential for fellowship with God. Nevertheless, original sin eventually manifests itself in the deliberate rejection of God and his ways.

Original sin creates a condition that theologians call "total depravity"— a term that needs to be carefully understood. "Total" means that sin has the ability to touch every part of a person's life and deeds, not that every person is as wicked as that person might be. Complete depravity is seen in Genesis 6:5, where, except for Noah and his family, every thought and plan that people had was evil. Total depravity is seen throughout Scripture in the many ways sin manifests itself in people's lives. The Old and New Testaments are rich both in the terms for different manifestations of sin and in the descriptions of sinful acts.

The need for redemptive grace is made clear by the Bible's teaching regarding sin. Whereas Genesis alone presents a wide range of personal wickedness and dysfunctional relationships, Romans 1 shows the downward moral descent into more and more wickedness by those who are determined to resist God and his ways.

Of course, the unborn, infants, and those who never become capable of moral judgment are not held accountable for Adam's sin; but they are, nevertheless, tainted with a sinful nature. In his hatred of anything that is morally imperfect, God cannot tolerate a tendency to do that which is ultimately destructive. If left unopposed, the presence of original sin, which warps the person against God, makes an individual unacceptable to God in the same manner that a contagious, debilitating disease is dangerous if not quarantined. There is abundant evidence for this truth in human history. God, who does not tolerate such a tendency within himself, cannot overlook this tendency in others. Commenting on Ephesians 2:3, Harold Hoehner wrote, "We were, because of our ancestors, children of wrath. It is the natural endowment or condition inherited from our ancestors, particularly from Adam (Rom 5:12-21), that brings wrath."[4] This requires the cleansing work of God.

The pollution of sin is even more important in those who *make themselves* morally accountable to God. Jesus taught that anyone who sins becomes a slave of sin (John 8:34). In Romans 7, Paul discusses how the pollution of his nature prevented him from obeying the Law of Moses even though outwardly he appeared blameless (cf. Phil 3:5-6). He fully agreed that the Law of Moses is holy and should be followed. Nevertheless, to his sorrow, he discovered there was another law within him undermining his ability to live according to that holy law (Rom 7:23).

In Romans 5:12-14, Paul teaches that death came upon all people because all—each person individually—committed sin. Although the sin that brought death to each one was not exactly like Adam's, it was, in some manner, a transgression of what that person knew God expected. It could be a sin of omission (like Cain's refusing to be his brother's keeper) or a sin of commission (the actual murder of Abel by Cain). The death referred to here is the same as that which is mentioned as the consequence of sin in Romans 6:23. John Wesley, commenting on this verse, describes this death as "temporal, spiritual, and eternal."[5] This death is not punishment for Adam's sin, but is the consequence of freely choosing sin for oneself, and its most troublesome consequence is spiritual death. To be "dead in trespasses and sins" is to be alienated from God and from the life of God, and therefore to live according to whatever impulses and desires present themselves (Eph 2:1-2; Col 2:13; Isa 53:6). Such a condition warrants the wrath of God for individual choices in addition to the pollution of sin (John 3:19-20, 36). God's wrath against sin must be placed in perspective, however, because God delays judgment and punishment, and implements a plan to rescue people from themselves.

The Nature of Sin

The portrayal of temptation and sin presented in Genesis 3 is no isolated case; it rings true with human behavior throughout history. The break with God led immediately to bad behavior and poor relationships—also

---

4. Hoehner, *Ephesians*, 323.
5. Wesley, *Explanatory Notes*, vol. 2.

corresponding to what we both commonly observe and frequently experience in daily life.

The Greek word *hamartia* is by far the most common word for "sin" in the New Testament. The original meaning of *hamartia* is "missing the mark," but that does not do justice to its meaning in the context of Scripture. It is important to understand that God is not asking people to meet some impossible standard of absolute perfection in all their thoughts and deeds. He is not looking for an excuse to accuse people; he is asking for what is, or should be, attainable. Micah asked, "What does the Lord require of you but to do justice (Hebr. ʿăśôt mišpāṭ), to love kindness (Hebr. wᵉʾahăbat ḥesed), and to walk humbly (Hebr. wᵉhaṣᵉnēaʿ leket) with your God?" (Mic 6:8). In the same vein, when God delivered the Law through Moses, he told the people it was something they could do (Deut 30:11–14).

Throughout the Scriptures, in both Testaments, there are many examples of sinful behavior, and many words that describe specific sinful behavior. The common factor is that every sinful act is in some manner a rejection of God—the symptom of a broken relationship with our Creator. This is seen most clearly, perhaps, in contrast to Jesus' manner of life.

All Gospels show the determination of Jesus to be faithful to what God the Father called him to do. This is emphasized most strongly in John's Gospel. Speaking of the Father, Jesus said, "My food is to do the will of Him who sent Me and to accomplish His work. . . . I always do the things that are pleasing to Him" (John 4:34; 8:29). Contrast this to the attitude of Adam and Eve when they ate the one food that was forbidden to them and the difference becomes obvious. Further, Jesus backed this up by the way he lived his life—with no exceptions.

Mark's Gospel describes Jesus' message as preaching "the kingdom of God" (Mark 1:15). There is a tendency to think of the kingdom of God as a territory, a geographical area, ruled by God. It is, rather, the personal rule of God in the life of an individual such as Jesus. Jesus told Pontius Pilate that his kingdom is "not of this world" (John 18:36). God's rule is personal before it becomes territorial.

John gives important insight into sin when he writes, "Everyone who practices sin (Gk. *tēn hamartian*) also practices lawlessness (Gk. *tēn anomian poiei*), and sin is lawlessness (Gk. *hē hamartia estin hē anomia*)" (1 John 3:4). The Greek word *anomia* means to be without law or to act as if there is no law—to be lawless. The lawlessness John speaks of here is not the failure to adhere to some abstract legal code, but the failure to submit to the rule of the Creator (cf. Matt 6:10). This aspect of sin is captured well in the words from Isaiah: "All of us like sheep have gone astray, each of us has turned to his own way" (Isa 53:6; cf. Judg 17:6; 21:25). The failure to submit to God's rule leads to chaos, and thus the destruction of everything God has for us that is beneficial.

In Romans 7:14-25, Paul gives a powerful personal testimony of the power of humanity's sinful nature to undermine our attempts to live for God. However, what God holds people accountable for is the choice they make to willingly surrender to temptation. As the author of Hebrews wrote in Hebrews 3:13, sin is deceitful, promising freedom and life, but bringing slavery and death. Temptation that is not resisted takes away our ability to make sound moral decisions. As James points out in James 1:13-16, the person who surrenders to temptation makes the decision to be deceived, to live according to a lie rather than to live according to the truth, and thus to reject God.

Jesus taught that the avoidance of God is due to the desire to protect one's independence from God, which is ultimately impossible because only the Creator can give true life and blessing. Those who do well come to the Lord because their works have been done in the Lord (John 3:21). Jesus showed us this way of life by the way he lived. Those who do evil, however, like Adam and Eve, avoid God in an attempt to hide the true nature of their actions (John 3:19-20). "This is the judgment," said Jesus, "that the Light has come into the world, and men loved the darkness rather than the Light, for their deeds were evil" (John 3:19). Sin breaks what should be a close Creator/creature relationship.

Unfortunately, sin also tends to mask this problem. As Proverbs says: "All the ways of a man are clean in his own sight. . . . Every man's way is right in his own eyes" (Prov 16:2; 21:2; cf. 12:15). Before people see their need for God, they need to recognize that their behavior, and their inner nature, is self-defeating. They will never come to that conclusion without intervention from outside themselves. Thus, the restoration of the proper relationship of people with God is impossible without a strong work by God. Fortunately, as Paul pointed out in his address to the philosophers on Mars Hill, it is a work in which God has already taken the initiative, with the goal that all people should find him (Acts 17:26-27).

10

Making It Personal

The Son of Man has come to seek and to save that which was lost.
LUKE 19:10

It is a trustworthy statement, deserving full acceptance, that Christ Jesus came into the world to save sinners.
1 TIMOTHY 1:15

CHRISTIANITY in general, and salvation in particular, provide the solution to a problem that most people do not believe they have. Just as every physician must identify the illness before explaining the treatment, people must understand the nature of the spiritual problem that afflicts the human race and understand that it affects them personally before they will embrace the divine remedy. This is highlighted by a conversation Jesus had with a Pharisee one evening.

Jesus and his disciples were the guests of a Pharisee named Simon. While reclining for dinner, a woman entered, then kissed and anointed Jesus' feet with precious perfume while weeping because of her sins. Simon thought Jesus should have sent the woman away because she had committed many sins. Knowing what was on Simon's mind, Jesus asked Simon to consider two people who owed money to a moneylender, one who owed a small debt and another who owed a much larger one (Luke 7:40–50). The moneylender knew they could not raise the money to repay him, so he forgave each their debt. Jesus asked Simon who would love the moneylender more: the person forgiven the small debt or the person forgiven the large debt. Simon responded that the person with the greater debt would love more, which Jesus said was the correct answer. Jesus then made clear that the lesson here was not about monetary debt, but the forgiveness of sins. Jesus pointed out that Simon had not honored Jesus as a special guest or even with the care usually given guests because Simon did not think his sins were great; but the woman honored Jesus because she knew her sins were great and needed God's forgiveness. Jesus told the woman that she was forgiven her sins because of her faith, adding, "He who is forgiven little, loves little" (Luke 7:47).

Simon's problem is not limited to first-century Pharisees. It seems one of the reasons Christianity is so little valued in our time is because so few feel the need for divine forgiveness. The Mosaic law was given precisely to remedy this problem. In Jesus' time, however, the Law itself became a problem for many—and still is today. Understanding how that problem developed helps us understand Jesus' message and the teaching of the New Testament.

The Giving of the Mosaic Law

The giving of the Law by God through Moses is one of the most important events in the history of Israel. The exodus from Egypt was about the founding of a nation in fulfillment of a promise made by God to Abraham hundreds of years before (Gen 15:12–21).

The deliverance of the Israelites from slavery in Egypt included multiple plagues and wonders, the leading of the Israelites out of Egypt by the Lord as a pillar of smoke by day and a pillar of fire by night, the crossing of the Red Sea, the defeat of Pharaoh's army, the provision of food and water in the wilderness, and the defeat of the Amalekites in battle by the power of God—surely some of the most dramatic events ever witnessed by human beings.

The exodus brought the Israelites to the base of Mount Sinai, where they made camp. Moses ascended the mountain. God told Moses that the Israelites were to become a nation of priests; in other words, they were to be a nation that would bring the people of other nations to the knowledge of God (Exod 19:1–6). Faithful Jews acknowledge this charge to this day.

On the third day at Mount Sinai, Moses led the people to the base of the mountain. God manifested his presence on the mountain in a dark cloud. Trumpet calls from the cloud indicated that God was coming nigh in a manner similar to the way people were alerted when an earthly sovereign was coming. *Yahweh's* coming was accompanied by lightning, thunder, fire, smoke, and earthquakes, demonstrating the reality and power of God in no uncertain terms. The God who had just delivered the Israelites from slavery in Egypt was no local deity, but sovereign over all the earth—a God to be reckoned with. No Egyptian god ever gave a display like this one! The people were warned that to come too close to God meant immediate death.

God then delivered the Ten Commandments audibly to all the people. This was to be the basic law that governed the lives of the people. After this, there were more manifestations of God's reality and power. The Israelites were so terrified they asked Moses to speak with *Yahweh* for them so they would not have to come directly before him again. Moses told them not to fear, that *Yahweh* was impressing them with his presence and power so they would know to obey him (Exod 20:18–21).

Honoring the people's request, Moses then approached God. God gave Moses more laws and promised to bring the people into the promised land. The laws God gave Moses in Exodus 20:22—23:33 are known as "the book of the covenant"—the ordinances that defined the covenant relationship between God and Israel (Exod 24:7). Moses told the people what God required, and the people agreed to obey. Moses then wrote down the book of the covenant. Although we are not told so, it would seem that the Ten Commandments were part of this book because they were the first part of the Law given to the Israelites, and they were given to them directly by God himself. They were surely not meant to be forgotten or ignored.

A covenant is a solemn and formal agreement. The use of blood in a covenant ceremony is foreign to us today, but it was important in ancient times. It was the assurance that both parties were making an unreserved commitment to a covenant agreement. The death of the sacrifice symbolized the fate that would come upon either party who broke the covenant. This was so central to covenants in the ancient Near East that the terminology for making a covenant was to "cut" (Hebr. *kārat*) a covenant (Hebr. *bᵉrît*). This terminology is used in both Genesis and Exodus, appearing multiple times in Exodus 34.

The author of the New Testament book Hebrews highlights the importance of sacrifice to covenant, underscoring the necessity of the blood of Jesus to the New Covenant by referring to this ceremony of Moses (Heb 9:15–22). Peter also recalls the Mosaic ceremony when he speaks of the sprinkling of the blood of Jesus in 1 Peter 1:2. The blood Moses sprinkled on the people in their covenant ceremony with *Yahweh* sealed their participation (Exod 24:3–8). It seems unlikely the people had multiple changes of clothing, so the spots of blood remaining on their clothing should have reminded them of their covenant obligations. It should not be lost that it was likely with the blood of the covenant on their garments that some of the people readily gave up on *Yahweh* and turned to sin not that long after.

Immediately after the ceremony, the drama of meeting God continued as Moses, Aaron, Joshua, Nadab, Abihu, and seventy elders came before *Yahweh* on Mount Sinai at *Yahweh's* request (Exod 24:1–2, 9–11). There, they saw a vision of God above a pavement that appeared like a transparent, deep-blue precious stone. While viewing this, they ate a meal. Then, as today, meals often celebrate fellowship. Meals were sometimes eaten on the upper floor of certain temples in the ancient Near East to celebrate fellowship with the god worshipped there. This meal on Mount Sinai celebrated the new covenant relationship with *Yahweh*.

After this, God invited Moses to come closer. Moses entered the cloud of God's presence, which seemed like fire to those who gazed from afar. At this time, Moses was given instructions how to build a tabernacle that would be the dwelling place of God among the people. Moses was shown a model of this tabernacle to ensure that it would be built exactly as *Yahweh* required. The remainder of the book of Exodus focuses upon the building of the tabernacle and the coming of God to dwell there. More laws and requirements would follow in the books of Leviticus and Numbers; then a summary and restatement of the Mosaic law would follow in the book of Deuteronomy.

The Makeup of the Mosaic Law

As seen in the history of its origin, the Law was more than a system of regulations; it was a central part of a covenant agreement that bound together God and the descendants of Abraham. This covenant was not racial, however. The covenant could be entered into by anyone willing to live under its requirements (Exod 12:48–49; Num 9:14; 15:14–16). Paul referred to this in Galatians 5:3.

The Galatian Christians Paul wrote to were Gentiles, yet they were being told by some—the Judaizers—that they needed to live by the Law of Moses to be acceptable to God; in other words, that they needed to enter into the Mosaic covenant to become Christians. The Judaizers would not have said this if it was believed that only blood descendants of Abraham could enter into covenant relationship with *Yahweh*. Paul's opposition to the Judaizers was not racial either. Paul did not say the Galatians could not enter into the Mosaic covenant. He reminded the Galatians that to commit themselves to the Mosaic covenant was to obey the entire law without exception. This leads to an important insight regarding the Mosaic covenant: it makes no difference which law is broken—if the covenant is broken anywhere, it is broken. In this respect it is like the anchor line for boat. An anchor line that is cut no longer holds a craft safely at its mooring. It makes no difference whether the cut is a small slice or a six-foot section of the line.

Nevertheless, the Law was not given to be burdensome. God told the Israelites that the doing of the Law was within their power (Deut 30:11–14). Jesus proved this when he lived blamelessly under the Law of Moses (Gal

4:4–5; Heb 2:17—3:6; 4:14–15; cf. John 8:45-46). However, the Law was never meant to be the end point of human morality. In the Sermon on the Mount, Jesus showed how the letter of the law was meant to be a starting point for people to learn the underlying spiritual principles that lead to true righteousness and peace.

In Deuteronomy 30:10, Moses refers to the Law as a whole—the Hebrew word *tôrâh*—as God's commandments (Hebr. *miṣôtāyw*) and God's ordinances (Hebr. *wᵉḥūqqōtāyw*). The word *tôrâh* is often used, as here, specifically for the laws and regulations given at Mt. Sinai; but it also came to be used for all of the material in the five books of Moses, which are referred to collectively as the Torah. In Hebrew, *tôrâh* has as its primary meaning "instruction" or "teaching." Obedience to the Law was essential, but there was a purpose beyond the legal application.

The ultimate goal of the Law was to inform the Israelites how to live righteously before the Lord so they would experience the benefits of righteousness. This is significant because the Egyptian culture that the Israelites had just escaped from thought that people were created to be menial servants of the gods. The Lord's people, however, are important to God in themselves. To show his kind intentions toward his people, Yahweh promised flourishing crops, security from enemies, and freedom from disease. The people would also be free from the burdensome consequences of immorality. Through these blessings, the people were to learn that Yahweh is a savior who is able to save them from harm and restore them to the life he created them to have.

Jewish rabbis determined that there are 613 separate commandments in the Law of Moses. However, there are better ways to understand its parts than counting laws. Jesus, for example, pointed to two commandments that contain the basic principles from which all the other laws derive. The first is found in Scripture that is commonly referred to as the *Shema*, the most sacred confession in Judaism: Deuteronomy 6:4-5: "Hear, O Israel! The Lord is our God, the Lord is one! You shall love the Lord your God with all your heart and with all your soul and with all your might." The second is found in Leviticus 19:18: "You shall love your neighbor as yourself; I am the Lord" (cf. Gal 5:14; Rom 13:9; Jas 2:8).

Jesus' teaching is helpful in understanding that the Law has a twofold purpose: showing how to relate to God properly and how to relate to other people properly. This difference does not mean that laws concerning our relationships with people are less important than laws concerning our relationship with God. Contrary to the laws of other nations at the time the Mosaic law was given, God himself is deeply concerned about our behavior toward other people. It is this aspect that ties both parts of the Law together.

In other cultures, people had the choice whether to enforce certain laws in civil relationships; in Israel, God was concerned that there be consistent and true justice at all times.

With respect to these two emphases, it is helpful to note that the first four of the Ten Commandments have to do with our relationship to God, and the remaining six to our relationship with people. This may be expanded to the entire series of laws. Laws concerning God may be divided into spiritual laws (e.g., Deut 5:7–15; 6:4–5), religious laws (e.g., Exod 12:14–27; 23:14–17; Lev 23; Deut 12:1–14), and ceremonial laws (e.g., Exod 12:3–11; Lev 1–7; Num 19). Laws concerning human relationships may be divided into moral laws (e.g., Deut 5:16–21; 18:9–14), civil laws (e.g., Exod 21:1—23:13; Lev 24:17—25:55), and health laws (e.g., Lev 11:1–15:33).

The two laws Jesus quoted apply to all people in all times. But, many laws in the books of Moses were, of necessity, related to the culture at the time they were given. This can lead to misunderstanding. For example, many claim that "an eye for an eye and a tooth for a tooth" is an example of the harshness of the Mosaic law (Exod 21:24; Lev 24:20; Deut 19:21). However, this law was designed not to promote injury, but to limit retribution. At the time this law was given, people, families, and tribes took their own revenge for real or imagined grievances. Violence often escalated without a stopping point as each individual or group tried to top the vengeance of the other. The principle behind this law, that punishment should always be proportional to the crime, should guide justice in all times. This removes the necessity for further retribution.

The Mosaic law limited revenge in another way: it took justice out of the hands of the individual or family and put it in the hands of the larger community. Justice is to be dispassionately dispensed by the community. This tends to limit the emotion that drives the escalation of vengeance in blood feuds. In addition, the Law required at least two witnesses and that no one "bear false witness" (Exod 20:16; Num 35:30; Deut 5:20; 17:6; 19:15–21). Both Jesus and Paul referred to the Law when teaching how to handle disciplinary matters among the followers of Christ (Matt 18:16; 2 Cor 13:1; 1 Tim 5:19).

The Israelite community was to enforce these laws without bias because God is always concerned with justice. No one was exempt from these laws, not even the king. The civil government was separated from the religious functions so that rulers could not use religion for their personal benefit. This also differed from other peoples of the ancient Near East, where the leader was generally the high priest and often considered a god. The principles regarding civil justice in the Mosaic law became part of the foundation of the justice system in Western culture.

Health is another area where the Law benefited the Israelites. The Law required care regarding diet, cleanliness, and the quarantine of those with disease. Of course, circumstances and culture have changed. Nevertheless, we can discern principles related to these restrictions that apply today even as then. One of the lessons of the these laws is that people often bring hardship upon themselves by poor choices—in this case, injuries and diseases. Such choices result either from carelessness or from a determination to indulge in behavior known to be risky.

The spiritual and moral laws of the Mosaic law also teach that bad conduct leads to undesirable consequences. These prohibitions do not pass away because they relate directly to the very nature of God as a righteous God, and because disobedience brings spiritual corruption. Some Christians point to the Jerusalem Council to argue that Christians are no longer subject to any of the Mosaic law, but that is not the case.

In the time of Jesus' ministry and the early church, Jews were dispersed to cities around the Mediterranean Sea. This dispersion was called the Jewish Diaspora. Many cities had a synagogue. Worship among the Jews of the diaspora was typically conducted in Greek rather than Hebrew, using a Greek translation of the Old Testament. Many Gentiles committed themselves to the moral and spiritual requirements of the Law of Moses without committing themselves to obey the entire law. These were called "God-fearers" (Gk. *phoboumenoi ton theon* or *sebomenois*). The first Gentile convert to Christianity, Cornelius, was a God-fearer, as were many of the Gentiles who first came to faith in Christ (Acts 10:1–2, 22; 17:4). Jews who became Christians tended to live by the Mosaic law just as they had done before. The rapid growth of Gentile Christians, partly due to the number of God-fearers present in the diaspora, brought about a crisis when Gentile Christians continued to ignore parts of the Law. What is commonly referred to as "the Jerusalem Council" was convened to resolve this problem (Acts 15). It demonstrated the unity of Christian leadership in seeking to do God's will.

The decision of the council was that Gentiles should abstain from four things that were either spiritually destructive or abhorrent to the Jews. Christians were told to avoid eating meat they knew had been sacrificed to idols, to avoid eating meat from an animal that had been strangled, to refrain from eating blood, and to avoid sexual immorality. Some interpret this to mean that the entire law of Moses was set aside except for these four prohibitions; but that is absurd. Can anyone honestly contend that the Jerusalem Council meant everyone to understand that it is acceptable for Christians to tell lies? Or to murder? To steal, to commit adultery, to covet, or to take the Lord's name in vain? Of course not. The purpose of the gospel was not to make pagans comfortable in their immorality, but to enable people to escape the corruption of the world's ways (1 John 2:17; 2 Pet 1:2–4).

No reading of the decision of the Jerusalem Council in the context of the rest of the New Testament justifies the interpretation that it is now acceptable to break the Ten Commandments or to participate in the occult (cf. Acts 10:34–35; 19:18–19; 24:14–16; 26:19–20; Rom 6:1–11; Gal 5:16–21). Early Gentile Christians would have interpreted that they did not have to accept the parts of the Law that were not moral and spiritual—such as circumcision, temple sacrifices, feasts, and dietary and health restrictions—but that they were to continue to live righteous lives before the Lord, this time with the aid of the indwelling Spirit of Christ.

The Mosaic Law in the History of Israel

Knowledge of, reverence for, and obedience to the Law of Moses varied greatly during the history of Israel. Most of the people could not read, and could not have their own copy of the Law even if they did. The priests were responsible to keep the scrolls and to teach the Law to the people. Certainly while Moses and Aaron lived, the Law was upheld, and to a certain extent during the time of Joshua as well. After that, there were long periods when the Law was not taught and little observed. The time of the Judges was one such period. The prophet Samuel taught righteousness and insisted the people practice it. Under David and Solomon, there was a renewed emphasis on worship at the tabernacle. The first temple was built in Jerusalem during the reign of Solomon. However, even Solomon went astray, taking part in the worship of false gods. Knowledge of and obedience to the Law when monarchs ruled Israel and Judah were spotty. The prophets cried out for righteousness and were sometimes heeded, but often ignored. Under King Josiah of Judah, there was a rediscovery of the scrolls of the Law and a renewed emphasis upon following the Law (2 Chr 34). Nevertheless, by Isaiah's time the people had largely hardened their hearts against the righteousness demanded by the Mosaic law. The nation of Israel was destroyed. Later, the neglect of true worship and righteousness led to the destruction of the nation of Judah as well. The Jews were then marched off to seventy-five years of captivity in Babylon.

While in captivity in Babylon with no tabernacle or temple, the Jews established synagogue worship. Prayer, song, and Scripture readings reminded the people of their covenant with God and the provisions of their covenant. When, under the Persians, Jews were allowed to return to Judah and rebuild Jerusalem, there was a renewed emphasis on temple worship and the Law (Ezra 5:1-2; Neh 8; 10:28-39). Following this, however, the Jews faced new trials as they were conquered by pagan powers.

During this intertestamental period, when the Old Testament had been written and the time of the New Testament had not yet come, the Jews came under harsh persecution for their faith. Only those truly devoted to the Lord practiced their faith openly, for which they were often tortured and killed. The Jews gained their independence for a while after the Maccabean revolt, following which they could practice their faith openly again. When the Romans later conquered Palestine, the Romans had no love for the Jews, but permitted them to practice their faith.

The period between the time covered in the Old and New Testaments brought three emphases. First, because those who were faithful during times of persecution showed their devotion to God by open adherence to the Law, there was a new stress on outward practice. Second, since most were no longer persecuted for practicing their faith openly, it became possible for someone who was motivated solely by outward appearance to make a show of living by the Law. Thus, Jesus would oppose those who had no love for God or for their neighbors, but sought the place of honor at banquets and in synagogues, dressed to impress others with their religious zeal, prayed long prayers to appear spiritual, and attracted attention to themselves in the market and when giving offerings at the temple (Matt 23:5-7). Third, the provision of blessing and cursing that was promised the nation of Israel for following the Law was wrongly applied to individuals.

Under the Mosaic covenant of *Yahweh* with the nation of Israel, *Yahweh* offered blessings to the nation for obeying his commandments and promised punishments if they did not. Portions of Old Testament Scripture that reflect this are often called Deuteronomic because it is in Deuteronomy that this is made most clear (cf. Deut 28). In the period leading up to the birth of Christ, the concept that obedience meant blessing and disobedience meant impoverishment was applied to individuals in a manner never meant under the Mosaic covenant. It is certainly true that anyone living according the ways of the Law will be better-off spiritually for doing so; however, when most people disobey, life can be difficult for the faithful (e.g., Ps 119:81-88, 145-168). This is seen, for example, in the lives of Jeremiah and Daniel.

The belief that wealth signified God's blessing but poverty signified God's judgment became widespread by the time of Christ. This belief fueled the greed and arrogance of the Sadducees, who thought in totally worldly terms—justified, they thought, by the Law of Moses. Most Jews seem to have accepted this logic even though most who lived in Palestine lived in poverty. The story of the rich man and Lazarus had the same function of opposing this prejudice as the story of the Good Samaritan had in opposing Jewish hatred of the Samaritans (Luke 10:30–37; 16:19–31).

Jesus faced an uphill battle trying to convince people that an individual's possessions had no relation to whether God approved of the way they lived. The account of the rich young ruler is perhaps the best illustration of how pervasive this misconception was. The wealthy young man who approached Jesus to ask what he had to do to inherit eternal life surely thought his wealth guaranteed there was nothing more for him to do (Mark 10:17–22). When Jesus told him to sell all of his possessions and follow Jesus, the man went away sad.

Jesus' demand confused his disciples as well. Even after hearing so much of Jesus' teachings, the disciples had not progressed beyond the young man's misunderstanding. They never expected Jesus to say that it was difficult for a *rich* person "to enter the kingdom of God" (Mark 10:23–27). "Then who can be saved?" the disciples asked Jesus, clearly thinking just about everyone was then disqualified (Mark 10:26). Yet, Jesus' teaching wasn't new. A look at Old Testament Scripture such as Psalm 37, Psalm 73, and the book of Job show that prosperity doesn't necessarily indicate faithfulness to the Lord, nor does suffering indicate rejection by the Lord—especially in the short run. Neither wealth nor poverty necessarily indicate a person's spirituality. Wealth isn't evil in itself and can bring many blessings, especially when it is used to serve the Lord. Nevertheless, both wealth and poverty bring their own unique stresses and temptations (Mark 4:18–19).

The renewed emphasis on the Mosaic law in the period between the Old and New Testaments led to further twisting of the Law. During this time, traditions were created as a guide to fulfilling the requirements of the Law. Unfortunately, some of these traditions went far astray from the intent behind the Law, promoting personal pride rather than true spirituality. Many of these traditions were self-seeking perversions of the Law designed to justify greed. Such traditions replaced the Law in day-to-day practice for many Jews. Jesus strongly opposed the emptiness and hypocrisy of such practices, as did the Apostle Paul (Mark 7:1–13; Col 2:8–17).

These trends produced a unique situation during the time of Christ. The knowledge of the Law among the people was probably as high as it had ever been because of the synagogues, temple worship, and pilgrimages from the diaspora to celebrate sacred observances and feasts in Jerusalem; nevertheless, the Law was often distorted far from what God intended. It is important to read the New Testament with this in mind. It is essential to distinguish the Law from the way it was abused at that time—to recognize that much of what was written in the New Testament was to oppose these errant practices rather than to impugn the Law of Moses itself—even though the practice of the Mosaic law was certainly always meant to be superseded by the New Covenant.

The Successes and Failure of the Mosaic Law

The dismal failure of the Israelites as a whole to follow the Mosaic law is often interpreted as a failure of the Law itself; likewise, the misapplication of the Law in New Testament times. Yet, Jesus lived his entire earthly life under the Law of Moses—an accomplishment that formed part of the basis for the effectiveness of his redemptive death on Calvary (Heb 7:26–27; 9:13–14; 1 Pet 1:18–19; 1 John 2:1). This could not have been true had the Law been inherently evil. Jesus taught that there was no portion of the Law that should be ignored. He preached that not only the smallest letters of the Scripture are sacred, the smallest marks that serve to distinguish one written letter from another are sacred (Matt 5:18; Luke 16:17). It is significant that Jesus speaks of the written law, appealing to the sacred documents in which each letter must be considered divinely inspired. Stephen would call these writings "living oracles" (Gk. *logia zōnta*, Acts 7:38).

Moreover, Paul, who opposed the false understanding of the Law with all his might, nevertheless also recognized the proper place of the Law. He wrote to the Romans that the Law is not sin (Gk. *hamartia*): "The Law is holy (Gk. *hagios*), and the commandment is holy (Gk. *hagia*) and righteous (Gk. *dikaia*) and good (Gk. *agathē*). . . . The Law is spiritual (Gk. *pneumatikos*)" (Rom 7:7, 12, 14). Later, he wrote to Timothy, "We know that the Law is good (Gk. *kalos*), if one uses it lawfully (Gk. *autōi nomimōs chrētai*)" (1 Tim 1:8). Why would Paul say these things?

First, the Law served to restrain the grossest sins, ensuring that there would be greater order and peace in society than if the Law were not in effect (1 Tim 1:9–10). Not only were limits set, there was an orderly way to handle infractions of the Law.

Second, the Law provided a framework for the behavior of those who were devoted to *Yahweh*. The teachings of the Law provided a better way of life than that of the pagan cultures surrounding the Israelites, one that could make them exemplary among other peoples. Individuals who wished to serve the Lord knew how to do so. From the time of Moses until the time of Jesus, there were many who were sincerely devoted to the service of God. This enabled not only the coming of Christ, but also the effectiveness of his ministry.

Among those who were shaped by the Law of Moses was Mary, Jesus' mother. Mary's devotion to the service of God makes her one of the most godly individuals of all time. Joseph, Mary's husband and Jesus' earthly father, was likewise devoted to the Lord. Zacharias and Elizabeth, the parents of John the Baptist, were chosen by the Lord because of their faithfulness—the foolishness of Zacharias at the announcement of the birth of John notwithstanding. Luke tells us: "They were both righteous in the sight of God, walking blamelessly in all the commandments and requirements of the Lord" (Luke 1:6). John the Baptist, in calling people to prepare themselves for the coming of the Christ, used the Law as the basis for his call to righteous living. Later, those who first received Jesus Christ as their Lord and Savior were either Jews or God-fearing Gentiles who had been prepared by the Law and the ministry of the prophets. That the Law is seen as having abiding value is shown by Jesus' use of the Law in the Sermon on the Mount and Paul's use of the commandment to honor one's parents in Ephesians 6:1–3.

Third, the Law existed so people would learn that they had a deep spiritual problem that only God can solve. Paul refers to this in Romans 7:5–24. He tells how the Law made him aware of sin because it showed him that desiring to live by the Law was not enough to overcome his tendency to disobey God. The Law isn't sinful, but it made the problem of inward sin obvious (Rom 7:7, 13). This revealed Paul's need for something more than the written law, something to change him inwardly and enable him to do what is right before God. This prepared him to receive Christ and the Holy Spirit, which Paul testified gave him victory over sin (Rom 7:25—8:17). As Paul told the Galatians, the Law was a schoolmaster that led to Christ (Gal 3:24). The woman who anointed Jesus' feet at Simon's dinner demonstrated that she understood this lesson.

Those who aren't serious about their relationship with God seek to do the minimum that seems to comply with the letter of the law. They view the commandments as the maximum they need to do rather than as starting points for understanding how to please God, viewing their minimal compliance as a source of pride. They, therefore, do not learn from the instruction of the Law as the psalmist did in Psalm 1 (cf. Ps 19:7–14; 119:1–16). Paul wrote, "The letter kills, but the Spirit gives life" (2 Cor 3:6). Only through the power of God's indwelling Spirit can inward sin be overcome, and that only for those who humbly seek to walk in fellowship with God (Isa 57:15).

In Paul's case, the utter wickedness of sin was demonstrated in that even his determination to observe the religious practices given by God were twisted into evil. Paul never forgot that in his religious zeal he persecuted the Christian church, making him, in his view, the "foremost" of all sinners (1 Tim 1:15).

Paul's teaching that the Law is a schoolmaster recognizes that God anticipated the failure of the people, using that failure to advance his plan.

Once this was achieved, the Mosaic covenant achieved its major purposes. The Mosaic covenant was then superseded by the New Covenant, even though the Law still has a purpose in the lives of those under the New Covenant.

The Law as a Gift of Grace

If the history of Israel under the Law of Moses is a record of the unfaithfulness of Abraham's children, it is equally a record of the long-suffering of a merciful God. As God said through Isaiah: "I have spread out my hands all day long to a rebellious people, who walk *in* the way which is not good, following their own thoughts, a people who continually provoke Me to My face" (Isa 65:2–3; cf. Rom 10:21). Though those who were given the Law were often stubborn in resisting God, God was more tenacious in working out his grace.

In the Old Testament, God sometimes called himself the "husband" of the Israelites, treating the Mosaic covenant as a marriage with the people of Israel (Isa 54:5–8; Jer 31:32; cf. Eph 5:25–32). The greatest example of this is seen in the book of Hosea. Hosea married a woman named Gomer who preferred the life of a harlot to a life of fidelity to her husband. In spite of Gomer's repeated rejection of Hosea's love, Hosea continued to pursue her with the hope of restoring their marriage. This is a metaphor of God's constant pursuit of Israel in view of God's covenant at Mount Sinai and his promise to Abraham (Gen 22:18). No matter how many setbacks, God would not be defeated in his plan to create a people for his own possession.

If the Law succeeded in accomplishing what God gave it for, it failed to be a solution to people's deepest spiritual needs; but then, it was never meant to be that. That is what many wanted it to be, and tried to make it. But that is not what God ever intended it to be. Even the best of God's people broke the Law at least once; and once broken, it was broken. No amount of faithfulness could fix the gulf created between a person and God if any portion of the Law was broken. God intended the Mosaic covenant as preparation for something greater. This was foretold by the prophet Jeremiah, who preached and wrote six hundred years before the birth of Christ.

Through Jeremiah, *Yahweh* foretold the coming of a New Covenant with the descendants of Abraham by the "husband" of Israel. This covenant, *Yahweh* said, would be unlike the one made with Moses—the covenant the people broke (Jer 31:31–32). "'This is the covenant which I will make with the house of Israel after those days,' declares the Lord, 'I will put My Law within them and on their heart I will write it; and I will be their God, and they shall be My people'" (Jer 31:33). This New Covenant would accomplish everything the earlier covenants had not. This covenant would be sealed by the blood of the Messiah and effected by the indwelling of the Holy Spirit.

11

COMPREHENDING THE TRIUMPH

For I delivered to you as of first importance what I also received, that Christ died for our sins according to the Scriptures, and that He was buried, and that He was raised on the third day according to the Scriptures.

1 CORINTHIANS 15:3-4

You were not redeemed with perishable things like silver or gold from your futile way of life inherited from your forefathers, but with precious blood, as of a lamb unblemished and spotless, *the blood* of Christ.

1 PETER 1:18-19

In this is love, not that we loved God, but that He loved us and sent His Son *to be* the propitiation for our sins.

1 JOHN 4:10

All of us like sheep have gone astray, each of us has turned to his own way; But the Lord has caused the iniquity of us all to fall on Him.

ISAIAH 53:6

AFTER two thousand years, the crucifixion of Jesus generally elicits no surprise. However, to the disciples first being told that Jesus would go to Jerusalem and die on a cross, the thought was unimaginable. Peter even tried to rebuke Jesus for saying it would happen (Matt 16:21-23). The thought was no less shocking when the crucifixion became reality, for according to the Mosaic law under which Jesus lived and died, a person hung on a tree was under the curse of God (Deut 21:22-23). To Jews who lived their lives avoiding anything "unclean," nothing could be more discouraging than the crucifixion of the person they loved and believed to be the Christ (Luke 24:18–21). It was no less problematic for those who were part of Roman culture, where crucifixion was reserved for the lowest class of criminals. Yet, something great and profound happened when Jesus was crucified and afterward. The cross became the symbol of Christianity because the crucifixion and the events following became the foundational events of the Christian faith.

The Unthinkable Becomes History

The arrest and crucifixion of Jesus of Nazareth was high drama even divorced from the supernatural events of the day. A high-profile religious leader popular with the crowds arrested at night by a large group armed with clubs and swords; falsely accused and abused by the highest ruling body in Judaism; paraded before the rulers of Palestine; consigned to death by a mob that couldn't honestly say what he had done to deserve it; then whipped, mocked, and crucified publicly by the Romans. But this was not all that happened—there were supernatural events as well.

In the hours before Jesus died an eerie darkness covered the land. At the time of his death, an earthquake shook the earth and the large curtain in the temple was rent from top to bottom. After the earthquake, a number of Jewish tombs were found open. The force of these latter events was so strong that even the Roman guard admitted that Jesus must have been a Son of God.

The crucifixion of Jesus was the result of the plan and actions of men. By delivering an innocent man to an agonizing death as a criminal, everyone involved—Jews and Gentiles alike—demonstrated the moral and spiritual bankruptcy of the human race. The darkness of their actions exposed the influence of spiritual powers of darkness of whose involvement they were largely unaware (John 13:21–30 with Luke 4:13; Eph 6:12). The crucifixion was the final attempt to eliminate Jesus by those human and spiritual forces that failed to defeat Jesus during his ministry. They failed then for the same reasons Jesus said they failed before: "not knowing the Scriptures nor the power of God" (Matt 22:29).

The situation is reminiscent of what happened to Joseph, who was given a many-colored robe by his father, Israel. Joseph's brothers were tired of Joseph's bragging and presence. They sold him into slavery to be rid of him forever, they hoped, telling their father that Joseph had been killed by a wild animal (Gen 37:18–36). However, God in his sovereignty worked through many difficult circumstances so that Joseph rose to become a ruler in Egypt. When a famine hit Palestine, Joseph was able to use his authority to bring his family to Egypt, and by doing so preserved their lives.

Joseph recognized that what his brothers had meant for harm, God used for the family's good (Gen 50:18-21). In much the same manner, through God's sovereignty, what started as an attempt to destroy Jesus resulted in a work of blessing for the entire human race; not because God caused the sinful behavior that took Jesus to the cross, but because God was able to use the circumstances created by sinful men to work out his plan. What started out as the sole work of men became a work of God.

This happened because God was not caught off guard by the actions of those who sought to eliminate Jesus. God foreknew what would happen, and had planned the divine response before the world was created (Acts 2:22-23; 1 Pet 1:20; Acts 4:24-28; Luke 22:22; 2 Tim 1:9). Indeed, many Scriptures in all four Gospels indicate that Jesus was well aware what was going to happen to him if he submitted to betrayal, trial, and crucifixion.

Jesus' teaching concerning his crucifixion and resurrection in fulfillment of Old Testament Scripture was, by their own admission, not fully understood by his disciples until after he rose from the dead (John 2:22; 12:16; Luke 9:43-45; 24:6-8; Mark 9:31-32). The authors of the New Testament make abundantly clear that the events at the end of Jesus' earthly life were foretold in the Old Testament Scriptures (e.g., Luke 24:25-27, 32; Acts 2:15-36; 3:18-26; 10:43; 17:1-3; 26:22-23; 1 Cor 15:1-4). This anchored the events at the end of Jesus' earthly life in the eternal plan of God.

Some of Jesus' foreknowledge came from Scriptures that foretold the events of his Passion and their meaning. Psalm 118, for example, foretold his rejection by the leaders of the Jewish religious community and his ultimate vindication. Isaiah 53 foretold in some detail his death and the redemptive purposes of the shedding of his blood. Other Scriptures provide examples of God's redemptive activity that foreshadow the work of Christ on Calvary, such as the priestly sacrifices of the Mosaic law. Finally, historical events recorded in Scripture presented circumstances that—like Joseph's experiences in Egypt in the time of the patriarchs—provided a pattern that would later be lived out by the Messiah (the Christ). All of these prepared Jesus for the events he would face. They also help us to understand what he accomplished by going to the cross.

The Purpose of the Atonement

A new covenant was promised in Jeremiah 31; however, the issue of sin had to be dealt with before this new covenant could come into effect. At his last supper, Jesus taught that the shedding of his blood would be for the forgiveness of sins (Gk. *eis aphesin hamartiōn*, Matt 26:28). This would institute the New Covenant (Gk. *hē kainē diathēkē en tōi haimati*, Luke 22:20; cf. 1 Cor 11:25). Paul wrote, "It is a trustworthy statement, deserving full acceptance, that Christ Jesus came into the world to save sinners" (1 Tim 1:15). This purpose was detailed in Isaiah 53:4-6 and 10-12. Before Jesus' birth, Joseph was told to name his son Jesus, "for He will save His people from their sins" (Matt 1:21).

During his ministry, Jesus also spoke of his work on Calvary as giving his life (Gk. *psychēn*) as a ransom (Gk. *lytron*, Mark 10:45; Matt 20:28). Jesus used the concept of a "ransom" to describe his work on the cross because a ransom is the price paid to free a captive or a slave. Jesus taught, "Truly, truly, I say to you, everyone who commits sin is a slave of sin. . . . If the Son makes you free, you will be free indeed" (John 8:34, 36). The concept of redemption is closely related in the New Testament. However, some Greek words for ransom, which are sometimes translated "redeem," relate to the Greek word for "loosing," "unfastening," or "delivering," *lyō*, and thus emphasize freedom; whereas other Greek words translated "redeem" relate to *exagorazō*, which has to do with buying at the marketplace, and thus emphasize the price paid (1 Pet 1:18; 1 Tim 2:6; Titus 2:14; Rev 5:9).

The Mosaic law taught that the forgiveness of sin requires sacrifice. According to Leviticus 17:11, the life of a sacrifice is in the blood; therefore, death by the shedding of blood is necessary to make an effective atonement for sin. The author of Hebrews sums up this teaching with the words: "According to the Law, *one may* almost *say*, all things are cleansed with blood, and without shedding of blood (Gk. *haimatekchysias*), there is no forgiveness (Gk. *aphesis*)" (Heb 9:22). Further, this fits with the custom of ratifying covenants by blood. This was part of the announcement of the New Covenant in Jeremiah 31:33. Where in the English translation God promises to "make" a covenant, the Hebrew says "I will cut (Hebr. *'ekrōt*)" a covenant— a reference to the sacrifice in a covenant ceremony.

The Old Testament also indicates that any atonement provided by human beings is inadequate to provide a remedy for the full problem of sin. Under the Mosaic law, people could come to the tabernacle to offer sacrifices for the forgiveness of confessed sin. These sacrifices were made on the alter in front of the tabernacle with the assistance of a priest. Also under the Mosaic law, the high priest would offer atonement for the sins of the nation on a day set aside for that purpose each year. To do so, he would bring the blood of the sacrifice into the very inner of the two rooms inside the tabernacle, the holy of holies, where the presence of God resided above the cherubim on the top of the ark of the covenant. The author of Hebrews reminds his readers that if the atonements offered under the Mosaic law were adequate, there would have been no necessity to repeat them again and again (Heb 10:1–7, 11). Further, the Mosaic law offered no sacrifice and no forgiveness for deliberate, intentional sin against the Lord (Num 15:22–31). The forgiveness offered was for unintentional infractions of the Law.

Given the inadequacy of the Mosaic sacrifices, what, then, constitutes an acceptable atonement for sin? In Micah 6:6–8, the question is asked:

> With what shall I come to the Lord
> *And* bow myself before the God on high?
> Shall I come to Him with burnt offerings, with yearling calves?
> Does the Lord take delight in thousands of rams,
> In ten thousand rivers of oil?
> Shall I present my firstborn *for* my rebellious acts,
> The fruit of my body for the sin of my soul?
> He has told you, O man, what is good;
> And what does the Lord require of you
> But to do justice, to love kindness, and to walk humbly with your God?

There is no answer here to the question of atonement. Confession and the determination to repent of sin are essential to the restoration of a broken relationship with God; but they are so much short of a sufficient atonement that they are not even mentioned here. Obedience to the Mosaic law with its rituals is a must for this individual, but the implication here is that the sacrifices and offerings mandated under this law are ultimately insufficient for anything more than an appeal. Micah's conclusion that he can only walk humbly with God suggests that he is dependent upon God for an atonement that is adequate.

The Nature of the Atonement Made by Christ

The first major conflict between human beings was between Cain and Abel, and it stemmed from methods of worship. God's warning to Cain indicates that Abel was offering worship that was acceptable to God, and Cain was not—thus illustrating that what constitutes acceptable worship and an acceptable atonement for sin is determined by God, not by human beings (Heb 12:28). This should make us cautious about using human wisdom to determine the nature and effects of the atonement provided through Jesus Christ. It should make us wholly reliant on what Scripture reveals and not go beyond. Through Isaiah, God declared that his thoughts and ways are far above those of human beings (Isa 55:8–9). Paul quoted Isaiah and Job to celebrate God's wisdom and knowledge, and to recognize that God's judgments are "unsearchable" (Gk. *hōs anexeraunēta ta krimata autou*) and his ways "unfathomable" (Gk. *anexichniastoi hai hodoi autou*, Rom 11:33–36; cf. Isa 40:13–14; Job 35:7; 41:11; 42:1–6).

The Atonement as a Work of God

Not only is the acceptability of any atonement determined by God, but also the nature of any atonement he makes, as well as its effects, are rooted in his character. The atonement made by Jesus Christ, as an act of God, was completely personal even though it touched creation. The atonement came from deep within the being and character of the Trinity—the fountain of God's love. Like the divine love that it expresses, the benefits of the atonement are only limited in efficacy and in extent by God's nature.

With regard to limitations, it is not controversial to say that God can always love more people. For example, to say God loves "the five people here" does not prevent him from loving "the ten over there." It would be silly to say that God is only capable of loving a certain number of people, but no more; just as it would be silly to say that God's love is like pie dough: the more it is spread out, the thinner it becomes. Certainly the living God is so great that his capacity to love is without bounds.

The atonement is analogous to love because the atonement is motivated by God's love. This is made clear by Jesus, John, and Paul (John 3:14–17; 1 John 4:9–10; Rom 5:6–8). It is God reaching out to bring his enemies into his fellowship (Rom 5:6–8; cf. Matt 5:43–48). Any limitation to the atonement also comes solely from God's nature: his refusal to let the destructiveness of unrighteousness exist without limitation. All attempts to analyze the atonement mathematically are doomed to failure in the same manner as all attempts to analyze God's love mathematically. In the arithmetic of the atonement, the atonement is always an undivided whole. The atonement addresses one problem: the problem of sin that breaks fellowship with the Creator; with one goal: the reconciliation of lost souls to their Creator (2 Cor 5:18–19; Eph 2:13–18). We cannot quantify the atonement, but we can confidently say that it is *sufficient* to accomplish God's purposes.

Because the atonement comes from the nature of God, we must not characterize it as pitting one member of the Trinity against the other. All members of the Trinity are equal in substance and character. Nor did God the Son change in his essential character because he became God incarnate (Heb 13:8). Therefore, the atonement did not pit the grace of God the Son against the wrath of God the Father, as if one is focused upon love and the other upon righteousness. All members of the Trinity are equally motivated by love and righteousness. John wrote, "God [the Father] so loved the world, that He gave His only begotten Son, that whoever believes in Him shall not perish, but have eternal life" (John 3:16). The author of Hebrews wrote that Jesus (the Christ, the "Anointed One") offered himself to God "through the eternal Spirit" (Gk. *dia Pneumatos aiōniou*, Heb 9:14). There is involvement by the entire Trinity with a single purpose, but with different roles.

The Trinity had the same roles in salvation as in creation: the Father wills, the Son mediates, and the Spirit effects the work. By this economy, the Son of God was willed to be the mediator of the New Covenant by God the Father. Paul wrote, "God was in Christ reconciling the world to Himself, not counting their trespasses against them" (2 Cor 5:19). This is not because the Son was forced to take this role by the Father and the Holy Spirit; the Son took this role upon himself voluntarily in response to the Father's will (Phil 2:5–11; Matt 16:21–23; 26:51–54; John 10:11, 15, 17–18). Further, although the Son made the sacrifice, all of the Trinity was involved in the event and its acceptance.

The Son Makes Atonement

It is certain from the Scriptures that the atonement must be seen as somehow bringing upon Jesus Christ the punishment for sin that sinners deserve. This is the teaching of the fifty-third chapter of Isaiah. Habakkuk wrote of God, "*Your* eyes are too pure to approve evil, and You can not look on wickedness *with favor*" (Hab 1:13; cf. Ps 34:15–16). God cannot simply overlook sin; the wrath of God against sin needed somehow to be propitiated (Rom 3:24–25; 8:1). Peter wrote, "For Christ also died for sins once for all, *the* just for *the* unjust, so that He might bring us to God" (1 Pet 3:18). The atonement made by Jesus is such that each person can look at Jesus' sacrifice and say: "Jesus died for me. Jesus died in my place; because of Jesus, I can be forgiven."

At the same time, it is important to recognize that Jesus did not die just for the individuals who will be redeemed; Jesus died as representative of the human race. John the Baptist pointed to Jesus and said, "Behold, the Lamb of God who takes away the sin (Gk. *tēn hamartian*) of the world!" (John 1:29, 36). John speaks of "the sin" singular, not plural, and he speaks of the world (Gk. *tou kosmou*), not individuals.

In a significant discussion comparing the effects of Adam's sin to the effects of Christ's atonement in Romans 5:12–21, Paul makes clear that the atonement is greater in every respect than the effects of sin on the human race. What is in view here is more than forensics, more than legal justification for those culpable before the throne of God. It reaches out to remove not only the penalty before the throne of God of those who choose to sin, but that sinfulness that is inherited as members of a sinful race, as well as the effects of sin that result from human ignorance and weakness.

Paul wrote that even when the presence of the Mosaic law increased sinfulness by making people aware of their sin, the grace of God based on Jesus' sacrifice was far, far greater (Rom 5:20). The Greek word Paul used for the increase in sinfulness is *pleonasē*. Paul used a different word for the increase in grace here, *hypereperisseusen*, indicating a superabundance of grace—grace that is beyond measure. The collective nature of the atonement is effective because the atonement is a work of God that touches all people for what they cannot control; it is God's work preparing the way for the forgiveness of sins for which people make themselves culpable. Any understanding of the teaching of the New Testament that portrays sin as more powerful than grace is not doing justice to what Paul says in this important passage of Romans. Paul makes clear that this grace comes by "the one Man, Jesus Christ" (Rom 5:15). For, as Paul wrote to Timothy, "there is one God, *and* one mediator also between God and men, *the* man Christ Jesus" (1 Tim 2:5).

Although Jesus died as a human being at Calvary, it was his unique identity that made the atonement effective. Jesus is often described by theologians as *theananthropic* to describe his dual nature as truly God and truly man, a word created by a combination of the Greek words for God (Gk. *theos*) and man (Gk. *anthrōpos*). Without this dual nature, Jesus could never have been the mediator who reconciled sinful human beings to a holy God. Although there are other reasons for the incarnation of the Son of God—such as identification, communication, and fellowship with human beings—the need for atonement made it a necessity for the Son of God to become the *theanthropic* Person. This would be the one Isaiah foretold would be named "Immanuel" ("God with us") and who, though a human child, would also be identified as "eternal Father" and "the Mighty God" (Isa 7:14; 9:6–7). Just how this dual nature served to bring about reconciliation is as wrapped in the divine mystery as is the incarnation itself. Nevertheless, we can be certain that no mere human being, especially a sinful one, could have fulfilled this role.

The author of Hebrews observes that as a priest of the order of Melchizedek, Jesus offered himself as a sacrifice for sin once for all (Heb 6:19—10:25). In this new priestly order of which Jesus is the only priest, the sacrifice is presented before God the Father in heaven. This happened in the real holy of holies where God the Father dwells, in contrast to the earthly holy of holies in the tabernacle of the Mosaic covenant (Heb 9:1–28). The author of Hebrews finds verification of this divine plan in the Psalms. In Hebrews 5:6 and 7:17 he quotes Psalm 110:4, "You are a priest forever according to the order of Melchizedek." In Hebrews 10:5-7, he presents David's words in Psalms 40:6-7 as prophetic of the attitude of the incarnate Son of God—Jesus, the son of David: "... a body you have prepared for Me ... then I said, 'Behold, I have come (in the scroll of the book it is written of Me) to do your will, O God.'"[1]

One of the reasons Jesus could provide a sufficient atonement is because he was without sin. Because his mother was human, he became fully human; and because his father was the Holy Spirit, he was without an inherited tendency to sin, just as was Adam after Adam was created. Jesus then lived a life that was blameless according to the Law of Moses (1 Pet 1:19; Heb 7:26; 9:14; John 8:46). He died, as Paul wrote, not as one who was sinful, but, "in the likeness of sinful flesh" (Gk. *en homoiōmati sarkos hamartias*, Rom 8:3). "He made Him who knew no sin *to be* sin on our behalf," Paul affirmed, "so that we might become the righteousness of God in Him" (2 Cor 5:21).

Jesus went to the cross as a man and suffered the excruciating torment and humiliation of crucifixion (Phil 2:5-11). Further, the place of the cross was, according to the Mosaic law, a cursed place. Paul wrote, "Christ redeemed us from the curse (Gk. *kataras*) of the Law, having become a curse (Gk. *katara*) for us—for it is written, 'Cursed (Gk. *epikataratos*) is everyone who hangs on a tree (Gk. *xylou*)'" (Gal 3:13; Deut 21:22-23).

As the *theanthropic* Person, there is another side to the crucifixion beyond the physical. It is the spiritual side of this event that made it something more than the crucifixion of a human being. This act affected God the Father as well as God the Son. The darkness that descended over the land during Jesus' crucifixion was a manifestation of this aspect of the crucifixion.

Just before Jesus died he proclaimed, "It is finished" (John 19:30). The atonement is a work that was finished with the death of Jesus on the cross. The author of Hebrews proclaims that this work is complete (Heb 7:27; 9:11-14, 26-28; 10:10). In this he is in harmony with all the authors of the New Testament. Although Jesus presented himself before the Father in heaven many days after his crucifixion, it was to present the results of the work, not to complete it.

The Atonement and Its Consequences

The nature of the atonement eliminates such pointless questions as: "If the atonement is a ransom, who was the ransom paid to?" Questions like this have taken too much time in Christian history. The concept of a ransom is an analogy that highlights the cost and efficacy of the atonement. The

---

1. On the use of Ps 40 in Heb 10:5-7, see the discussion by Guthrie in *CNTUOT*, 975-78.

important points made by ransom/redemption terminology are that atonement for sin is costly, the price was paid, the price was paid in full, and the payment of this cost brings freedom to the redeemed (Rev 5:9). While the atonement releases the sinner from any claim Satan might have on that individual, the reconciliation of the sinner is wholly God's work. It has nothing to do with Satan except to deprive him of a claim that the sinner belongs to him rather than to Christ (Col 1:13–14).

The release of an individual from Satan's realm is because God has freed the sinner from the consequences of his or her sin, not because Satan was owed or paid anything. It is the effect of the atonement that has a direct relationship to Satan. Satan's works, in terms of corrupting human beings and moving them farther away from fellowship with God, are nullified for the redeemed (1 John 3:8). Jesus' triumph over the cross reveals the wickedness of Satan and his followers, and shows the power of God to defeat them even when they do their worst (Col 2:13–15; cf. John 13:21–30).

Ransom terminology has the benefit of differentiating the atonement from other works of God. The purchase of an item moves it from storage to make it available for use; but it is up to the new owner to actually make use of that item. A person redeemed from slavery is freed to do other things, but the ransom doesn't accomplish those things, it makes them possible. Similarly, the atonement should not be confused with the opportunities for God's further work that it enables. The atonement is an undivided whole, but it enables multiple blessings to follow. A key unlocks a door, but the door must still be opened and people must pass through the door along with whatever they wish to bring with them, or the open door has no benefit. In like manner, the atonement opens the way for God to work out his purposes in the lives of those who have been redeemed; but that doesn't remove the need for further work, it enables it.

Jesus Christ Risen and Glorified

On the first Easter, Jesus rose physically and bodily from the dead. Luke tells us that Jesus then presented himself to his followers over a period of forty days with "many convincing proofs" (Gk. *pollois tekmēriois*, Acts 1:3). Richard Thompson observes of the word translated "convincing proofs," *tekmēriois*: "In Greek rhetoric, it describes compelling evidence that results in defensible or irrefutable conclusions."[2] John begins his first letter by declaring that he and the other apostles had direct experience with the resurrected Christ. Paul provides a list of those who were witnesses to the

---

2. Thompson, *Acts*, 58.

resurrected Christ, including, on at least one occasion, a group of more than five hundred of Jesus' followers—many of whom were alive and able to be interviewed at the time Paul wrote (1 Cor 15:1–8).

It is important that Jesus' resurrection was of his physical body (Luke 24:39). A purely spiritual afterlife was characteristic of Greek rather than Hebrew thought. Where this is present in certain Jewish writings in the centuries surrounding the life of Christ, it was due to Greek influence on Jewish writers rather than the writings of our Old Testament.

Hebrew writers did not view the physical world or the physical body as unworthy of God. Their conviction has its basis in Genesis, which tells us that at the end of the sixth day, when creation was complete, "God saw all that He had made, and behold, it was very good" (Gen 1:31). The translation "very good" for the Hebrew *ṭôb mᵉʾōd* in our English Bibles does not communicate the full meaning suggested by the Hebrew phrase. The Hebrew adjective *ṭôb* in the Old Testament may mean any or all of the following: "good, pleasant, beautiful, delightful, glad, joyful, precious, correct, righteous."[3] This meaning is intensified by the Hebrew *mᵉʾōd*, meaning "very" or "exceedingly." Given this, it seems best to take the meaning of *ṭôb* in Genesis 1:31 in its broadest possible sense: that God was declaring there to be nothing lacking in the whole of the new creation—including human beings—that would make it less than wholly pleasing.

Hebrew thought also considered every person as a whole rather than a collection of parts. The concept of separating the spirit and the physical body was unnatural, something not envisioned in the original creation that was "very good." Therefore, in Hebrew thought the bodily resurrection of the dead was an absolute necessity for any meaningful afterlife, as reflected in Paul's discussion in 2 Corinthians 5:1–10. In contrast, Greek thinkers tended to see the physical world and physical bodies as not only inferior to the spiritual sphere, but essentially restricting, and even evil, and thus as something to be escaped. The concept of bodily resurrection was thus abhorrent to the Gentiles.

The Jewish Sadducees were steadfast in resisting the idea of any kind of afterlife. In sharp contrast, the Pharisees were just as insistent that there would not only be an afterlife, but a resurrection of the dead as well (Acts 23:8). Paul was a Pharisee before his conversion. Given that the Pharisees insisted on a strict manner of life, it seems likely there were those who didn't identify as Pharisees who nevertheless shared belief in a bodily resurrection. Although Jesus only spoke of his upcoming passion and resurrection to the inner circle of his disciples, Jesus taught publicly that the story of Jonah is

---

3. Bolling, "*ṭôb*," in *TWOT*, 1:345.

analogous to his resurrection from the dead (Matt 12:39–40). Later, apparently based on what Jesus taught them, Christians perceived the foretelling of Jesus' resurrection and eternal reign in such passages as Hosea 6:1–2; Psalm 16:7–11; Psalm 110:1 and 4; Psalm 132:10–11; and Isaiah 9:6–7 (cf. Acts 2:22–36).

Jesus' resurrected body was more than just revivified in the manner of the resurrection of Lazarus (John 11:38–45). Lazarus's resurrection was a reprieve. Afterward, Lazarus aged and died like everyone else. Jesus' resurrection body, on the other hand, was glorified. Glorification transformed his mortal body to last forever. The resurrected Lazarus was still part of the current creation of the present age; the glorified Jesus was part of the new creation of the age to come.

The historical fact of Jesus' resurrection is of primary importance in Christianity. If his resurrection had not been bodily, the Romans and the Jewish authorities could have simply produced his body and refuted the Christian movement before it had a chance to take root. Even the disciples would have been discouraged had this happened. As it was, the Apostle Paul, who was a part of the Jewish religious leadership before his conversion, would have known the resurrection of Jesus was a fraud and would never have been converted. Instead, he devoted his life to proclaiming Jesus as risen from the dead.

There would have been theological ramifications, as well, had Jesus not risen. Paul told the Corinthians that if Jesus did not rise from the dead, Christianity has no value because they were still in their sins (1 Cor 15:12–19). This would also eliminate any hope of resurrection and glorification for the redeemed. The witness of the documents of the New Testament, however, is that Jesus has risen bodily from the dead. Peter wrote that because of this, we have in Jesus a "living hope" (1 Pet 1:3). In a similar vein, Paul wrote that if we were brought into fellowship with God through the death of Jesus, the living Son of God provides even more assurance of his saving grace (Rom 5:8–10).

Indeed, Jesus of Nazareth was one of many thousands of individuals crucified by the Romans in the first century. Had he not risen bodily from the dead, it is difficult to imagine how his followers would have been convinced that he is the Christ. Paul reminded Festus and Agrippa that the events of Jesus' life, death, and resurrection had not taken place in a secret place (a corner), but in Jerusalem when there were thousands of visitors from every corner of the Roman empire, not to mention the presence of the Roman government and the Jewish ruling body, the Sanhedrin (Acts 26:26).

Jesus Christ as Priest and Intercessor

After meeting with his followers on the last day he was with them, the resurrected Christ gave final instructions, then ascended into heaven (Acts 1:9–11). Jesus would continue his work through his followers, who would be empowered for this by the Holy Spirit. John the Baptist said that while he baptized with water, the Christ would baptize with the Holy Spirit. This could not happen, however, until the priestly work of Christ was complete (Acts 1:4–5).

There is an interesting passage in John's Gospel regarding the ministry of the Holy Spirit. Jesus said that those who followed him would have rivers of living water flowing from them. John explained that Jesus "spoke of the Spirit, whom those who believed in Him were to receive; for the Spirit was not yet *given*, because Jesus was not yet glorified" (John 7:39). The Greek here is literally: "the Spirit was not yet" (Gk. *oupō gar ēn Pneuma*). Taken out of context, this seems to state that the Holy Spirit either didn't exist or wasn't in the world yet. But that would be nonsense since it is obvious from Scripture that the Holy Spirit was involved in creation and had been working in the world, and especially since the anointing that made Jesus "the Christ" was the anointing of the Holy Spirit. What John spoke of was that the Holy Spirit would come with a new role. The "Promise of the Father" was that the Holy Spirit would come to exalt Jesus Christ, to enable his followers to live for him under the New Covenant promised in Jeremiah 31:31–34, and to bring the gospel of Jesus Christ to the world (Acts 1:4–8; cf. Gal 3:13–14). However, before this could happen, Jesus had a priestly role to complete.

As we have discussed, the author of Hebrews explains that Jesus, as a priest of the order of Melchizedek, had to bring his sacrifice before God the Father. This was similar to the way the high priest went before the Lord in the holy of holies once a year for the nation of Israel to be forgiven their sins. Jesus, however, only needed to present himself once. Further, after Jesus did this, he sat down at the right hand of God the Father in fulfillment of Psalm 110:1.

The seat at the right hand of God is the place of honor. That Jesus is said to sit there indicates that his work as priest is both complete and successful. The Promise of the Father could now be fulfilled. The Holy Spirit was poured out upon God's people at Pentecost, and the church of Jesus Christ was born.

Jesus interceded for others with God the Father during his earthly ministry. We see this in his words to Peter in Luke 22:31–32 and in his prayer in John 17. However, having completed his work to reconcile sinners to God, Jesus now takes on the role of intercessor with God the Father for all who appeal to him for aid. The author of Hebrews rejoices that Jesus, having lived in the world as a human being, understands the trials of earthly life, and so is well equipped to be a merciful intercessor to help us with our problems (Heb 2:17–18). Further, Jesus knows from experience what it is to be tried and tempted as a human being, so we can have confidence that we will receive mercy and grace if we go to him with our trials (Heb 4:14–16; cf. 1 Pet 5:6–7). Everything is now in place for his people to receive the benefits of the salvation Jesus purchased with his blood and to enable his people to bring many others into the kingdom of God (Heb 13:13–14, 20–21).

12

Recognizing the Provision

"I have no pleasure in the death of anyone who dies," declares the Lord God. "Therefore, repent and live." . . . "As I live!" declares the Lord God, "I take no pleasure in the death of the wicked, but rather that the wicked turn from his way and live."

EZEKIEL 18:32; 33:11

He made from one *man* every nation of mankind to live on all the face of the earth, having determined *their* appointed times and the boundaries of their habitation, that they would seek God, if perhaps they might grope for Him and find Him.

ACTS 17:26–27

So then as through one transgression there resulted condemnation to all men, even so through one act of righteousness there resulted justification of life to all men.

ROMANS 5:18

We have fixed our hope on the living God, who is the Savior of all men, especially of believers.

1 TIMOTHY 4:10

Providential Grace

MUCH of pagan religion was about keeping nature functioning normally so people could meet their basic needs. The pagan gods of the ancient Near East, often thought to be parts of nature, were believed to need the services of human beings to maintain both their own well-being and the cycles of nature. To this end, pagans created idols and provided acts of worship (Isa 44:9–20). Priests not only maintained certain temples to house the idols, in some cases they dressed, bathed, and provided food offerings to the idols—all to keep the god it represented happy so nature would be hospitable and human beings would prosper. The concept of a Creator above creation who maintained the natural order to meet people's needs without their intervention was unique to the Hebrews.

All living things exist because it was God's will to populate the earth with plants, animals and human beings. When he did so, he provided for the needs of each creature to be met, as Jesus underscored in his teaching (Matt 6:25–33; Luke 12:22–31).

All creatures, including human beings, are dependent upon God for everything they have. The reverse is not true. God has no physical needs for people to fulfill (cf. Ps 50:10–12). The one, true God, *Yahweh*, gains nothing from the existence of human beings except the fellowship of the creatures he has created and his joy in their happiness. It is he who gives life and the means to sustain life to all creatures. The goodness of God is described as his benevolence, and his provision for human needs is his providence.

Moses, desiring to know God better on Mount Sinai, asked God to come near. *Yahweh* obliged, passing before Moses and giving a grand statement describing his divine nature. In Exodus 34:6–7 we read that *Yahweh* declared himself to be:

> The Lord (Hebr. *Yahweh*), the Lord God (Hebr. *Yahweh ʾĒl*), compassionate (Hebr. *raḥûm*) and gracious (Hebr. *wᵉḥannûn*), slow to anger, and abounding in lovingkindness (Hebr. *ḥesed*) and truth (Hebr. *weʾĕmet*); who keeps lovingkindness (Hebr. *ḥesed*) for thousands, who forgives iniquity (Hebr. *ʿāôn*), transgression (Hebr. *wāpešaʿ*) and sin (Hebr. *wᵉḥaṭṭāʾâ*); yet He will by no means leave *the guilty* unpunished.

Some of the Hebrew words in this passage are of particular interest. We've encountered the word *ḥesed* before, noting that it is one of the most important words in the Old Testament, and that its meaning is not easy to capture in English. "Lovingkindness" is a good translation here, but the concepts of "steadfast love," "mercy," and "covenant faithfulness" are conveyed as well. The ideas of dependability and steadfastness stand behind the Hebrew word *ʾĕmet*, which thus connotes faithfulness and truth.[1] The

---

1. Scott, "*ʾĕmet*," in *TWOT*, 1:52.

word for graciousness here is *ḥannûn*, which is used only of God in the Old Testament.[2]

The concept of God presented in this passage is reinforced by the rest of Scripture; divine providence is the activity of a gracious, divine Creator. As Paul noted, we brought nothing into the world, and we can take nothing out of it (1 Tim 6:7). Everything we have or can ever have that is to our benefit comes from God.

Redemptive Grace

The generosity of the living God did not end with the entrance of sin into the world. The Apostle Paul explained to the pagans of Lystra that the existence of the necessities of life indicated the providence of the Creator of all things (Acts 14:14–17). The "Most High," Jesus taught, "is kind to ungrateful and evil *men*" (Luke 6:35). The evidence of this is that "your Father who is in heaven . . . causes His sun to rise on *the* evil and *the* good, and sends rain on *the* righteous and *the* unrighteous"; for in this manner, God reaches out to his enemies (Matt 5:45). However, God's providence, which was bestowed at the time of creation, was never designed to deal with sin and its consequences.

Yahweh's words to Moses on Mount Sinai declare that he will bring the consequences of sin upon the sinner; but they also make clear, by stating it first, that he prefers forgiveness to punishment. Three Hebrews words are used in Exodus 34:7 for sin that *Yahweh* is willing to forgive. The word *ḥaṭṭāʾâ* is a general term for sin, the root meaning to "miss a mark or a way."[3] The word *ʿāôn* denotes the twisting of something good into something evil and deserving of punishment, therefore, iniquity.[4] This word is sometimes used to indicate punishment for the sin rather than the sin itself. The word *pešaʿ*, which has the meaning "transgression" or "rebellion," carries the underlying concept of a broken relationship.[5]

A negative effect on personal relationships cannot be divorced from the concept of sin anywhere in the Old or New Testament. Sin is never just the violation of some specific legal demand or abstract ideal—although it often involves that. Sin always breaks a person's relationship with his or her Creator, and often their relationship with other people as well. It is the restoration of that person's relationship with God that opens the way for the

---

2. Yamauchi, "*ḥannûn*," in *TWOT*, 1:303–4.
3. Livingston, "*ḥaṭṭāʾâ*," in *TWOT*, 1:277–78.
4. Schultz, "*ʿāwōn*," in *TWOT*, 2:650–51.
5. Livingston, "*peshaʿ*," in *TWOT*, 2:741–42.

presence and power of God in a person's life. This requires grace that goes beyond divine providence to grace that leads to and provides redemption and reconciliation.

The Universal Reach of Redemptive Grace

Paul did not write Romans 5:12–21 to proclaim the power of sin, but to proclaim the greater power of God's grace in dealing with sin. Paul makes clear that whatever resulted from the sin of Adam is more than covered by the grace that was brought through Jesus' obedient, righteous act of going to the cross. Through Jesus' "one act of righteousness there resulted justification of life to all men (Gk. *di' henos dikaiōmatos eis pantas anthrōpous eis dikaiōsin zōēs*)" (Rom 5:18). It is significant that the "to all men" from Adam's sin is matched by the "to all men" from Jesus' act of going to the cross in v. 18. In v. 20, as we have seen, Paul points out that even though the Mosaic law increased sin, "where sin increased (Gk. *epleonasen hē hamartia*), grace abounded all the more (Gk. *hypereperisseusen hē charis*)."

By the time we come to vv. 5:12–21 in Romans, Paul has already established the effectiveness of God's saving grace provided through Jesus Christ. The primary thrust of Romans 5:12–21 is, therefore, also on salvation. Because of this, many interpreters argue that the effects of grace described here are solely in relation to those who receive salvation from sin. However, it seems that to argue in this manner is to fail to see the forest for the trees. Paul's argument is that the *full* affects of Adam's sin, and thus sin in humanity, is more than superseded by the provision of God's grace through the atonement made by Jesus Christ. Paul is not writing to exalt the triumph of sin, but to proclaim the complete triumph of God's grace over the damage caused by sin.

John Fletcher, a prominent leader in early Methodism explains:

> But the moment we allow, that the blessing of the second Adam is as general as the curse of the first; that God "sets" again "life and death" before every individual; and that he mercifully restores to all a capacity of choosing life, yea, and of having it one day more abundantly than Adam himself had before the fall; we see his goodness and justice shine with equal radiance, when he spares guilty Adam to propagate the fallen race, that they may share the blessings of a better covenant. For according to the Adamic law, "judgment was by one sin to condemnation; but the free gift of the Gospel is of many offences to justification. For if through the offence of one the many be dead, much more the

grace of God, and the gift by grace, which is by one man, Jesus Christ, hath abounded unto the many."[6]

The intention of God to make all human beings the objects of his saving grace is seen in Jesus' teaching as recorded by Matthew in his gospel. Jesus taught that the "eternal fire" to which the sinful would be condemned was "prepared for the devil and his angels," not human beings (Matt 25:41). A similar point is made by Paul, who notes in Ephesians 6:12 that while Christians may be persecuted by human beings, "our struggle is not against flesh and blood, but against . . . the spiritual *forces* of wickedness in the heavenly *places*," who are servants of Satan.

God is determined to work out the plan he had for each person when he created the human race. God does not take pleasure in the death of the wicked (Ezek 33:11). His desire is for all people to come to the truth (2 Pet 3:9). To make his work effective, he must counteract the effects of original sin. This is a general, universal benefit of the atonement of Christ. It is perhaps most clearly seen in 1 Timothy 4:10, where Paul writes, "We have fixed our hope on the living God, who is the Savior of all men (Gk. *sōtēr pantōn anthrōpōn*), especially of believers (Gk. *malista pistōn*)." The term *malista* is important, differentiating the way God is the Savior of those who are believers from those who are not.

John writes about Jesus that "He Himself is the propitiation (Gk. *hilasmos*) for our sins; and not for ours only, but also for *those of* the whole world (Gk. *ou peri tōn hēmeterōn de monon alla kai peri holou tou kosmou*)" (1 John 2:2). Similarly, in Hebrews 2:9, we read that Jesus submitted to the cross, "so that by the grace of God He might taste death for everyone" (Gk. *hopōs chariti theou hyper pantos geusētai thanatou*). These verses describe a unified work of God flowing from the atonement touching all the children of Adam; however, they do not ensure a universal reception of the full benefit of Christ's saving work.

This universal aspect does not mean that God fails if individuals reject his grace. Rather, if God did *not* provide such universal benefits, his work would be seriously deficient. If he were unable to mitigate the full effects of sin in his plan of salvation, he would not be sovereign over all people and all things; but he is both able and sovereign (Rom 11:32–36).

For God to provide salvation to anyone caught up in sin requires both that there be grace to draw people to God and time for them to realize their need for God: "For he who comes to God must believe that He is and *that He is a rewarder of those who seek Him*" (Heb 11:6). For God not to provide

---

6. Originally written in Madeley, Shropshire, England, February 3, 1772. Fletcher, "Third Check to Antinomianism," in *Works*, 1:147.

a way for people to come to him *before* they receive salvation would be like his building an eternal home without providing a door for people to enter, or putting the entrance to the home one hundred stories in the air without providing a way to reach it. Shortly before Romans 5:12–21, Paul observes that "while we were yet helpless (Gk. *asthenōn*), at the right time Christ died for the ungodly (Gk. *hyper asebōn apethanen*). . . . God demonstrates His own love toward us, in that while we were yet sinners (Gk. *eti hamartōlōn ontōn*), Christ died for us" (Rom 5:6, 8). Helpless, ungodly, sinners—notice carefully that this includes everyone under sin—these are those Paul says Christ died for. For *anyone* to achieve salvation from sin, the way must be opened to *everyone* in some way. The atonement opens the way for the grace necessary to enable those caught up in sin the opportunity, though certainly not the guarantee, to find and receive salvation. This is provided by grace that is universally available.

Redemptive grace has a single source in the atonement of Christ and a single goal: saving people from sin and its consequences. It enables a close, blessed, personal relationship with God. As such, there are no divisions in redemptive grace. However, it does result in different benefits that may be viewed individually. It is helpful to categorize the various ways that God uses redemptive grace to achieve his goal of creating a people for his own possession.

Common Grace

Common grace includes the continuation of providential grace to sinful people. In addition, if there is to be an opportunity for people to discover both their need of God and the gospel, the Spirit of God must restrain both the spiritual forces of evil and the human tendency to wickedness. This is generally referred to as common grace. Common grace counteracts the presence of sin so that society is able to function. It enables the organization of society under leaders and enables systems of trade so that people may meet their basic needs (Rom 13:1–7; 1 Pet 2:13–14). Without this benefit of the atonement, the world would be completely depraved, chaos would reign everywhere, and only the very strongest would survive. Even under common grace, there are times when some human groups and nations come close to this level of wickedness.

Common grace does not rid the world of hardship, injustice, injury, disease, death, or wickedness. Our mortality and pain are to remind us that we are mortal and need to have the life and peace that only our Creator can provide. This is not unlike pain in our physical bodies, which, when working normally, helps us to know that something is wrong so we can correct it.

People are stubborn in their resistance to God as it is; if God were to make this a perfect world, no one would realize their dependence upon their Creator. Further, death ensures that there is a limit to how much sin anyone becomes responsible for before the throne of God.

God works to bless his people in many ways, but they are still subject to the same trials as those who are not his own (John 16:33). If God were to remove all difficulties for Christians, they would not have the opportunity to show the strength of their faith and hope in God, which would reduce the effectiveness of their witness to the reality of the gospel (1 Pet 1:6–9; Rom 8). In addition, God blesses Christians through times of hardship; God uses suffering to build faith and character (Rom 5:1–5). That doesn't make trials easier or pain less painful. It does mean no one needs to be defeated by difficulty, and everyone can look forward to ultimate victory over the troubles of this age in the same way Jesus endured the cross (Heb 12:1–2).

Common grace is not saving grace. However, it provides time for people to learn their need for God and to turn to him, as Peter explains in 2 Peter 3:8–9.

Prevenient Grace

In his sermon on Mars Hill, Paul said that God

> made from one *man* every nation of mankind to live on all the face of the earth, having determined *their* appointed times and the boundaries of their habitation, that they would seek God (Gk. *zētein ton theon*), if perhaps they might grope for Him and find Him." (Acts 17:26–27)

For this to happen, God has to provide grace that counters the resistance to God that comes from the sinful nature inherited as part of Adam's race (Rom 5:12). This grace awakens people to their need of God and enables them to receive the message of the gospel. This grace is called "prevenient grace." There is a sense in which this is like common grace in that it is a universal benefit of the atonement of Christ. However, prevenient grace is redemptive because it opens the way for further grace (Rom 5:20–21).

God does not hold people accountable for being born part of a sinful race because they did not choose to do so. *Yahweh* makes clear in Ezekiel 18 that he does not hold children responsible for the sins of their fathers; in fact, he is deeply offended that anyone would accuse him of doing so. Nevertheless, because of God's holiness, there must be justification for God to work in the lives of those who inherited a sinful nature from Adam; justification that is provided by the atonement of Christ. This grace ensures that those who are miscarried, stillborn, or die in infancy—indeed, all human beings who never develop the moral judgment to be responsible for their own actions—are never excluded from God's presence now or in the future (Matt 18:10; cf. 2 Sam 12:21–23). For all others, this grace prepares for further grace. Part of this is ensuring the ability to make moral judgments.

It is the nature of human beings to have a conscience (Rom 2:15). It is part of what makes human beings unique. The conscience was affected, but not eliminated, by Adam's fall from grace. The evidence for this is that both Adam and Eve tried to hide from God after they sinned. Since human beings live in spiritual and moral darkness apart from the work of God, the source of this conscience is the grace of God to sinners (Rom 3:9–18).

In the second chapter of Romans, Paul recognizes that everyone has a concept of morality. He observes that some who do not have the Law "do instinctively the things of the Law" (Gk. *physei ta tou nomou poiōsin* , Rom 2:14). The Greek word translated "instinctively" here is literally "by nature (Gk. *physei*)." Paul teaches that it is conscience that persuades some Gentiles, who may have no knowledge of the Law of Moses, to act in accordance with the Law (Rom 2:14–16). He is not saying that Gentiles live according to the entire Mosaic law—certainly not its many regulations for civil life, diet, and worship—but that they sometimes live according to the morality demanded in the Mosaic law. For example, they may be careful never to be guilty of dishonesty, theft, adultery, or murder. Referring to the time when such Gentiles come before God in final judgment, Paul writes: "They show the work of the Law written in their hearts (Gk. *hoitines endeiknyntai to ergon tou nomou grapton en tais kardiais autōn*), their conscience (Gk. *syneidēseōs*) bearing witness and their thoughts (Gk. *logismōn*) alternately accusing or else defending them" (Rom 2:15). On these grounds, even those without the Law of Moses may be held accountable for whether or not they follow what they consider to be the highest standards of behavior.

Guilt is a common human experience. However, the conscience is often a less than perfect guide, and especially so for those who aren't in fellowship with God. It may be distorted, misshaped by the surrounding culture, repressed, ignored, and in some people, completely silenced (1 Cor 8:7–12; 1 Tim 4:2; Titus 1:15). Though imperfect, its presence often guides people to curb the tendency toward their worst behavior, and sometimes helps them to exhibit their best. Consider the Assyrians, a severe, warlike people, repenting under the preaching of Jonah. Jonah did not work alone—God worked through him. In fact, Jonah was actually hoping the Assyrians would *not* repent so they would be punished. If it depended solely upon him, that is exactly what would have happened. It was the presence of God already working with the people of Nineveh *before* and *when* Jonah preached that convicted them of behavior God would no longer tolerate. It was the Spirit of God that brought repentance. This episode illustrates not only the universal work of God but also the impossibility of escaping the presence of God (cf. Ps 139:1–12).

The morality Paul has in mind in Romans 2 is more than a concept of strictly human social standards and rules. People motivated by social standards might not go against the rules made by a leader because they fear punishment. Some people might comply with certain types of behavior—social mores or customs—because they don't want to be rejected by the people they know: their relatives, neighbors, employers, or members of some other group they belong to. Whereas lower animals like bees are completely governed by instinct, higher animals, such as wolves, are capable of social standards. Animals, however, are incapable of moral and spiritual judgment. This capability is part of the image of God unique to human beings. The moral behavior Paul refers to here recognizes standards of behavior that are universal and binding, often related to a deity or deities. The motivation to follow these standards is inward. It is conscience that informs the intellect here, not vice versa.

When informed by religion, conscience looks beyond behavior to some form of accountability from a higher power of some sort, be it pagan gods, karma, or the true God. Some religions, like Hinduism and Buddhism, which maintain that natural cycles govern human life, nevertheless have a moral component to them. They teach that behavior, in some way or another, affects the outcome of people's lives, including their existence after death. This awareness of ultimate moral values, especially when linked to some form of accountability after death, indicates the work of the God's Spirit. Prevenient grace thus prepares for the reception of the gospel by countering the influence of sin and creating a hunger for the one, true God and his saving grace.

Election as a Means of Grace

The direct, universal ministry of God through his Spirit is only part of God's plan for redeeming sinners; the other is the more particular work of God through human servants. This work, of necessity, involves specific individuals and groups of God's choosing: election. The goal of this particular work of God also has universal goals that fit with the more universal ministry of his Spirit. The Bible is a record of sacred history, which is God's work through history to bring redeeming grace to all people.

Election is seen in the choice of Abram, who lived in the city of Ur, to be the father of all after him who would become God's people. Before

Abram, God dealt with humanity as a whole. That ended with the fall of the tower of Babel, after which people were scattered into different nations.

A simplistic reading of the account of the Tower of Babel in Genesis sees it as an attempt to climb from earth to heaven in a manner not wholly dissimilar from the fairy tale of Jack climbing to the realm of giants on a huge beanstalk. The reality is that ziggurats—the sacred pyramids of ancient Mesopotamia—were believed to raise worshippers to the realm of a god at the top level, whereas the bottom level was sometimes believed to extend to the underworld. The tower of Babel was apparently an attempt to reach the level of the one, true God using a similar tower. Construction was stopped to teach that the true God cannot be reached this way. In any case, after people were scattered into separate nations, it was necessary to raise up a nation to reach the other nations.

Genesis makes clear that Abram and Sarai (later called Abraham and Sarah) were specifically chosen by God for their part in his universal plan. The migration from Ur to Palestine began under Abram's father, Terah; but it was Abram and Sarai who would complete the journey. God promised Abram: "I will make you a great nation . . . and in you all the families of the earth will be blessed" (Gen 12:2–3). Impatient for Abram to have a son after many years of waiting, Sarai gave Abram her slave Hagar, who bore a son named Ishmael. This was according to a custom of the time, where a woman who was unable to bear children and feared divorce would give her slave to her husband to produce offspring in her place. Nevertheless, Abram and Sarai were renamed Abraham and Sarah by the Lord, and were told that it was through Sarah, not Hagar, that God would bring about Abraham's descendant: Isaac (Gen 17:15–19; 18:1–15).

Abraham was told that his descendants would go from Palestine to another land where they would become slaves, but after four hundred years they would return to Palestine (Gen 15:13–21). This gave the people time to grow in number so they were no longer a small clan, but a people. Abraham's descendants became the nation of Israel when they emerged from Egypt to worship God at Mount Sinai. At Mount Sinai they were chosen—elected—to become God's "own possession among all the peoples . . . and you shall be to Me a kingdom of priests and a holy nation" (Exod 19:5–6). Moses was elected to be their leader, and Aaron and his descendants were elected to become the priests in Israel. But all the people of Israel were chosen to become priests in the sense that through them others in the world would learn of God and come to him. Later, God would elect David to be the king of Israel and the one whose descendant would reign on the throne over all mankind forever (Isa 9:6–7; Mic 5:2).

It is important to remember that Abraham's descendants were those who followed him in faith in the one, true, living God, not those who were simply blood descendants (Rom 2:28–29; 4:1–17; Matt 3:9; Luke 3:8). Though his blood descendants constituted the natural group for God to work in and through, his descendants were not limited to or defined by his biological progeny; others could become part of Israel by committing to live in compliance with God's requirements for those faithful to him (Exod 12:37–38, 43–48; Num 9:14).

Throughout the history of Abraham's descendants, God not only chose leaders, he also chose individuals to speak for him. These prophets would record his works and make his will known. It was through the preaching and writing of the prophets that God laid the groundwork for the ministry of his Messiah: Jesus. The earthly ministry of Jesus was primarily to the descendants of Abraham, that they might fulfill their role in God's plan. At Pentecost, God blessed Jesus' disciples with a ministry of the Holy Spirit that was more complete than ever experienced before. After Pentecost, with the establishment of the church of Jesus Christ, the church became the primary instrument for the spread of the gospel (1 Pet 2:9–10). Jesus commanded his followers to "make disciples of all the nations (Gk. *panta ta ethnē*)" (Matt 28:19). The church then became the elected nation through which God would invite people of all the world to enter into his saving grace (Acts 1:8; Rev 5:9–10).

Election and the Unreached

Election has been God's means to reach out to all people through certain people to accomplish his goals. Of necessity, this means working in some individuals and groups rather than others in certain periods of history. This leads to a question concerning those outside election.

The thrust of the Old and New Testaments is that people must be brought specifically and unambiguously to the one, true God for salvation. There is certainly no way to come into saving grace in any age apart from the grace provided through Jesus Christ. The purpose of prevenient grace is to prepare for the preaching of the gospel and the acceptance of Jesus Christ as Savior. Those in the time of the Old Testament who came to *Yahweh* came to the one, true God. Although they did not know the identity of his Messiah, they nevertheless humbled themselves before God and trusted in his provision for their needs. Because it is clear that God judges those who both have and do not have the Law, there is no universal salvation. As a result, some people will be lost who have not had the opportunity to worship *Yahweh* or to receive a presentation of the gospel. Does this mean there is absolutely no hope for the many who have not had a chance to hear God's Word and to express faith in the one, true God?

Only Jesus is qualified to determine who receives saving grace and who does not. We are not knowledgeable, wise, righteous, or impartial enough to make that determination about others or ourselves. It is also his rightful place as the Christ of God (John 5:22, 26–27; Acts 10:42).

Clearly God, in his mercy and justice, neither leaves the wicked unpunished nor does he bring judgment without weighing people's lives (Rom 2:11–16). The death of Christ demonstrates that he is neither vicious nor uncaring, and that his desire is to extend grace. Here and there, the Scriptures seem to suggest that the grace of God *may* be wide enough to encompass some of those who have not had a chance to respond to *Yahweh* under the old or new covenants.

Jesus said, "From everyone who has been given much, much will be required," indicating that God is completely fair in his determinations of culpability for people's deeds (Luke 12:48). Paul wrote to the Romans, "Where there is no law, there is no violation" (Gk. *hou de ouk estin nomos oude parabasis*, Rom 4:15). Paul told the pagans of God in Lystra, "In the generations gone by He permitted all the nations (Gk. *panta ta ethnē*) to go their own ways" (Acts 14:16). Later, he told the Athenians, "Having overlooked the times of ignorance (Gk. *tous men oun chronous tēs agnoias hyperidōn*), God is now declaring to men that all *people* everywhere should repent" (Acts 17:30). Jesus' parable of the laborers who were all paid the same no matter how long they worked may hint that God's grace toward some of those in the "times of ignorance" *may* be different from what we might expect (Matt 20:1–15).

Just as the Jewish Christians after Pentecost were surprised that Gentiles qualified for God's grace without being circumcised and without adhering to the Mosaic law, we may well be surprised that God has opened the life-gate to those who did not have a chance to know God's Word or to come to him in this life, but commended themselves to God's saving grace in ways of which we are currently ignorant. That *possibility*, however, is best left in God's capable, righteous, and merciful hands. Either way, it is not our decision to make.

Meanwhile, the Scriptures do not primarily concern themselves with those who are past hearing or cannot hear the gospel, but with those who can or should—those who might be reached by our evangelistic and missionary efforts. The focus of the Scriptures is the knowledge of Jesus Christ, the opportunity for salvation through him, and the offering of saving grace to others who live in our time. That is where our concern should be because those are the only things we can do anything about. "I urge that entreaties *and* prayers, petitions *and* thanksgivings, be made on behalf of all men. . . . This is good and acceptable in the sight of God our Savior . . . who desires all men to be saved and to come to the knowledge of the truth" (1 Tim 2:1, 3–4).

Election and Saving Grace

Those who receive saving grace are sometimes referred to in Scripture as "elect" (e.g., *eklektoi tou theou*, Rom 8:33; Col 3:12; Titus 1:1). Unlike the election of leaders and others chosen to be his servants, the election of these individuals is based upon *their* choice to reach out to God for his saving grace.

The designation "elect" in Scripture is meant to convey the assurance that the redeemed have blessings that were planned for them before the foundation of the world (Eph 1:3–21). Some Christians go far beyond this. They believe that the election of those who receive saving grace indicates that God made a choice before the foundation of the world to provide salvation to certain individuals and not to others; to provide salvation not because of a person's response to his offer of grace, but simply as a random choice. According to this understanding of Scripture, prevenient grace is given only to those individuals God has randomly chosen to save. This interpretation of divine election is contradicted by passages that state God's desire to save all and that indicate his provision of preparatory grace to all people. If true, it would also make his offer of salvation an empty offer to those God did not give the power to accept. At a more basic level, this interpretation is at odds with the understanding of God given throughout the Scriptures.

Suppose some adults went out on a charter boat that was drastically overloaded. The capacity of the boat was listed on a sign with large letters that was directly in front of every person who boarded the vessel. As the boat became full, it was obvious to everyone that the number onboard greatly exceeded the capacity the vessel could safely hold. Imagine that during the excursion, the boat struck a rock some distance from shore and sank, leaving all passengers in life-threateningly cold water. What would be the reaction to a nearby Coast Guard or police rescue vessel saving some at random and leaving others to die in the water "to show the justice of laws against the life-threatening overcrowding of charter boats"?

In a different scenario, what would be the reaction to some doctors randomly giving life-saving medication to those who carelessly contracted a life-threatening disease while denying the medication to others? Is the standard of decency required of individuals higher than that which would be expected of God? Certainly not! The issue is not that this would mean

God falls short of some high standard of decency outside of God, but that if this were the way God behaved, God would fall short of *his own*, *revealed* standard of love, compassion, mercy, and grace. God, himself, is the measure of love and mercy (1 John 4:7–11).

Aside from this, when "election" is interpreted as special privilege reserved for an elite, the result is often arrogance and self-righteousness. The Gospels give multiple examples of people who thought they were entitled to salvation because as descendants of Abraham they thought they were "of the elect" (e.g., Matt 3:7–9; Luke 3:7–8; John 8:39–40). The New Testament makes clear that God is not a respecter of persons (Rom 2:11; Acts 10:34; Eph 6:9; Col 3:25; cf. Jas 2:1). Election plays a role in God's choice of people to serve him in his broader role of bringing salvation to the world. Saving grace, however, is offered to all.

Convincing Grace

All grace may be resisted. God's presence is persuasive rather than controlling. Those who choose to reject God may reach the level Paul describes in Romans 3:10–18: acting as if there is no God, and often manifesting this in evil and even murderous ways (cf. Ps 5:9; 10:7; 14:1–3; 36:1; 53:1–3; 140:3; Isa 59:7–8). Though this is the natural state of all people who live totally apart from the influence of God, and though no human being is free from at least the tendency to turn away from God, it is obvious from Scripture that this is not descriptive of the lives of all people.

In spite of the strong tendency to sin in human beings, there *are* seekers after God. This is seen in the Scriptures and it is seen in the world today. In the time of Jesus, great crowds of people, both Jews and Gentiles, went to see John the Baptist in their search for fellowship with God. Likewise, large crowds gathered to hear Jesus preach. In Acts, Luke tells us about an Ethiopian eunuch who traveled to Jerusalem to draw closer to God (Acts 8:27–34). Luke also tells us about Cornelius, a Roman centurion who worshipped the God of the Jews and lived an exemplary life (Acts 10:30–33). As we've seen, Cornelius, the first Gentile convert to Christianity, was a known as a "God-fearer" among the Jews—someone who did not obey the entire law of Moses, but who worshipped God in the Jewish synagogue and tried to live a moral life before the Lord. Luke tells of another such centurion in his gospel (Luke 7:2–5). These people sought God because of the influence of God's Spirit.

There is a limit to how far a person can go without the Scriptures and without someone explaining its message to them, as exemplified by the Ethiopian eunuch and by Cornelius. They had come to the place in their spiritual lives from which they could go no farther without human assistance. First the nation of Israel, and then the church of Jesus Christ, fulfill this need. It is prevenient grace that creates both the interest and the desire to come close to God, and to recognize that he can be known through Jesus Christ. This grace then makes the message of the Old and New Testament Scriptures ring true in the minds of seekers, motivating and enabling them to respond to God's invitation to fellowship.

Jesus said the Holy Spirit would "convict the world concerning sin and righteousness and judgment" (John 16:8–11). The word "convict" here is the Greek verb *elenchō*, which often means to bring remorse, but also carries the meaning "convince." In this case, the world will be convinced of the sin of rejecting God and his Christ. They will be convinced because Jesus, who was innocent of all crime, was isolated from all other people and condemned to die on the cross. The world will also be convinced of the righteousness of Jesus because of his resurrection and ascension into heaven—which indicate that he is fully acceptable to God the Father and is with the Father. Finally the world will be convinced of judgment upon the current, corrupt world order because the righteousness of Christ means that the ruler of the present world order, Satan, has been condemned and cast out.

The Holy Spirit will convince people not only of the sin of rejecting Jesus, but also of their own individual sinfulness and acts of sin, and the belief that they will be held to account before the throne of God (Ezek 18). This brings each person to the point of decision. Each person may decide to cry out to God for help or to reject God entirely. This is not because of any natural ability to choose, but because God, by his grace, restores the ability of each person to decide whether to seek and petition God for saving grace. It is not a decision to save oneself by one's own effort, but a decision whether to ask God for salvation.

Saving Grace

Salvation is the goal of all redemptive grace, and is accomplished with saving grace. "Saving grace" is often called "particular grace" because it is only given to some.

A person who receives saving grace enters into the New Covenant sealed by the blood of Jesus Christ (Luke 22:20; 1 Cor 11:25; Heb 13:20–21). This is the covenant promised in Jeremiah (Jer 31:31–34). The Lord promises to those who enter into this covenant:

I will forgive (Hebr. *'eslaḥ*) their iniquity (Hebr. *la'ăônām*), and their sin (Hebr. *ûlᵉḥaṭṭāʾtām*) I will remember no more (Hebr. *lōʾ 'ezkār-'ôd*) no more." (Jer 31:34)

Every benefit that comes through God's saving grace follows logically from the forgiveness of sins promised in this passage and by Jesus at the Last Supper. Forgiveness is a term often associated with indebtedness in the New Testament. In this passage, however, the Hebrew *sālaḥ* is more closely associated with the legal concept of pardon. Further, it is a word used only of *Yahweh* in the Old Testament.[7]

Paul wrote that Christians are

> justified (Gk. *dikaioumenoi*) as a gift by His grace through the redemption (Gk. *apolytrōseōs*) which is in Christ Jesus; whom God displayed publicly as a propitiation (Gk. *hilastērion*) in His blood through faith. *This was* to demonstrate His righteousness (Gk. *dikaiosynēs*), because in the forbearance of God He passed over the sins previously committed; for the demonstration, *I say*, of His righteousness (Gk. *dikaiosynēs*) at the present time, so that he would be just (Gk. *dikaion*) and the justifier (Gk. *dikaiounta*) of the one who has faith in Jesus. (Rom 3:24–26)

It is important to note that "to be justified" and "to be righteous" are communicated in Greek by similar terms. It is often the context that determines whether they are interpreted "justify" or "righteous." There is thus a close relationship between the two concepts; but especially in Christian usage, they must not be confused.

Righteousness has to do with correct attitude and behavior; justification has do with the pronouncement of a court of law. God is always righteous, and thus always acts in a manner that is just—that is in accordance with his perfect righteousness—in all his relationships. In his earnest desire to offer forgiveness to sinners, *Yahweh* cannot simply forgive and remain righteous. However, through the righteousness of Jesus Christ, and Jesus' righteous act at Calvary, he can be the justifier of those who appeal to him to be restored to his fellowship. What God offers is a pardon for past sin. "Therefore there is now no condemnation for those who are in Christ Jesus" (Rom 8:1).

When God forgives and justifies a sinner, as promised in Jeremiah, God no longer remembers his or her sin; but because God is omniscient, this cannot mean that God becomes unaware of that sinner's former unrighteous attitudes or deeds. It means that God no longer holds the sinner

---

7. Kaiser, "*sālaḥ*," in *TWOT*, 2:626.

accountable on the basis of Jesus' redeeming work at Calvary. Forgiveness by one human being to another is similar in that the wrongful attitude or behavior is known to both parties, but the value of the relationship now comes to the fore and the offending action or attitude is relegated to the past. Similarly, the sinner who is justified by God is forgiven and will not come before the throne of God with past sins on his or her conscience (Rom 8:1). Instead, the justified sinner is forgiven past sins and accepted *as if* righteous.[8]

Before saving grace is experienced, however, each person who is able must make use of the prevenient and convincing grace God provides to respond to God's offer of salvation appropriately.

---

8. Wiley, *Christian Theology*, 2:393.

13

Responding to Grace

I call heaven and earth to witness against you today, that I have set before you life and death, the blessing and the curse. So choose life in order that you may live.

DEUTERONOMY 30:19

For by grace you have been saved through faith; and that not of yourselves, *it is* the gift of God; not as a result of works, so that no one may boast.

EPHESIANS 2:8–9

When the kindness of God our Savior and *His* love for mankind appeared, He saved us, not on the basis of deeds which we have done in righteousness, but according to His mercy, by the washing of regeneration and renewing by the Holy Spirit.

TITUS 3:4–5

Jesus answered and said to him, "If anyone loves Me, he will keep My word; and My Father will love him, and We will come to him and make Our abode with him."

JOHN 14:23

Work out your salvation with fear and trembling; for it is God who is at work in you, both to will and to work for *His* good pleasure.

PHILIPPIANS 2:12–13

Receiving Grace

THE grace provided by God through the work of Jesus Christ on the cross and the ministry of the Holy Spirit requires a response. In fact, the grace that precedes saving grace is meant to bring people to the point where they choose to receive God's saving grace. Only by this preparatory grace may individuals recognize their need and appeal to God for saving grace.

Some believe that if God gives a choice to individuals, they have earned merit before God that entitles them to saving grace. Such a view of merit, however, is entirely foreign to Scripture.

Jesus taught us to pray to the Father: "Your kingdom come, Your will be done, on earth as it is in heaven" (Matt 6:10). "Kingdom" here means the rule of God. In heaven, obedience to God is the base for behavior because obedience to a benevolent, sovereign God is expected—it is not special, not unique. There is no legitimate reason to question whether God's judgments are favorable to his creatures. Therefore, no merit or praise is deserved by those creatures who choose to do the will of God and actually do it.

Jesus reinforced this teaching when he spoke of servants who did everything that was expected of them (Luke 17:7-10). Jesus said their masters would not thank their servants for doing their master's will. "So you too, when you do all the things which are commanded you, say, 'We are unworthy slaves; we have done *only* that which we ought to have done'" (Luke 17:10).

The reason Jesus is "highly exalted" by God is because he took upon himself that which he did not deserve; he took upon himself a role that caused him to receive the suffering that was deserved by others for their sinfulness (Phil 2:5-11). Human beings who commit sin, making themselves accountable to God, are in a far different situation. Even if, contrary to the Scriptures already considered, there were merit of any kind for choosing to accept God's offer of grace, that merit would pale in comparison to the enormity of the guilt they brought upon themselves by choosing to sin in the first place. Isaiah compared the righteousness of the people to a filthy garment (Isa 64:6). Through Isaiah, God told the people: "I will declare your righteousness and your deeds, but they will not profit you" (Isa 57:12).

Clearly, one righteous choice or one righteous act does not earn salvation in the sight of God. However, it is possible to appeal to God for his gift of saving grace, and to receive it. One must approach God as a supplicant—a beggar if you will—humbly beseeching God for that which he alone is able to provide.

The requirements for receiving saving grace are repentance and faith. These must always be viewed in relation to the living God, not as separate acts that, like magic, have power in themselves. Each begins with a change in how an individual thinks about God and themselves, which then manifests itself in changes in outward behavior. Due to differences in culture and personality, each person may experience these differently and the changes in behavior will often vary. For some, there is a process over time that results in repentance and faith; for others, they come much more quickly. What is most important is where a person is in their spiritual life rather than how they got there. God is waiting to respond graciously to all who seek him (cf. Jer 29:11–13).

Repentance

The first requirement for receiving grace is repentance. It comes first because repentance is preparing for a new relationship with God, and there cannot be a new relationship with God without a change in attitude. John the Baptist preached repentance in preparation for the ministry of Jesus, the ministry of Jesus began with the preaching of repentance, and the preaching of the gospel on the Day of Pentecost exhorted people to repent. Repentance is turning to God and away from sin in preparation for the presence of the Lord (Isa 40:3–4). It is akin to marriage in the sense of "forsaking of all others" to be faithful to God.

Repentance may or may not be accompanied by strong emotion. It comes from an awareness of the reality and perfection of God, one's own inadequacy, and the sense that one will be held accountable by God. It may include a general sense of unworthiness or it may follow from awareness of the wickedness of certain acts and attitudes. The essence of repentance is humility before God, a sense of accountability to God, and the desire and willingness to change. It is a cry for assistance and an appeal for grace. It is a recognition that one has reached the end of one's human capability and must have God's work to be complete.

At the same time, it is a commitment—with God's enabling—to live faithfully under God's authority (Phil 2:12–13). The act of submission to God as Creator and Sovereign over the universe is the restoration of the correct Creator/creature relationship. This entails ridding oneself of anything that is against God and his ways, including bad attitudes.

John the Baptist insisted that his hearers demonstrate that they had repented, often providing specific instructions how they should live (Luke 3:7–14; Matt 3:7–8; cf. Acts 26:20). The Prodigal Son exemplified true repentance in the way he returned to his father's house, putting his unrighteous lifestyle behind him (Luke 15:17-21). The change brought by genuine repentance was demonstrated by Zaccheus when he promised to provide for the poor and give restitution to anyone he had defrauded, and by the Ephesians when they rid themselves of their occult books (Luke 19:8-10; Acts 19:18-20).

With the ministry of Jesus, repentance also necessarily involves recognition of Jesus as the Christ. A person who truly repents has come to understand that rejecting Jesus is rejecting God (John 16:8-9). There is a commitment to a new way of life as a result of seeing Jesus in a new way (2 Cor 5:14-17). Thus, repentance involves turning to God through Jesus Christ (1 Pet 2:25; John 10:1-10). A thief being executed with Jesus, for example, recognized the sinfulness of being a thief, recognized Jesus' Lordship, and humbly asked to be part of his kingdom. The Apostle Paul not only repented after his encounter with Jesus, he preached repentance from the time of his conversion (Acts 26:12-20).

True repentance removes any sense of superiority over others for whatever reason. The Prodigal Son dropped all thought of sonship, intending only to become a hired worker on his father's farm. Our dependency as creatures, shame for personal sin, and the knowledge that we are completely dependent upon the work of God for redemption precludes all pride. Isaiah wrote, "Thus says the high and exalted One Who lives forever, whose name is Holy, 'I dwell *on* a high and holy place, and *also* with the contrite and lowly of spirit in order to revive the spirit of the lowly and to revive the heart of the contrite'" (Isa 57:15).

The most appropriate form of reverence and submission is prostration. The Greek word *proskyneō* is one of the most common words for worship in the New Testament. Its literal meaning is to fall face down in worship, as with the magi before the Christ child, those convicted of their sinfulness by Christian prophets, and the elders surrounding the throne of God in heaven (Matt 2:11; 1 Cor 14:24-25; Rev 4:10; 5:14). This word is also used to identify worship in general where there is an attitude of submission and reverence even if the worship is falsely or wrongly directed, and even when physical prostration is not in view (John 4:20-24; Acts 7:43; 8:27). Thus the posture is less important than the inner attitude. "The Father seeks to be His worshippers (Gk. *tous proskynountas auton*)," Jesus taught, those who "worship (Gk. *proskynein*) in spirit and in truth" (John 4:23-24).

Jesus told the story of the Pharisee and the tax collector to emphasize the importance of humility (Luke 18:9-14). When one's face is literally or metaphorically in the dirt asking for forgiveness, it is only possible to look to one side or the other to those who have likewise admitted their need; it is impossible to look down on anyone else for whatever reason—physical characteristics, intelligence, race, national origin, gender, occupation, wealth, life accomplishments, or anything else—none of these matter when a sinner comes before the Lord to ask for mercy.

Paul started his adult life thinking he was the prime example of a person dedicated to God; after he met Christ, he considered himself the "foremost of all sinners" (1 Tim 1:15–16). Although repentance is a humbling experience, the humiliation is in proportion to one's past choices, and its end is not endless sorrow, but mercy and life from a gracious God (2 Cor 7:9–10). As David wrote in Psalm 32, the person who confesses his or her sin and finds forgiveness is blessed.

A relationship with God is no different in some respects from any other relationship we might have. Honesty is at the very base of that relationship. Accordingly, although the person who turns to God confesses and turns away from sin, repentance does not end there.

Whenever something is discovered that might come between the redeemed and God, confession and repentance are in order. It was to Christians John wrote: "If we confess our sins, He is faithful and righteous to forgive us our sins and to cleanse us from all unrighteousness" (1 John 1:9; cf. Rev 3:14–19). The opposite is true of unconfessed sin; it hinders our relationship with God (1 John 1:6–10).

A bad habit or addiction does not necessarily prevent one from coming to God, for it is expected that all sinners will need to struggle with some tendencies as long as they live in this age. But it is incumbent upon each person to seek strength and healing from the Lord, to resist temptation, and if possible, to put any such habit behind. God is not mocked: the sincere will find grace; those who seek to "use" God will find that God is no fool (Gal 6:7–8).

Faith

The second requirement for receiving saving grace is faith. Faith is simply believing in God, simply trust. For example, you believe that the floor or earth you are standing or sitting upon will support your weight. You trust the floor. Until I mentioned it, it probably never crossed your mind to even question that the floor would support you. In reality, this faith is not so much in the floor as it is in the people who constructed the floor and the people who certified that it is sufficiently well constructed to allow occupancy of the building. Biblical faith is similar in that it is not faith in salvation, a thing, but faith in the God who provides that salvation. Biblical faith always has a personal component. It is trust in God as a living person similar to the trust you put in someone else who is close to you.

In this case, saving faith is not just to the conviction that God exists, but that God provides salvation that is effective for you, personally (Heb 11:6). Paul wrote: "Even though we have known Christ according to the flesh, yet now we know *Him in this way* no longer" (2 Cor 5:16). In other words, we no longer see Jesus the way the world sees him, as just another human being whose teachings have no consequence for us. Therefore, "the love of Christ controls us" (2 Cor 5:14). Faith leads to a different kind of life because Jesus "died for all, so that they who live might no longer live for themselves, but for Him who died and rose again on their behalf" (2 Cor 5:15). Unfortunately, many today do not see faith in this straightforward manner. To understand why, it will be necessary to make a brief review of history.

We have discussed the overreach of the Roman Catholic and state churches in the sixteenth and seventeenth centuries that brought about a strong reaction against Christianity. Gotthold Ephraim Lessing (1729–1821) was a German playwright and scholar who was part of the German Enlightenment. He thought that it is impossible to know the past because there is no way to go back and observe it. On this basis, he argued that there is a great chasm between the past and the present that we cannot breach. The distance between a person and the past came to be called "Lessing's ditch." Lessing was wrong, very wrong. Through documents and the exploration of archaeological evidence we can know a great deal about the past. However, his thought was popular with those who wanted to undercut the historicity of the Christian faith because of their resentment of the church or their commitment to pagan beliefs.

The Danish Christian Søren Kierkegaard (1813–1855) was deeply troubled by the corruption of the Danish church because it catered to and ignored the misbehavior of royalty. He accepted Lessing's view of history. Further, he believed that much in the Bible is irrational. He also believed that God hides himself so that only those fully determined to seek him will find him. Kierkegaard argued that it is necessary to make a "leap of faith" to cross Lessing's ditch and believe the Gospels. His view flies in the face of the biblical concept of faith. Whereas Christianity invites people to explore the facts and come to belief, Kierkegaard encouraged people to assume that what they want to be true is true. Whereas Christian faith involves the mind, the Kierkegaardian concept of faith is primarily irrational and emotional.

Kierkegaard's writings remained largely unknown until the early twentieth century. When they became available, they became popular, as did the phrase "leap of faith." Today, the acceptance of Kierkegaard's concept of faith is virtually ubiquitous. Unbelievers, liberal Christians, and many who are committed to biblical Christianity think that faith requires them to "throw caution to the wind" and go with their emotions. It is even found in the writings of some scholars who are committed to traditional Christianity. Nevertheless, it makes Christian faith seem to be a wild guess or wishful thinking rather than a rational decision based upon historical evidence.

Hebrews 10:32 through 12:2 is an important portion of Scripture regarding faith. Hebrews 10:38 quotes Habakkuk 2:4, in which God says: "My righteous one shall live by faith; and if he shrinks back, My soul has no pleasure in him." The Hebrew word often translated faith in Habakkuk, *'ĕmûnâ*, places an emphasis upon faithfulness, as seen in some English translations. Hebrews 10:38 quotes from the Greek Old Testament (the Septuagint) rather than the original Hebrew text. The Greek word *pistis* found there emphasizes faith, belief. The concepts of faith and faithfulness are closely related, and are encompassed by both words. Scripturally, it is impossible to be faithful without faith, or to have true faith without exhibiting faithfulness. So there is a difference in emphasis but not a contradiction between the Hebrew and the Greek texts.

Faithfulness is the fruit of faith. It is a gift to be received from God, but it is also a choice. Faith is described in the New Testament as a "walk" rather than a one-time commitment (2 Cor 5:7; cf. Rom 4:12; 8:4; 13:13; Gal 5:16, 25; Eph 2:10; 4:1, 17; 5:2, 8, 15; Phil 3:17; Col 4:5; 1 Thess 2:10–12; 4:1; 1 John 1:6–7).

Hebrews 11:1 gives not so much a definition of faith as a description of what faith looks like in the lives of the faithful. The examples that follow Hebrews 11:1 clarify what the author intended to teach. Faith (Gk. *pistis*) that God will bring about something in the future is hope (Gk. verb: *elpizō*, noun: *elpis*; cf. Rom 8:24–25). Hebrews 11:1 tells us that true faith is acting as if what is hoped for already exists. We then see this exemplified by Noah, Abraham, Sarah, Isaac, Joseph, Moses, and Jesus. Hope seems to be a major emphasis in this passage because the readers needed to have their focus changed. They had apparently been focusing on a world that does not recognize the triumph of Christ; they needed to focus on Jesus and what he accomplished.

The second aspect of faith that Hebrews 11:1 highlights is the conviction that spiritual realities that are unseen are real. Paul wrote that as Christians, "we look not at the things which are seen, but at the things which are not seen; for the things which are seen are temporal, but the things which are not seen are eternal" (2 Cor 4:18). Our faith, for example, should be in the invisible God who made all things (Heb 11:3). This aspect of faith is exemplified by Abel, Enoch, and Moses, as well as those mentioned above. We learn that Moses "endured, as seeing Him who is unseen," and this is true of all who rest in faith in the one, true God (Heb 11:27; cf. Heb 3:12—4:11).

For Christians, the source of this faith is Jesus and those who testified to his life accompanied by manifestations of God's reality and power (Heb 1:1–3; 2:1–4). The invisible God has made himself known in creation and throughout history, especially the history involving Jesus and the founding of his church. Focused upon this, God's people are enabled through the Holy Spirit to have the conviction that he is real and that their present and future are blessed in him.

This faith is akin to the faith we place in others in that it follows our conviction that the other person is trustworthy. It is demonstrated in that we live our life based on that trust. Saving faith differs in that it is also a gift that we receive from God as we ask God for faith and open ourselves to his work in our lives. It cannot be based simply on a feeling or we make ourselves vulnerable to feelings; true faith in someone else is never just a matter of feeling. Nevertheless, for those who open themselves to the love of God, as Paul says: "The Spirit Himself testifies with our spirit that we are children of God" (Rom 8:16). However, we dare not "get the cart before the horse" here. A person who bases their faith on feelings effectively commits themselves to doubt, and is continually challenging God to overcome their doubt with feeling; whereas, the person who lives by faith commits themselves to live in trust and finds the witness of the Spirit inevitably follows. It is the difference between focusing upon God and his promises, and focusing within ourselves. True assurance requires that our feelings be linked to the firm, outward reality of a living God and his work in our lives so that the witness that follows has meaning beyond ourselves.

The Benefits of Saving Grace in the Lives of the Redeemed

The goal of salvation is saving individuals from themselves. This may sound strange; but the reality is that were God to forgive us without changing us, the corruption of our inner nature would only grow worse, bringing misery to ourselves and others. Therefore, saving grace is more than just a forensic work before the throne of God, it is a transformative work whereby God cleanses the redeemed and, over time, makes their character like his own. This is the only way to escape the consequences of sin.

Like common grace, saving grace is indivisible. Nevertheless, it works in various ways to bring about the unified goal of delivering an individual from the effects of sin. Some blessings of saving grace are instantaneous; others work over time. They are often, but not always, concurrent. Nevertheless, while keeping the unified nature of this grace in mind, it is helpful to look at the various ways this grace works in the lives of the redeemed.

Adoption

Justification enables a restored relationship with God. The redeemed are adopted by God the Father and transferred from the kingdom of darkness into the kingdom of Light, becoming members of the household of God and citizens of the kingdom of God (1 John 3:1; Rom 8:15; Col 1:13; Eph 2:19). This also brings the redeemed into a close personal relationship with every other person who has experienced saving grace, not only in this age, but in past ages as well (Heb 12:18–24).

Every person who receives saving grace does so solely for him or herself; however, every person who receives saving grace does not remain alone, but becomes part of the universal church of Christ. This accomplishes God's purpose to create "a people for his own possession" (Titus 2:14; 1 Pet 2:9–10; Exod 19:5; Deut 4:20; 7:6; 14:2; 26:18; cf. Hos 1:10; 2:23). While being a possession might seem intimidating—as if God's goal is to control us as puppets—God's goal for his people is that "in the ages to come He might show the surpassing riches of His grace in kindness (Gk. *en chrēstotēti*) toward us in Christ Jesus" (Eph 2:7). The goal is *not* for the redeemed to lose their personal identity, individual thoughts, or the characteristics that make each individual unique. The goal is the fulfillment of all that God planned for each individual before creation. This is the personally fulfilling life promised by Jesus (John 10:10). There is, therefore, a social aspect because no human being is fulfilled in the absence of either divine or human relationships.

The most commonly used Greek term for "church" in the New Testament, *ekklēsia*, is not a new word coined by Christians. It refers to a public assembly, and is used in this manner in Acts 19:32, 39, 41. Elsewhere in the New Testament, it always refers to the assembly of Christians, with the exception of Acts 7:38 where it refers to the congregation of Israelites assembled with Moses at Mount Sinai. The New Testament meaning of "church" refers to people, not a building where Christians meet.

Christians could have chosen the more general Greek terms *sunagōgē* or *sullogos* for their assemblies. The Greek word *ekklēsia* was perhaps more attractive because in the Greek Old Testament used at the time of Christ it was often used to translate the Hebrew *qāhāl*, especially when translating "assembly of *Yahweh*" (Hebr. *biqʿhal Yahweh*) as "assembly of the Lord" (Gk. *ekklēsia Kuriou*; Deut 23:2–4; Mic 2:5).[1]

A desire to emphasize divine calling may also have created the preference for *ekklēsia*. The Greek verb *ekkaleō*, to "call out" or to "call from," is the product of the prefix *ek-*, "from," and the verb "to call" or "to summon":

---

1. Lewis, "*qāhāl*," in *TWOT*, 2:790.

kaleō. An assembly of the "called out" is *hē ekklēsia*. Just as the Israelites were called out from slavery in Egypt into fellowship with God, sinners are called out from slavery to sin into fellowship with God through Jesus Christ. Those individuals who respond are referred to as *klētoi*: "called" (Rom 1:6–7; 8:28; 1 Cor 1:2, 24; Jude 1; Rev 17:14). This is consistent with the prominent place of divine calling not only in the Old Testament, but in the New Testament as well.

Jesus taught that his earthly ministry in service to God the Father was "to call (Gk. *kalesai*) . . . sinners to repentance" (Luke 5:32; cf. Matt 9:13; Mark 2:17). God continues to call people through the gospel (2 Thess 2:14). Paul wrote that God is *ho kalōn hymas*, "He who calls you" (1 Thess 5:24). He "called us with a holy calling" (Gk. *kalesantas klēsei hagia*) because he is "the God who calls you (Gk. *tou theou tou kalountas hymas*) into His own kingdom and glory" (2 Tim 1:9; 1 Thess 2:12; cf. 2 Thess 2:14; Heb 3:1). It is a calling that those who respond need to strive to be worthy of (Eph 4:1–2; Phil 3:13–15; Luke 3:8).

This calling is first and foremost a call to fellowship with the Lord. Jesus said, "Where two or three have gathered together in My name, I am there in their midst" (Matt 18:20; cf. Matt 28:20). Both Paul and Peter conceive of the church in terms of a temple in which God's people represent the walls and God is present in the midst of his people (Eph 2:19–22; 1 Cor 3:9, 16–17; 2 Cor 6:16–18). Peter envisions Christians as "living stones" making up a dwelling for the Lord with Jesus as the cornerstone (1 Pet 2:4–6). There is a blessing that comes upon God's people as a group that they cannot experience alone.

However, this does not take anything away from each Christian becoming a temple of God's Spirit individually. Jesus promised: "The Spirit of truth . . . abides with you and will be in you" (Gk. *par' hymin menei kai en hymin estai*, John 14:17). Paul wrote that if someone does not have the Spirit of God, they are not saved (Rom 8:9; cf. 1 Cor 6:17–20). John is in complete agreement, writing of the Holy Spirit as the indwelling Spirit of Christ, "He who has the Son has the life (Gk. *ho echōn ton huion echei tēn zōēn*); he who does not have the Son of God does not have the life" (1 John 5:12; cf. John 14:23). It is because of the presence of God in the redeemed that the church of Jesus Christ is more than just a group with a membership.

The presence of God in the life of the believer brings new life and the transforming presence of the Holy Spirit.

Regeneration

The plan of God, the Creator of all things, is to make all things new through Jesus Christ (Rev 21:5). Underlying God's ability to re-create is his original role as Creator. The church of Christ is the beginning of this new creation. The work whereby God re-creates an individual is known as regeneration, new birth.

The Greek word *palingenesia* is formed from the prefix *palin*—meaning "again"—and *genesis* from the verb *ginomai*—"to become" or "to be born." It appears only twice in the New Testament. In Matthew 19:28, it is used to identify the time when all creation is made new and Jesus sits on his throne over all creation. In Titus 3:5, Paul uses it to refer to the regeneration of an individual made new in Jesus Christ. The first takes place in the age to come; the second takes place in the present age, here and now. A similar Greek term in Peter's first letter, *anagennaō*, indicates regeneration by virtue of the prefix *ana-* which often means "up," but can also mean "again," as it does in Peter's letter (1:3, 23).

When the Prodigal Son returns to his father's house, the father says that the son was dead (Gk. *nekros*), but has become alive again (Gk. *anezēsen*, Luke 15:24). This is consistent with the way the New Testament speaks of regeneration. It is a renewed relationship with the God the Father, but it is more than that. Jesus promises that those who hear his words and believe the message he brings from the Father pass from death to life (Gk. *metabebēken ek tou thanatou eis tēn zōēn*, John 5:24). Paul speaks of the new birth as a resurrection in Ephesians 2:1–7 and Colossians 2:13–14.

When Jesus tells Nicodemus that no one sees the kingdom of God without being "born again" (Gk. *gennēthēi anōthen*), he also stresses the source of that birth (John 3:3). This becomes clear in the wider context of John 3:3. The Greek adverb *anōthen* has a range of meanings, which can include "again," "anew," and "from above." Later in John 3, John the Baptist refers to Jesus as "He who comes from above" (Gk. *ho anōthen erchomenos*, John 3:31). This is significant because in his conversation with Nicodemus, Jesus asserts authority for his teaching because as the Son of Man, Jesus has come down from heaven (John 3:13; cf. 6:38). When Jesus teaches that another birth is necessary, he is not only saying there must be a second birth, he is also saying that it must come from above. In John 3:7, Jesus repeats that Nicodemus must be born from above (Gk. *gennēthēnai anōthen*). In both cases, being born is passive, meaning the birth is something that happens to someone, not something someone does. This fits with the prologue to John's Gospel, where John writes that those who receive Jesus (the Word, Gk. *ho logos*) are born of God (Gk. *ek theou egennēthēsan*, John 1:12–13).

Paul wrote that anyone in Christ is a "new creature"—literally a "new creation" (Gk. *kainē ktisis*, 2 Cor 5:17). He told the Ephesians that as a gift of God's grace they had been "created in Christ Jesus" (Gk. *ktisthentes en Christōi Iēsou*, Eph 2:10). He told the Galatians that for those who followed Christ, what mattered was not some outward "badge of faith" like circumcision or uncircumcision, but the reality of a "new creation" (Gk. *kainē ktisis*, Gal 6:15).

Paul uses the word *kainos* for "new" when he writes about the new creation because unlike the other Greek word commonly used for "new," *neos*—which indicates something new in time—*kainos* can indicate something that has existed before that has in some way been renewed.[2] Because God has life in himself, he is able to communicate "eternal life" to the redeemed (John 5:25-26). This is how our Creator can re-create us, transforming, but not replacing the personality of the redeemed.

The beginning of this work is communicating life to the inner spiritual life of the individual. Although the indwelling Spirit is able to communicate life to the physical body, and sometimes the Holy Spirit brings healing from injury or disease, the complete transformation of the physical body awaits "the redemption of our body" at the return of Christ (Rom 8:11, 23).

The presence of God, nevertheless, brings a "down payment" or "earnest" of the completion that will occur at Christ's coming (Eph 1:13-14). The resurrected, glorified Christ is an even greater assurance for the redeemed than the crucified Christ, because the fact that Jesus is alive guarantees that the work at Calvary is effective forever (Rom 5:8-10). Accordingly, Peter notes that because of Jesus, the redeemed have been "born again (Gk. *anagennēsas*) to a living hope" (1 Pet 1:3). The Spirit of Christ within communicates this assurance of salvation to the minds and hearts of those who are his (Rom 8:15-17).

Sanctification

Paul told the Romans that they were "called *as* saints" (Gk. *klētois hagiois*, Rom 1:7). The Greek word *hagios* is used frequently in the New Testament to refer to Christians, those who are members of the church of Jesus Christ. Although used most frequently by Paul, it is also used in this manner by Luke, John, Jude, and the author of Hebrews. The plural *hagioi* literally means "holy ones," which is translated "saints" in our Bibles due to the influence of Latin. The process of making one a "holy one" is called "sanctification" in English for the same reason.

---

2. Behm, "*kainos*," in *TDNT*, 3:447.

We have seen that the meaning of the word "holy" depends upon the deity the holiness relates to. To be made holy in the New Testament sense is, first of all, to be set apart to God. Second, it is to be purified. And third, it is to be made *like* God in character. Peter exhorted his readers to be holy in the way they live their lives because God is holy and he demands that his people be holy (1 Pet 1:15–16; 2 Pet 3:11–12; Lev 11:44; 19:1–2; 20:7, 26). This involves more than just outward behavior. The goal is not just for the people of God to appear righteous, but to become righteous—to be sanctified.

Paul's personal goal concerning Christ was that he "may be found in Him, not having a righteousness (Gk. *dikaiosynēn*) of my own derived from *the* Law, but that which is through faith in Christ, the righteousness which *comes* from God (Gk. *ek Theou dikaiosynēn*) on the basis of faith" (Phil 3:9; cf. 2 Cor 5:21). This is a goal that cannot be achieved apart from the work of God.

Paul described salvation as "the washing of regeneration and renewing by the Holy Spirit" (Gk. *loutrou palingenesias kai anakainōseōs pneumatos hagiou*, Titus 3:5). This is the initial act of sanctification that makes every Christian a "holy one." In the New Covenant promised through Jeremiah, *Yahweh* promised his people: "I will put My law within them and on their heart I will write it" (Jer 31:33). Through Ezekiel, *Yahweh* promised: "I will cleanse you from all your filthiness and from all your idols. Moreover, I will give you a new heart and put a new spirit within you . . . I will put My Spirit within you and cause you to walk in My statutes, and you will be careful to observe My ordinances" (Ezek 36:25–27). *Yahweh* promised that as a result of his work, the people would become his people and he would be their God (Jer 31:33; Ezek 36:28).

Paul reminded the Christians in Rome that when they received salvation, the love of God was poured into their hearts (Rom 5:5). This is not only the love of God toward us, but the love of God in us, changing us so that, in the words of Jeremiah and Ezekiel, God's Law is now within our hearts and we walk in his ways. Jesus taught that the Law of Moses is fulfilled by loving God with all of our hearts and loving our neighbor as ourselves (Matt 22:34–40; Mark 12:28–34; Luke 10:25–28; Deut 6:4–5; Lev 19:18). The love that God implants within us by his Spirit is the fulfillment of the Law. It fulfills God's promise: "I will remove the heart of stone from your flesh and give you a heart of flesh," which is the heart God intended those to have who have been created in his image (Ezek 36:26).

We have observed that when Scripture speaks of the heart, it is referring to the entire inner life of an individual. The cleansing and renewing that the Spirit of God performs in this age is primarily moral and ethical in nature. Paul exhorted his readers to submit to God's transformation of their thought and values. "Do not be conformed to this age (Gk. *aiōni*), but be transformed by the renewing of your mind (Gk. *metamorphousthe tēi anakainōsei tou noos*), so that you may prove what the will of God is, that which is good and well-pleasing and perfect (Gk. *to agathon kai euareston kai teleion*)" (Rom 12:2; cf. Eph 5:7–10; Acts 23:1; 24:14–16). This results from submitting to and cooperating with the work of God, for, "the fruit of the Spirit is love, joy, peace, patience, kindness, goodness, faithfulness, gentleness, self-control" (Gal 5:22–23).

Peter rejoiced that through the promises of God we escape the corruption that is in the world that comes from evil desires, God perfecting his image within us so that our nature becomes like his (2 Pet 1:4; cf. 2 Cor 3:18). It was Adam and Eve's desire for the one thing they were told they could not have that caused the corruption of man's nature in the first place. It is that tendency to sin that, when indulged by pursuing that which is contrary to God's character, brings increasing corruption of a person's moral and spiritual nature (Jas 1:13–15; Eph 2:2–3; Rom 1:18–32; 1 John 2:16–17; Matt 12:33–35). By the work of God, the redeemed are cleansed from these desires and given new ones (John 7:38–39; 15:5; 1 John 1:9; Titus 2:11–14). Indeed, through the work of God: "His divine power has granted to us everything pertaining to life and godliness, through the true knowledge of Him who called us to His own glory and excellence" (2 Pet 1:3).

Entire Sanctification

The ultimate goal of saving grace in this age is entire sanctification. The clearest teaching on this work is found in Paul's First Letter to the Thessalonians.

As Paul closes his letter to the Thessalonians, he writes: "Now may the God of peace Himself sanctify you entirely; and may your spirit and soul and body be preserved complete, without blame (Gr. *amemptōs*) at the coming of our Lord Jesus Christ. Faithful is He who calls you, and He also will bring it to pass" (1 Thess 5:23). It is important to notice that this is a desire for God, himself, to do something for the Thessalonian Christians, not an appeal for the Christians to do something themselves as, for example, in 1 Thessalonians 4:3.

What Paul wants God to do for the Thessalonians is to sanctify them entirely (Gr. *hagiasai hymas holoteleis*). It is something that God himself (Gr. *autos de ho theos*) will do (Gr. *poiēsei*, 1 Thess 5:23–24). There is abundant evidence in this letter that Paul considers the Thessalonians to have received saving grace, even considering them to be examples to other believers of how to live (1 Thess 1:6–10). Therefore, this is not the initial sanctification that they received that qualified them to be saints—literally "holy ones" (Gr.

hagioi)—it is something more (1 Thess 3:13). It is also a desire for God to do something here and now that will be in effect when Christ returns bodily—not when or after the return of Christ; a state of grace in which Christians may be "preserved"—kept (Gr. *tērētheiē*[3]).

The Greek word translated "entirely" is a combination of the word for "whole" (Gr. *holos*) and the word for "perfect" or "complete" (Gr. *telos*): *holoteleis*. The Greek word later translated "complete" is a combination of "whole" (Gr. *holos*) and "portion" (Gr. *klēros*). The extent of this completeness is the whole portion (Gr. *holoklēron*) of a person's spirit, soul, and body (Gr. *to pneuma kai hē psychē kai to sōma*); so it touches every part of a person's inner and outer existence. We learn several things from Paul's letters to the Thessalonians that help us to understand the nature of this sanctification.

First, although it involves the physical body, it does not mean the physical body is prepared for eternity (cf. 1 Cor 15:35–57). Paul speaks to the bodily resurrection of believers as a future event in 1 Thessalonians 4:13–18. In 2 Thessalonians 2:14, Paul affirms that through the gospel these Christians will "gain the glory of our Lord Jesus Christ" at his coming. So the completeness spoken of here is something attainable in this age. Still, after this work, Christians will age and die; they will still be prone to illness.

Second, we observe that blamelessness is Paul's ultimate goal. It is the goal of blamelessness that ties Paul's desire in 5:23 to Paul's desire in chapter 3. In chapter 3, Paul expresses the hope that "He [God] may establish your hearts without blame in holiness before our God and Father at the coming of our Lord Jesus with all His saints" (1 Thess 3:13). Jude also shares this vision. At the close of his letter, Jude celebrates that the Lord "is able to keep [literally 'guard'] you from stumbling, and to make you stand in the presence of His glory blameless with great joy" (Jude 24). This helps us understand what this means for the physical body in this age: that it be disciplined so as not to lead to sin (1 Cor 9:24–27; cf. 1 Cor 6:19–20; Rom 6:12). Legitimate human desires are to be met in ways that are pleasing to God, and this work helps Christians to do that.

Finally, we learn from 1 Thessalonians 3:12 regarding the goal of blamelessness that Paul hopes God may "cause you to increase and abound in love for one another, and for all people." Entire sanctification must be seen as affecting not only the whole person, but whatever a person thinks and does. At the same time, it does not bring a person to absolute perfection, but to the point where a person is best able to grow. Spiritual growth

---

3. Third-person singular aorist optative passive, which indicates that the "keeping" here is done by God, but is contingent upon a person's faith and faithfulness. Note "kept" and "keep" in Jude 1, 20–21.

is not only possible, it is desirable and expected even if what Paul hopes for, entire sanctification, is accomplished.

The sanctification thus available is a moral/ethical sanctification. It is entire in the sense that it affects every part of a person's nature and existence, not in the sense that it removes the need for spiritual growth or the eventual glorification of the physical body. It does not remove the need for self-discipline. It is not a source of pride, but a state of dependence upon God (Isa 57:15). It is not a freedom from misunderstandings or poor judgments. It does not eliminate unworthy thoughts from coming to mind, but it helps Christians to reject them. It does not eliminate emotions, nor is it limited to emotions. It does not make a person faultless, but blameless in love (properly conceived) toward God and man (Matt 22:36–40). This is the state Paul was in and desired for others (Phil 3:12–21). It is available by faith to all those who love the Lord and trust him.

Faith in God for entire sanctification is no different from faith in God for saving grace; it is trust in God to do this work. Christians who notice that there is inner resistance to doing God's will in their lives may seek a deeper cleansing and the fullness of the Holy Spirit (1 Thess 5:23–24; Acts 15:7–9; 1 Tim 1:5; 2 Tim 2:20–22). Those who seek this work of God should be aware that they will still need to continue to increase in their knowledge and understanding of God's Word, they will still have the full range of human emotions, and they will still be subject to temptation.

Some will be especially prone to the temptation of pride; but genuine sanctification precludes arrogance. Any sin, quickly confessed and repented of, will not forfeit this state of grace. Those who give in to such temptations and do not repent, or who lose faith, may lose this state of grace; but it may be regained through commitment and faith.

Becoming spiritually mature takes time. Personal discipline will be required just as before. It will still be challenging, at times, to do God's will. However, inner resistance to making God's will the governing principle of life will be gone. Therefore, growth will take place at the greatest possible pace because the greatest inner hindrance to doing God's will have been overcome.

Those who are entirely sanctified, though they will not tolerate willful sin, will become even more aware of their failings and weaknesses, of past mistakes and things they need to change in their lives. There will be resistance to denying the reality of these moral and spiritual infirmities. Both honesty and faith are required to prevent the knowledge of these weaknesses from taking over and to allow the Holy Spirit to use this knowledge to refine behavior (1 John 1:9). Satan will seek to use this knowledge to defeat a Christian and burden that person with guilt. Faith in God, here as elsewhere, requires paying more attention to God's grace than to our weaknesses. For the Christian who is entirely sanctified and focuses on the Lord, knowledge of human weaknesses not only spurs further growth, it also deepens awareness of and faith in God's love and redeeming grace.

14

Bearing Fruit

I am the vine, you are the branches; he who abides in Me and I in him, he bears much fruit, for apart from Me you can do nothing.

JOHN 15:5

The hard-working farmer ought to be the first to receive his share of the crops.

2 TIMOTHY 2:6

I planted, Apollos watered, but God was causing the growth. So then neither the one who plants nor the one who waters is anything, but God who causes the growth. . . . For we are God's fellow workers; you are God's field . . .

1 CORINTHIANS 3:6-7, 9

For we are His workmanship, created in Christ Jesus for good works, which God prepared beforehand so that we would walk in them.

EPHESIANS 2:10

You will know them by their fruits.

MATTHEW 7:16

For Martin Luther, salvation brings a privileged way of life, living with the gracious presence of the Lord only available to those who are in Christ. Luther called this living *coram Deo*—living *before God*. The Latin phrase *coram Deo* has roots in Scripture.

The Hebrew phrase *lipᵉnê Yahweh*, "before the face of the Lord," is a metaphorical expression for coming before God and being in his presence (e.g., Gen 18:22; Deut 4:10; 6:25; Ps 95:6; Dan 9:20). The authors of the Greek New Testament use several words to communicate a similar meaning. The most common is *enōpion*, notably in Luke 1:75, where the salvation provided by the "Lord God of Israel" will enable his people to "serve Him without fear, in holiness and righteousness before Him all our days" (cf. 2 Cor 4:2; 1 Tim 5:4; Heb 13:20–21; Jas 4:10). Other words are *emprosthen*, *katenanti*, *katenōpion*, and *enantion* (1 John 3:19, 22; 2 Cor 2:17; 12:19; Eph 1:4; Luke 1:6). The presence of the Lord opens new possibilities for spiritual blessings and growth, but only when the redeemed recognize and cooperate with the Lord (Phil 2:12–13). Fortunately, the Scriptures teach that there are ways to ensure that God's work in our lives is always fruitful.

The Means of Grace

Jesus' teaching is filled with examples and parables that have to do with agriculture. Agricultural references are seen in many other places in Scripture as well. For example, the very first psalm in the book of Psalms compares the person who avoids sin and focuses on God's Word to a fruitful tree.

Certainly these references were appropriate in a time when most people were, in one way or another, involved in farming plants or herding animals, as was true into the early twentieth century as well. Today, only a small percentage of the population in advanced societies is involved in farming. However, there are more enduring reasons for these teachings. First, they are easily understood by all, and second, bringing about spiritual growth is very much like farming.

A farmer cannot force plants or animals grow. Tugging on a young stalk of wheat, for example, will not make it more mature, it will simply pull it out of the ground. What a wise farmer does is to provide the conditions appropriate for growth: preparing the soil, making sure animals have adequate food and water, watering plants if necessary, and preventing bugs, vermin, and predators from destroying the yield. A plant, tree, or animal then grows and bears fruit because it has the God-given ability to grow and be fruitful. Fruitfulness is inevitable given the right conditions—including the appropriate length of time. Farming takes time and patience. It also requires the farmer to exercise faith in God that the crop will come, as it predictably will as long as the conditions are right.

Similarly, people cannot force spiritual growth by their own effort. However, God has provided the ability for spiritual growth to take place if the proper conditions exist. Thus Psalm 1 talks about the tree bearing fruit "in its time" or "in its season" (Hebr. *be'ittô*, Ps 1:3). These conditions are called "the means of grace." There are no shortcuts to spiritual maturity. Using the means of grace is an act of faith in God "who causes the growth"—to speak in terms of Paul's teaching in 1 Corinthians 3:7. The means of grace ensure that spiritual growth takes place "in its time" whether it is an individual seeking spiritual growth or a spiritual leader seeking to help others to grow.

The discipline of the means of grace should not be seen as earning salvation. Their is no cost to the redeemed for saving grace—that cost was paid in full by Christ. However, there is a cost to devotion just as there is a cost to not being devoted (Matt 16:24–27; 25:14–46).

In the Parable of the Sower, Jesus taught that those who respond to the gospel may be divided into four groups (Matt 13:1–23). The first group carelessly allows Satan to cause them to forget the truth of the gospel. The second group does not value salvation enough, and falls away when affliction or persecution arises. The third group places their focus on the things of this world, and allow riches or the troubles of life to squeeze out any devotion to the Lord. The fourth group focuses upon God's Word, believes what God has said, devote themselves to the Lord, and live fruitfully as described in Psalm 1.

It is important to understand that this parable does not teach that exactly one-fourth of hearers in any specific time or place will respond in each of these four ways. It depends upon the hearers. What Jesus teaches is that overall there will be these four types of outcomes for those who claim faith in Christ. Jesus also teaches that not everyone will produce the same amount of spiritual fruit (Matt 13:23). Fruitfulness depends upon a person's personality and circumstances, as well as their level of faithfulness.

God generally uses means to accomplish his work. This is seen clearly in Romans 10:14–15, where Paul points out that unless preachers are sent and the preachers present the gospel, there will be no knowledge of the work of Christ and no one to respond with faith. Preachers are the means God uses to bring people into his fellowship through saving grace. Peter, for example, was the means God used to bring people to Christ on the day of Pentecost and when he brought the gospel to the Gentiles for the very first time (Acts 10:1–48). Deacons became the means whereby Christians cared for their widows (Acts 6:1–6). Paul and Barnabas exemplified this not only by becoming missionaries from the church at Antioch, but by collecting and presenting an offering to the Christians in Palestine on more than one occasion (Acts 11:27–30; 13:1–4; 24:17). The offerings they brought were the means God used to relieve the suffering brought by famine. The offering brought late in Paul's ministry was the means Paul used to promote fellowship between Jewish Christians and Gentile Christians (2 Cor 8:1—9:15).

The founder of Methodism, John Wesley (1709-1791), taught that it is fanatical (the terminology of the time was "enthusiastic") to expect the end without the means.[1] One reason people become discouraged in their relationship with God is that they expect the Holy Spirit to do things they, themselves, should be doing. Certainly, God can work immediately—in other words, directly and without means—to accomplish whatever he wants at any time. For example, he can heal any illness whenever he chooses to do so. But it is no less a healing from the Lord to use medical professionals and appropriate medical treatment inasmuch as there are no means available to God's creatures that God the Creator did not enable. Since God generally uses means to accomplish his work in the world, Christians should expect that most often one or more means will be used to accomplish God's work in their lives.

The primary means of grace are: prayer, Scripture reading, worship, good works, and abstaining from evil. Using the means of grace is an act of faith, faith similar to that of a farmer who works toward a harvest with confidence in his plants and animals. Those who practice the means of grace will reap rewards that those who do not use them will forfeit (Gal 6:9; Heb 12:11).

Worship

Worship is the natural response of a person who has received grace from God (Ps 63:1-8; 27:4). A person who has received the gift of salvation and understands what that means cannot help but express their gratitude in worship. Those who feel no need to worship have forgotten both the condition of their souls apart from saving work of God and the cost of their salvation at the cross of Christ (Jas 1:22-25; 2 Pet 1:2-11).

Jesus said, "God is Spirit, and those who worship Him (*tous proskynountas auton*) must worship (*proskynein*) in spirit and truth," and God seeks these people to worship Him (John 4:24). By "worship in spirit," Jesus taught that God must be worshipped by the inner person, not just in outward ceremonies. The belief that we can affect our lives by the equivalent of incantations and ceremonies without the appropriate attitude and goals is pagan magic or sorcery. Even the ceremonies given by God have no value if not performed with the proper attitude (Matt 9:13; 12:1-7; 23:23; Hos 6:1-6; Isa 1:10-23; 58:1-14). To "worship in truth" is to give worship in a

---

1. Wesley, "Nature of Enthusiasm," in *Wesley's 52 Standard Sermons*, 360, 367.

manner that recognizes the true nature and character of God as well as the true nature of what we are doing. Just as every good gift is designed to please the one who receives the gift, to have true value, worship must be given in a manner that is pleasing to God, not just to ourselves.

Knowing that God does not change in his essential nature, the authors of the New Testament recognized a definite pattern of divine behavior in the sacred history of the Old Testament that has significance for Christians. The exodus was seen as a metaphor for escaping the slavery of sin into the freedom of God's kingdom (John 8:33-36; Rom 6:3-18; 8:2). The crucified Jesus was understood to relate to the Passover Lamb (1 Cor 5:7; 1 Pet 1:18-19). The "sprinkling" of Jesus' blood brought people into the New Covenant just as Moses initiated the Old (1 Pet 1:2; Exod 24:8). The Christian walk was viewed as analogous to the journey through the wilderness to the promised land (1 Cor 10:1-13; Heb 3:12—4:11). They also pointed out differences, perhaps most visibly in Hebrews, where the author emphasizes the superiority of the New Covenant over the Old. Nevertheless, they knew that a careful study of the Old Testament reveals insights for Christian worship.

We have already seen how the Greek word *proskyneō*—to do obeisance by prostrating oneself—describes the proper inward attitude of humility before God. Certainly this is the correct attitude with which to approach God in worship. Two related New Testament words for worship, the verb *latreuō* and the noun *latreia*, cannot be easily translated into English. It is helpful to take a brief look into the background of these terms.

Moses demanded that Pharaoh release the Israelites so they could serve the God of the Hebrews with sacrifices and feasting (Exod 3:12, 18; 4:23; 5:1, 3, 8, 17; 7:16; 8:1, 8, 20, 25-29; 9:1, 13; 10:3, 8-9, 11, 24-26; 12:31). The Hebrew verb ʿābad and the Hebrew noun ʿăbôdâ in these Old Testament passages are often translated "serve" and "service." Inherent in these words is the concept of obedience to the one served (Deut 10:12-13). When used for the service of a deity—whether *Yahweh* or a false god—these words describe the service performed as a act of worship (Exod 23:24-25, 33; Deut 4:16-19, 28; 5:8-10; 6:13).[2] The services to be performed for *Yahweh* consisted of sacrifices dedicated to *Yahweh*, the celebration of the Passover, the construction of the tabernacle, the sacred activities at the tabernacle, and even choral singing at the tabernacle (Exod 10:24-26; 12:23-26; 13:1-5; 30:16; 35:21; 36:1, 3; 39:42; Num 3:7; 4:4-49; 1 Chr 25:1-7; 2 Chr 35:15).

In addition to the more formal religious worship at the tabernacle, the words of *Yahweh* to Moses and the events at Sinai indicate that continued obedience in daily life is integral to true worship (Exod 19:4-6; 24:1-8; Deut

---

2. Walter C. Kaiser, "ʿābad," in *TWOT*, 2:639.

5:1–33; cf. Ps 24). The obligation to serve God by living according to his moral requirements broadens the time of worship from specific ceremonies to one's entire life. There is, then, a problem for translators of the Hebrew text as to whether to emphasize service or worship when translating these words for the English text. Often they will return to the basic meaning of service, in which case only the context indicates whether the service rendered is an act of worship.

The Greek Septuagint translation of the Old Testament used *latreuō* and *latreia* to translate ʿ*ābad* and ʿ*ăbôdâ*. The writers of the New Testament applied the Greek terms to all Christians, not just to the services of the Levitical priests, retaining emphases upon obedience, worship, and service (Rom 1:9; 12:1; Luke 1:74; Acts 24:14; 27:23; Phil 3:3; Rev 22:3). As before, the terms involve life in general as well as acts of worship (Rom 12:1; Heb 12:28). Also following from the Old Testament is the problem of translating *latreuō* and *latreia* into English; translations vary as to whether they should be translated "service" or "worship" in certain verses. Given the basic meaning of the words, again, modern translators often seem to prefer "service."

Not so obvious from the New Testament texts, perhaps, but implied by the terms, is the connection between obedience and worship. Jesus said, "Your Father has chosen gladly to give you the kingdom" (Luke 12:32). In view of this, the author of Hebrews exhorted, "Since we receive a kingdom which cannot be shaken, let us show gratitude, by which we may offer to God an acceptable service with reverence and awe" (Heb 12:28). The service we are to give is indicated here by the Greek verb *latreuōmen*, which carries the connotation of worship. Similarly, when Paul encourages Christians to present their bodies as living sacrifices, he declares this is "your spiritual service of worship" (Rom 12:1). "Worship" here is the Greek noun *latreian*, which is often translated "service." Both verses indicate a way of living in addition to the proper approach to acts of worship.

"Reverence and awe" (Gk. *eulabeias kai deous*) in Hebrews 12:28 are appropriate because God is the exalted sovereign of all things and deserves to be recognized as such. A close relationship with God as "Abba, Father" does not require or condone treating God in a trite, frivolous, or childish manner (Rom 8:15; 1 Cor 13:11). John rightly recognizes that perfect love casts out fear of the Lord because faith in our Redeemer eliminates fear of eternal punishment (1 John 4:18). Reverence for the Lord, which may be described as godly fear, is nevertheless appropriate because it recognizes our creaturely dependence upon our Creator, not only for but especially for salvation from sin (1 Pet 1:17–21; Acts 9:31; 2 Cor 5:11; 7:1; Phil 2:12–13; Ps 111:10; Prov 9:10). True worship recognizes the closeness of the redeemed to the Lord—a God who reaches out to us in love and rejoices when we respond with love. At the same time, God is worthy of, and demands, the highest level of respect, as exemplified in Abraham's intercession in Genesis 18:22–33 and in Jesus' prayer in John 17. The demeanor of Jesus, the sinless Son of God, toward God the Father is especially noteworthy.

Although Christian worship demands humility and reverence before the Lord, and much of what Christianity teaches and celebrates in worship demands appropriate solemnity, Christian worship is uplifting rather than burdensome. This is because freedom from guilt and the love of God fill the worshipper with peace and joy (John 14:27; 16:33; Acts 8:39; 9:31; Rom 1:7; 8:6; 12:12; 14:17; 15:13; Phil 4:4; 1 Thess 5:16; 1 Pet 1:8). True worship is a joyous celebration of our relationship with the Lord.

Personal Worship

The Protestant Reformation emphasized the priesthood of believers: that every Christian has the privilege of going directly before the Lord. Both Peter and John recognized the status of all Christians as "priests" (1 Pet 2:9; Rev 1:6). No longer required to worship through the Levitical priesthood of the Old Testament, Christians may go directly to the Lord both for themselves and as intercessors for others.

Prayer

The person relieved of the burden of sin may take immediate advantage of their new state of grace by speaking to the Lord in prayer. It is significant that all prayers we find in Scripture are in a language known to the person praying. Jesus, himself, prayed and taught his followers to pray in a known language. Prayer that is silent rather than spoken will, nevertheless, involve words.

Prayer is a form of fellowship with God, similar to the way conversation is a form of fellowship with other people. God knows our needs and desires, but he often will not act upon them apart from our prayers to bring us closer to himself (Matt 6:8).

The Psalms are a good resource for learning about prayer. The prayers in the book of Psalms were spoken by people who, like us, were struggling to live for the Lord in a fallen world. We can appreciate their emotions as well as the content of their prayers.

In these and other prayers recorded in Scripture, we should notice the five major parts of prayer: praise, confession, intercession, petition, and thanksgiving. Not all prayers contain all five parts, but all five parts should be in at least some of our prayers. Praise recognizes the greatness of God and celebrates specific aspects of his nature and character. Confession is twofold: confessing our faith in God, his works, and his Word; and confessing our weaknesses, sins, and need for saving grace. Intercession is prayer for others and their needs. Petition is asking God to work in our own lives. Thanksgiving is first an expression of gratitude for the Lord's changeless reality, holiness, and love; second for his works in the past, present, and future that benefit us; and last, for specific ways he has blessed us. Thanksgiving is thus not dependent upon our circumstances.

It is in intercessory prayer for the lost that we most act as priests, standing between God and those who need to know him (e.g., Rom 10:1; Eph 3:14-20). It is important to pray for God's work in the lives of those who are apart from God, and to persist in prayer by name for those we know (1 Tim 2:1-6). Evangelists and missionaries also depend on our prayer support to be effective and fruitful (Rom 15:30-32; Eph 6:18-20; Col 4:2-4; 1 Thess 5:25).

Several scriptures refer to "praying without ceasing." Paul encourages this (1 Thess 5:17; cf. Rom 1:9-10; 2 Tim 1:3). It is important to understand that while our fellowship with God is continuous, these Scriptures do not mean that we should provide spoken prayer without rest. Obviously, we will be doing many things other than formal worship during the day, and some of those things will require our complete attention. What the Scriptures describe and Paul encourages is that we never come to the place where we cease returning to God in prayer. It is natural to pray many times in a day—and these prayers will often be brief. Frequently, even on a daily basis, we should remember those close to us and other Christians before the Lord—more often when they have special or serious needs (Eph 6:18).

There is no sin reading a prayer written by someone else if we really mean what it says. Repeating the Lord's Prayer, for example, is often helpful. However, God is a living Person. He is not a vending machine that one puts in the correct input and counts on a particular outcome. There are no "special phrases" that bring results. In fact, Jesus warned against "meaningless repetition" (Matt 6:7). We should speak to God naturally and honestly. We may expect him to respond to us individually, but also consistent with his ways (cf. Jas 4:3). Accordingly, it is always appropriate to pray for God's will to be done above our own, just as Jesus did in Gethsemane, because God always knows what is truly best for all.

Jesus taught us to persist in prayer; however, we need to do so with respect for God and faith in his love for us (Luke 11:5-13; 18:1-8). Repeating the same prayer over and over obsessively may be treating God as if he doesn't care (Matt 6:7; John 14:1). This can result from a lack of faith in his wisdom or goodness, or a refusal to accept his answer. Nevertheless, as long as we approach God with the appropriate reverence, there is no limit to how often we may speak with him, and no limit to what we may discuss. Nothing is too great or too small to bring before the Lord. Peter exhorted us to "humble yourselves under the mighty hand of God . . . casting all your anxiety on Him, because He cares for you" (1 Pet 5:6–7). The author of Hebrews reminds us that Jesus is our high priest; having lived life as a human being, he understands the pressures, problems, and pains of life, and so is able to intercede effectively to God the Father on our behalf (Heb 2:17–18; 4:14–16). The indwelling Holy Spirit also intercedes on our behalf (Rom 8:26–27). God will answer according to his love and his power, and according to his plan for us and for all people.

With this in mind, we should always be willing to be part of the answer to our prayers. If there are things that only God can do, then surely we must leave the results to him. This is also true when we go to the Lord to ask him to intervene in a situation, but don't know exactly what to ask for. While we should look for an answer, we should leave the answer to him, especially in cases such as these. However, in many cases we should see ourselves partnering with God in bringing about what we are asking God to accomplish. God will generally not do for us what we ourselves should do. If we are praying for the salvation of someone we know, for example, we should also be praying about what we might do to help that person come to know God through Jesus Christ.

Scripture Reading

We should expect God to give us guidance for life (Rom 8:14). All Christians agree that the Holy Spirit provides guidance to the redeemed; the central issue is not whether the Holy Spirit gives guidance, but how. In the Scriptures, we observe that God gave guidance by speaking directly to some individuals. At Mt. Sinai, the Lord spoke audibly to the entire nation of Israel (Exod 19:18—20:22; Deut 5:4–27). At various times, God communicated through dreams, visions, and angelic messengers; he also communicated by his actions (Heb 1:1; 2:1–4). God is not restricted from speaking in any of these ways today. However, the principle that "we should not expect the end without the means" applies here as well; it does not exclude divine guidance.

The primary means whereby God gives guidance today is the Holy Scriptures. They came about through the work of the Holy Spirit (2 Tim 3:16–17; 2 Pet 1:20–21). The Scriptures contain truths (e.g., God's acts in history, God's words to us); general principles (e.g., love, righteousness, justice); specific commandments (e.g., love God with all your heart, mind, and soul; love your neighbor as yourself; do unto others as you would have others do onto you); and examples of both good and poor conduct (cf. Rom 15:4; 1 Cor 10:11). These provide guidance for all people in the present age. We are warned not to add to these (Rev 22:18–19). By studying and prayerfully considering what is written, we can determine what to believe and how to live. The process of interpretation is not left to individual judgment, however (2 Pet 1:20).

Peter wrote that those who misunderstand Scripture include those who are untaught and those who are not firmly committed to following the Lord (2 Pet 3:16). The Greek word for "untaught" in this passage is *amatheis*. It is related to the word for disciple in the New Testament: *mathētēs*, and the verb form for making disciples: *mathēteuō*. This is because a disciple is simply someone committed to learning. The charge from Jesus to the apostles was to "make disciples"—those willing to learn his teachings and his ways— and we see this happening in Acts (Matt 28:19). A Christian disciple is one who is eager to learn rather than one who is simply wise in him or herself (Prov 3:5–6). This learning is a lifelong process. To refuse to spend the effort to learn from others is to refuse to be a disciple of Christ.

Jesus' promise that the Holy Spirit would remind of Jesus' teachings and guide into Truth was given to Jesus' apostles, not to all Christians (John 14:25–26). Their teaching, collected in Holy Scripture by the work of the Holy Spirit, forms the tradition on which the Christian faith is communicated. For all who come after, the Holy Spirit distributes spiritual gifts to the church of Jesus Christ, his *ekklēsia*, and some of those gifts have to do with the interpretation of Scripture (1 Cor 12:4–11; Eph 4:11–12; 1 Pet 4:10–11; Rom 12:6).

Orthodox teachings (small *o*) constitute the consensus of long, hard consideration of the true meaning of Scripture by Christian scholars and leaders gifted by the Holy Spirit throughout the early centuries of the Christian era. To contradict their teachings is to insist that an individual in a short period of time can do better scholarship than a number of learned and devout individuals over many years. It is both humble and prudent to be careful of any interpretation of Christian faith and morals that runs counter to traditional, orthodox Christian teaching.

The Scriptures must be interpreted carefully because they are the Word of God (cf. 2 Tim 2:15; 3:16–17). The best way for new Christians to interpret Scripture is to follow more mature Christians, either ones they know, or through reading books written by mature Christians who are faithful to the Scriptures according to the traditional understanding of the faith.

Finally, with all of this in mind, there is a place for personal study and understanding of the Scriptures. By no means should the need for carefulness hinder Christians from reading the Scriptures frequently—daily if possible. The Holy Spirit illuminates the mind of a Christian who studies and meditates upon the Holy Scriptures (Eph 1:18–23; 3:14–19; cf. 2 Tim 2:7). The clarity (the fancy theological word is "perspicuity") of Scripture does not mean it can be read once and always understood, and it does not mean everything is easy to understand; but it does mean that the average individual can, with diligent study, correctly understand the basic teachings of Scripture. There is also a place for freedom of judgment in those matters not covered by the basic, orthodox, traditional teachings of the faith (Rom 14:5). Such issues are often the reason for different denominations within the Christian church.

Direct, Personal Guidance

While the Scriptures provide general guidance to all Christians, God is just as able to provide individual guidance today as at any time in the past. However, circumstances have changed since the early church because the New Testament is available. In certain circumstances, God still uses visions, dreams, angelic messengers, and the direct communication of wisdom and knowledge to guide his people. Nevertheless, great caution needs to be exercised in this area.

John Wesley explained,

> Though the Spirit is our principal leader, yet He is not our rule at all; the Scriptures are the rule whereby he leads us into all truth. Therefore, only talk good English; call the Spirit our *guide*, which signifies an intelligent being, and the Scriptures our *rule*, which signifies something used by an intelligent being, and all is plain and clear.[3]

The wisdom the Holy Spirit brings to Christians who are determined to do God's will is an opening of the mind to understand the teachings of Scripture and to have the same perspective as God (Jas 1:5–7). The assurance that we understand what Scripture requires of us in a particular matter Wesley calls "conviction":

> I fear you do not in anywise understand what the being "moved by his Spirit" means. God moves man, whom he has made a reasonable creature, according to the reason which he has given him. He moves him by his understanding, as well as his affections; by light, as well as by heat. He moves him to do this or that by conviction, full as often as by desire. Accordingly, you are

---

3. Wesley, "A Letter to a Person Lately Joined with the People Called Quakers," in *Works*, 10:178. Emphasis his.

really "moved by the Spirit" when he convinces you you ought to feed him that is hungry, as when he gives you ever so strong an impulse, desire, or inclination so to do.[4]

In Deuteronomy 18:20–22, God warns that those who speak for him when he has not commissioned them will be liable to punishment. This passage directly follows Moses foretelling of the coming of the greatest prophet, Jesus, which serves to underscore its importance (Deut 18:15–19; Acts 3:22–23; 7:37). Deuteronomy 13 requires God's people to listen to his voice and to obey his commandments. God told the Israelites that even if a prophet's prediction seems to come true, what that prophet says isn't necessarily of the Lord; sometimes God is testing to see if those hearing the prophet are truly faithful to him and his Word (Deut 13:1–4). Everything we do should be measured against the principles and guidelines he has given us in his Word. It is not wrong to pray for divine guidance and to expect help from the Lord. However, if we believe God has communicated to us apart from Scripture, we should understand it and state it as our belief rather than as fact, and be careful to test our belief by the teachings of Scripture.

Wesley saw great danger in treating impressions or circumstances as divine guidance, especially in comparatively small matters. He wrote,

> I have often found an aptness both in myself and others, to connect events that have no real relation to each another. So one says, "I am as sure this is the will of God, as that I am justified." Another says, "God as surely spake this to my heart as ever he spoke to me at all." This is an exceedingly dangerous way of thinking or speaking. We know not what it may lead us to.[5]

Most of the Lord's guidance apart from Scripture comes in ways that aren't obvious or felt. The experiences of Abraham, Moses, Job, Jeremiah, Jesus, Peter, and many others teach us that God's will isn't always comfortable.

Wesley taught that in decisions of life where the Scriptures give no direct counsel, there is the general principle that God wills our sanctification—our holiness (1 Thess 4:3). He taught that on this basis, we should use experience and reason to carefully evaluate what promotes the most holiness—the most good—for ourselves and others, believing in the assistance of the Holy Spirit through this process to help us arrive at a decision.[6] In some matters, this may involve consulting mature Christians to examine

---

4. Wesley, "A Letter to a Person Lately Joined with the People Called Quakers," in *Works*, 10:181.

5. Wesley, Letter 567, "To Miss. Bolton," in *Works*, 12:485–86.

6. Wesley, "On the Nature of Enthusiasm," in *Wesley's 52 Standard Sermons*, 365–66.

whether our understanding has merit (Prov 12:15). Study, planning, and consultation with others are, therefore, the means God uses to guide his people.

The Apostle John explains why such a careful approach is necessary. John wrote, "Beloved, do not believe every spirit, but test the spirits to see whether they are from God" (1 John 4:1). John wrote in a time when it was common for Christians to receive guidance directly from the Holy Spirit because the Scriptures of the New Testament did not yet exist or weren't widely available. His warning recognizes that even if we believe we have been given spiritual knowledge, our mind and feelings may have been affected by our own spirit or even an unclean spirit rather than by the Holy Spirit.

Paul recognized that Satan often presents himself as "an angel of light" (2 Cor 11:14). Thus, Paul told the Christians in Corinth that any message thought to have come from God should be evaluated by more than one person, because, "the spirits of prophets are subject to prophets" (1 Cor 14:32). As Wesley taught, carelessness in this area can lead to many woes. If Satan cannot get us to ignore God's will, he may try to get us to jump to false conclusions regarding what God wills. Sadly, many have fallen victim to this kind of deception. Unless there is immediate and apparent danger, the Holy Spirit will not prompt us to rush into action (Prov 19:2; 21:5; 29:20).

Corporate Worship

Corporate worship, the worship of Christians with other Christians, is important because God is gathering "a people for his own possession," which is the church, the *ekklēsia*. Jesus said, "Where two or three have gathered together in My name, I am there in their midst" (Matt 18:20). Jesus' teaching here opened public worship to any meeting of Christians. The two could be two friends, two acquaintances, or even two strangers who are followers of Jesus. The two could be a couple; the three could be a couple and a child.

To meet in Jesus' name is much more than simply invoking the name "Jesus." His name should not be treated as a magical incantation. Jesus warned that a perfunctory citing of his name would have no value (Matt 7:22–23; cf. Acts 19:13–17). The concept of meeting "in Jesus' name" goes back to the concept of the name of *Yahweh* in the Old Testament.

In the Old Testament, the name (Hebr. *šēm*) of God was associated with his presence (e.g., Deut 12:11; 14:23; 26:2; Ezra 6:12; Jer 7:12). To do anything in the name of the Lord is to represent him; those who acted in a manner worthy of him under the Mosaic law received blessings, while those who acted in an unworthy manner brought God's wrath upon themselves (Exod 20:7, 24; Deut 5:11; 12:5, 10–14, 28–32; cf. Mic 4:5). Similarly, to meet in the name of Jesus is to represent him, his character, and his redemptive mission (cf. 1 Cor 15:34). Those who gather to pray may expect an answer when they meet in Jesus' name, and thus pray in accordance with his holiness and his plan to bring all people into his fellowship (Matt 18:19–20; 1 John 5:14).

Traditional Christian worship generally follows the model of the synagogue. This is partly based on Jesus' custom to worship at the synagogue (Luke 4:16). An important difference is that Christian worship takes places on "the Lord's Day" rather than the sabbath (the last day of the week), because Jesus rose from the dead on the first day of the week—the day we call "Sunday" (e.g., Rev 1:10; cf. Acts 20:7). The activities of corporate worship include prayer, Scripture reading, the singing of hymns and spiritual songs, and a discourse upon Scripture or a scriptural theme. There is a great deal of freedom within this model for Christians, embracing formal liturgical worship at one end of the spectrum and a more free style of worship on the other (cf. Col 2:16–17).

Although worship is a form of witness to the gospel, and evangelism is a natural part of any service of worship, evangelism should not *govern* Christian worship. Certainly Christian worship has the ability to draw unbelievers into fellowship with God through Christ. However, Christian worship is not given to please the preferences and sensibilities of the unbeliever, but to please God. A congregation should see themselves as before the Lord in the same sense that one might have an audience before a king in a royal court rather than to see themselves as the audience for a presentation to themselves. The primary purpose is to give worship to God rather than to receive anything. On the other hand, participation in worship with other Christians builds faith and encourages us to live for Christ (Heb 10:24–25).

Because worship is given to God, all parts of a worship service involve the participation of those gathered for worship. In the earliest days of Christianity, meetings tended to be informal, governed by the contributions of all gathered for worship (1 Cor 14:26). Nevertheless, worship is not open to whatever might enter people's minds. There is a requirement for all things to be done "properly (Gk. *euschēmonōs*) and in an orderly manner (Gk. *kata taxin*)" (1 Cor 14:40). This reflects the nature of God, "for God is not *a God of confusion but of peace, as in all the churches of the saints*" (1 Cor 14:33). Worship involves the mind, not just the emotions (1 Cor 14:15, 19).

If it is inappropriate for unbelievers to *govern* what takes place, it is nevertheless necessary that worship be conducted in such a manner that everyone is able to understand what is being said and done—thus the emphasis in the Protestant Reformation that worship be conducted in the language of the people (1 Cor 14:7–9, 23). Paul summarized: "Let all things be done for edification (Gk. *oikodomēn*)" (1 Cor 14:26).

The Greek word *oikodomē* is basically a construction term, a term that would usually be applied to building or repairing a house or some other structure. Used metaphorically, it has to do with that which builds-up and strengthens Christians. Taking a cue from 1 Corinthians 13:13, this would be anything that increases faith, hope, and love. Activities that advance God's purposes may be entertaining, but entertainment for its own sake is ruled out. On this point Norman Snaith cautions: "As soon as the aim of hymns and songs and music generally becomes aesthetic, it is time to beware."[7] Praise, prayer, instruction, exhortation, encouragement, testimony, warning, and reminding all qualify, as do those ceremonies that are uniquely Christian. Thus, worship that is given to God advances God's work in the lives of his people.

Christian Ceremonies

The two most important Christian ceremonies are baptism and the Lord's Supper. Traditionally referred to as "sacraments," but now often referred to as "ordinances" in Protestant churches, they are important because they were clearly instituted by Jesus himself.

Baptism witnesses to a person's commitment to God through Jesus Christ. Jesus commanded his disciples to baptize "in the name of the Father and the Son and the Holy Spirit" (Matt 28:18). Acts testifies to the obedience of early Christians in baptizing converts. This goes beyond the baptism of John because it is post-Pentecost and invokes the Trinity.

The Lord's Supper is a remembrance of the sacrifice of Jesus that took away the sins of the redeemed. Jesus commanded his followers to do this in remembrance of him (Matt 26:26–28; Mark 14:22–24; Luke 22:19–20; 1 Cor 11:23–26). It is to be celebrated with careful examination of one's life and commitment to Jesus (1 Cor 11:27–30). Therefore, preparation should include a time for confession and repentance.

These ceremonies need to be engaged in with appropriate gravity, generally in the presence of a local congregation of believers, and generally administered by a duly prepared and appointed spiritual leader. However, there is no magic in the ceremony itself. Grace does not come simply because someone participates. Jesus promised that those who obey him would be blessed; accordingly, those who participate in a worthy manner gain a spiritual blessing. It is in this manner that they become means of grace

---

7. Quoted in Smith, *Micah-Malachi*, 51, from Snaith, *Amos, Hosea, Micah* (London: Epworth, 1956), 104.

(John 14:23-24). The social aspect is part of the blessing that comes upon the participants.

The testimony to the redemptive work of Christ in the life of an individual is the most important aspect of Christian baptism. Baptism by immersion for those who confess faith in Christ is a meaningful form for those old enough to make a decision for Christ, where modesty can be assured, and where there is plenty of water (Col 2:12). In many cases, however, the candidate is sick or older or extremely young, there is insufficient water or a lack of clean water, or there are other circumstances that make immersion impractical or even impossible. In such cases, given the importance of baptism in the life of all believers and given Christian liberty, the ceremony is more important than the mode. Those who are baptized by sprinkling or pouring make no less a confession of faith in Jesus Christ.

Infants are proper candidates for baptism when raised in a Christian family. Such baptisms are an important witness to the prevenient grace by which infants are not held accountable for being part of Adam's race. It is because of prevenient grace that baptism is superior to a dedication ceremony. Baptizing infants is consistent with the practice of circumcision, which was performed on infants and also required children to affirm the faith for themselves when they came of age. In both cases, parents are expected to communicate the faith in such a manner that their children desire to follow the Lord as adults. It is important here that Jesus was circumcised (Luke 2:21, 39).

There is the requirement for infant baptism that at least one parent or guardian be a Christian. Paul taught that the believing spouse sanctifies (Gk. *hēgiastai*) the unbelieving spouse in the sense that the child may be considered holy (Gk. *hagia*, 1 Cor 7:14). Thus, given the commitment of the parents and prevenient grace, the child may be considered part the church (Gk. *hē ekklēsia*)—those called to be made holy in Christ Jesus, and thus called to be holy ones (Gk. *hēgiasmenois en Christōi Iēsou, klētois hagiois*, 1 Cor 1:2). In this case, as with circumcision, the parents are the *means* God uses to bring blessing to the child when they lovingly raise the child "in the discipline and instruction of the Lord" (Eph 6:4; cf. Prov 22:6; Ps 78:1-4; Deut 6:4-7; 2 Tim 1:5; 3:14-15). The people of the church are also a means to grace for the child when they aid parents in this task by their example, teaching, and prayers.

Marriage of one man with one woman was established by God with the first couple, and affirmed by Jesus (Matt 19:3-9; Mark 10:2-9). Because of its roots in the relationship of Adam and Eve, it was established for all people, and therefore is not a sacrament or ordinance. Nevertheless, this ceremony is of central importance to the church, having special meaning for Christians (Eph 5:22-33). The family is an important institution because it is in the family that the best opportunity exists to communicate the faith to children. Christians should take note that the importance of the family has remained a key institution maintaining Judaism as a distinct religion for thousands of years.

Similarly, God's providence for human beings began with Adam and has never eased. Therefore, though Christians should be exemplary in giving thanksgiving to God at meals and for other blessings, all people owe and should render gratitude to God (cf. Rom 1:20-21).

Those who practice the washing of feet as a Christian ceremony do nothing wrong, just as other ceremonies consistent with Scripture may be established by Christians. However, the example Jesus gave by washing the disciple's feet was not restricted to foot-washing, so it should not be considered at the same level as baptism and the Lord's Supper (John 13:1-17). Jesus used this act to help his disciples understand what he was going to do at the cross, and to communicate that a life of love and service was to be the hallmark of his followers. To raise this to the level of baptism and the Lord's Supper seems to detract from the general significance of his act. However, using this ceremony to draw attention to his teaching is certainly appropriate for those who choose to do so.

15

Living Redemptively

You know how we *were* exhorting and encouraging and imploring each one of you as a father *would* his own children, so that you would walk in a manner worthy of the God who calls you into His own kingdom and glory.

1 THESSALONIANS 2:11–12

For the kingdom of God is not eating and drinking, but righteousness and peace and joy in the Holy Spirit.

ROMANS 14:17

Whether, then, you eat or drink or whatever you do, do all to the glory of God.

1 CORINTHIANS 10:31

Become sober-minded as you ought, and stop sinning; for some have no knowledge of God. I speak *this* to your shame.

1 CORINTHIANS 15:34

My beloved brethren, be steadfast, immovable, always abounding in the work of the Lord, knowing that your toil is not *in* vain in the Lord.

1 CORINTHIANS 15:58

THE means of grace bless not only the Christians who live by them, but others as well. It can be said that to use the means of grace is to live redemptively: to live in such a manner that God is able to work out his redemptive purposes in people's lives. That purpose includes not only restoring fellowship, but transforming a person's character to be like Jesus (2 Cor 3:18). Because this touches the entire personality, it touches all of life. The means of grace, therefore, are not restricted to acts of worship, but involve the things we do in our everyday lives. Good works and abstaining from evil are important means of grace in the life of every Christian.

Good Works

The author of Hebrews wrote that "the blood of Christ" is able to "cleanse your conscience from dead works (Gk. *apo nekrōn ergōn*) to serve the living God" (Heb 9:14). Paul wrote that God purified "a people for His own possession, zealous for good deeds (Gk. *zēlōtēn kalōn ergōn*)" (Titus 2:14). He wrote of the redeemed that "we are His [God's] workmanship (Gk. *poiēma*), created (Gk. *ktisthentes*) in Christ Jesus for good works (Gk. *epi ergois agathois*), which God prepared beforehand so that we would walk in them" (Eph 2:10).

Good Works and the Redeemed

There is, of course, the important matter of not mistaking good works as a requirement for salvation. This does not become a problem if certain Scriptures are kept firmly in mind. It is not those who need to be saved that Hebrews identifies as able to do good works, but those who have had their consciences cleansed by the blood of Christ—the redeemed (Heb 9:14). In John 15, Jesus taught that he is the vine and his people are the branches; those who abide in him bear much fruit. It is essential to observe the order here. Abiding in Christ is not the result of good works; good works flow from abiding in him. This is consistent with Psalm 1, where the righteous man is the one whose life bears fruit in due season.

The legitimate determination to see faith as the sole requirement for receiving saving grace has caused many to ignore or to misinterpret essential teachings on works in the New Testament. Jesus came to be a servant, and taught his followers that the greatest among them would be a servant of others (Matt 20:20–28; Mark 10:35–45; Luke 22:24–27). He demonstrated this by washing the disciples' feet and by going to the cross (John 13:1–17; Phil 2:3–11). The twenty-fifth chapter of Matthew's Gospel describes a man judging his servants on the basis of what they had done with the wealth he had given them; the one who did nothing was cast aside (Matt 25:14–30). Immediately following, Jesus speaks of the final judgment of souls upon his return, and his judgment is based on what people have done to nourish the hungry, provide clothing for the poor, and visit Christians who were in prison (Matt 25:31–46). In both teachings, it is what people *did* that disclosed the true nature of their relationship with Christ.

The teaching is similar in John's Gospel. Jesus said the time would come when the dead would hear his voice "and will come forth; those who did the good *deeds* (Gk. *ta agatha poiēsantes*) to a resurrection of life, those who committed the evil *deeds* (Gk. *ta phaula praxantes*) to a resurrection of judgment" (John 5:29). In all of these teachings, as well as with false prophets, Jesus taught "you will know them by their fruits" (Matt 7:16, 20). Jesus explained that a good tree cannot bear bad fruit, and a bad tree cannot bear good fruit. Each person reveals their own nature by what they think and do; therefore, people may be judged even by the words that they speak (Matt 12:33–37). Jesus taught that people are drawn to God or avoid God because of their deeds (Gk., *ta erga*, John 3:19–21). Keep in mind that the Greek word translated "deeds," *erga*, may also be translated "works." In physics, the word "erg" based on the singular Greek *ergon*, is a measure of work done.

The teaching in the epistles is consistent with the Gospels. James taught that Christians are not just hearers of the word, but doers of the word (Jas 1:23–25). Such people show that they practice true religion by bridling their tongues and by caring for widows and orphans (Jas 1:26–27). He asks what good it does to say "be warmed and be filled" to someone who is cold and hungry; they need to be properly clothed and fed (Jas 2:15–16). In agreement with Jesus' teaching, James insisted, "I will show you my faith by my works" because faith without works "is dead" (Jas 2:17–18).

John creates a unique expression to describe the life of faith. He writes that the person in fellowship with God "practices the truth" (Gk. *poiōn tēn alētheian*, John 3:21). Those who "walk in the darkness" are those who "do not practice the truth" (Gk. *ou poioumen tēn alētheian*," 1 John 1:6). The Greek word translated "practice" here is *poieō*, which identifies action—doing. This phrase is all the more interesting because the first is found in the Gospel of John and the second in the first epistle of John. John writes that "the love of God" does not "abide" (Gk. *menei*) in those who have "the world's goods" but ignore those in need (1 John 3:17).

The author of Hebrews encourages his readers to "not neglect doing good and sharing, for with such sacrifices God is pleased" (Heb 13:16). He encouraged Christians to "stimulate (Gk. *paroxysmon*) one another to love and good deeds (Gk. *kalōn ergōn*)" (Heb 10:24).

Paul encouraged Titus to be an example in "good deeds" and to teach clearly that all of God's people should engage in good deeds for the benefit of all people (Titus 2:7; 3:8, 14). He told Timothy that the Scriptures provide preparation for good works (2 Tim 3:16–17). The rich should be instructed to use their wealth for the benefit of others (1 Tim 6:17–19). Women should "adorn themselves" with "good works" (*ergōn agathōn*, 1 Tim 2:9–10; cf. 5:9–10).

All of this may seem intimidating to those who forget that good works flow from those who have been redeemed and reconciled with God. The good works done by the righteous stand in stark contrast to the self-seeking legalism so prevalent in the Jewish community at the time of Christ. Paul's encouragement to do good to all is in his letter to the Galatians, his strongest letter condemning legalism and the misuse of the Mosaic law (Gal 6:9–10). Those who ask "how much is required" or "how much is enough" are asking the wrong questions. Serving God is a privilege; it is entering into his work of providing redeeming grace to all. The picture we have in Scripture is not of Christians worried about whether they have done enough to be saved, but whether they have served the Lord in gratitude for the way he has served them (2 Cor 8:9).

As a means of grace, good works bring meaning, purpose, and fulfillment to the lives of Christians. Just as with other means of grace, service is a means of growing closer to God by adopting the same attitude and commitment to the Father that was shown by Jesus, "the author and perfecter of faith" (Heb 12:2).

Good Works and Spiritual Gifts

What kind of fruit comes from good works? Certainly growth in personal holiness (Gal 5:22–24; Heb 5:14; Phil 3:8–21). However, we can expect fruitfulness in the lives of other people as well. There is a difference in what we should expect from each, however. The former benefit depends upon the diligence of a disciple of Christ in their personal devotion to the Lord, the latter is highly dependent upon the gifts, time, and opportunities available to each person.

Scripture teaches that the Holy Spirit gives gifts to Christians to help them serve the Lord. The church, the *ekklēsia*, is the body of Christ in the world: his hands, feet, and mouth. As such, the church goes into the world to serve the Lord, serve others, and proclaim the gospel and the teachings of Christ. The spiritual gifts that enable the church to do this are described in 1 Corinthians 12–14; Romans 12:4–9; Ephesians 4:4–16; and 1 Peter 4:10–11.

Spiritual gifts may be new abilities, or they may be natural talent or abilities enhanced by the aid of the Holy Spirit. There are many varieties of gifts, and the lists in Scripture are probably partial rather than comprehensive. Some Christians may have more than one. Some gifts may seem modest, others more visible. For example, not everyone is gifted to provide leadership in the church. Nevertheless, every gift is vitally important (1 Cor 12:11–31). The Holy Spirit distributes gifts as he sees fit to glorify Jesus Christ and to build his church, his Body in the world (1 Cor 12:11). The distribution of gifts may, therefore, change from place to place and in different periods in history according to the needs of each place and time.

The good works done by a particular person will often reflect that person's spiritual gifts, though good works are not restricted to that person's gift or gifts. For example, a person who has a gift for teaching and not for giving can still give alms; a person without the gift of evangelism can still lead others to Christ. Zeal comes from the desire to show love and gratitude to the Lord and from the desire to spread his love to others. Love is implied or discussed in or near all of the passages where spiritual gifts are discussed. First Corinthians 13 is in the midst of the longest.

The ability to do good works varies greatly because some people will always have more opportunities to express their gift than others. Place in the world and time in history affect each person's opportunities. Because gifts are individual and God does not expect anyone to do more than they are able, comparison with others is self-defeating, leading to inappropriate pride on the one hand or discouragement on the other. The important thing is for each person to make use of whatever gifts and opportunities are uniquely available to him or her.

Paul's teaching in Ephesians 2:10 that God has prepared good works for each Christian to "walk in" raises the question whether God has created a precise schedule of specific works for each person to do, or whether he has created certain categories of good works from which we are to choose. In other words: does God have a specific plan for each moment of our day? Or does God simply ask us to look for ways to serve others? Certainly, there are specific tasks that God plans for some to do, and there are clear examples of this in the Bible. However, this question does not need to be answered; either way, it doesn't matter.

God is well aware that in a practical sense, we cannot try to meet a schedule of tasks that is not provided to us. If God has something specific for us to do, he will lead us to it and make it obvious. All that is necessary is to look for opportunities to serve that are within our ability, and to follow the advice in Proverbs: "Do not withhold good from those to whom it is due, when it is in your power to do *it*" (Prov 3:27). In a similar vein Paul wrote, "Let us not lose heart in doing good, for in due time we will reap if we do not grow weary. So then, while we have opportunity (Gk. *hōs kairon echomen*), let us do good to all people, and especially to those who are of the household of the faith" (Gal 6:9–10). Certainly Jesus gave an example of this kind of service, since much of his ministry to individuals was done while he was on the way to do something else.

Giving

The expectation regarding giving is similar. The Mosaic law used the tithe as a rule for giving, and it is still a good rule today. However, the tithe was instituted when agriculture was the primary means for people to support themselves. It was also instituted in a system where God promised rewards of health, welfare, prosperity, and security to those who were faithful to him in their obedience to the Mosaic law. Since the Israelites failed to be faithful to the Mosaic law as a nation, these rewards are no longer automatically part of the New Covenant. That doesn't mean the tithe should be done away with. It is still a sound basic measure of giving. However, we are now under the New Covenant, which is not tied to the civil and ceremonial requirements of the Mosaic law. In addition, the tithe seems to be an inappropriate guide for both the impoverished and the affluent.

Paul taught a way of thinking about giving more in line with the New Covenant. Paul makes several points about giving. First, our example is Jesus, who became poor that we might become rich (2 Cor 8:9; 9:15). Second, the more liberality there is, the more blessings that result (2 Cor 9:6–14). Third, each person should give not as mandated by others, but as they decide before the Lord, "for God loves a cheerful giver" (2 Cor 9:7). Fourth, the appropriate measure is not some hard and fast standard, but how much a person is able to provide: "For if the readiness is present, it is acceptable according to what *a person* has, not according to what he does not have" (2 Cor 8:12). It is obvious from this measure that those in strict poverty are not expected to give away what they need to maintain their health or welfare—although they may choose to do so (2 Cor 8:1–5; Luke 21:1–4). However, by this rule, a family should not take food or medical care away from children to provide a tithe to the church. On the other hand, those who have plenty should not feel that a tithe is necessarily sufficient. Paul referred to God's provision of manna in the wilderness: "He who *gathered* much did not have too much, and he who *gathered* little had no lack" (2 Cor 8:15; Exod 16:13–21). By this rule, some who have been greatly blessed may need to give much more than a tithe to shoulder their part of the burden of supporting the work of the church and providing alms to care for those in need.

John Wesley believed money provides a means to serve the Lord as well as a means to provide for our needs. He taught that the Christian approach to money should be: "Gain all you can. . . . save all you can. . . . give all you can."[1] By "gain" he meant that Christians should earn money by any honest means. This is consistent with Paul's instruction that Christians should work to meet their own needs and to provide for others (2 Thess 3:12; Eph 4:28).

Whether giving money, time, or skill to honor God, the example of David is also important. When David was instructed to build an altar to the Lord, he went to purchase a threshing floor from Ornan (also known as Araunah) the Jebusite (1 Chr 21:18–30; 2 Sam 24:18–25). Ornan prostrated himself before King David and offered to give David the threshing floor without cost. David, however, responded: "No, but I will surely buy *it* for the full price; for I will not take what is yours for the Lord, or offer a burnt offering which costs me nothing" (1 Chr 21:24; 2 Sam 24:24). There are many rewards for giving. Jesus said, "It is more blessed to give than to receive" (Acts 20:35). Nevertheless, true giving is that which costs. As with all good works, giving for the work of the Lord and giving to relieve the needs of others brings spiritual blessings that are real, but often not financial. Giving to the Lord as an investment for a financial return isn't giving. True giving costs. It is part of the cost of devotion.

Righteous Relationships

Righteous living, simply conforming to God's will for the way we live our lives, is, in itself, a form of witness, especially social righteousness. People need to be loved into the kingdom of God. We witness by our actions as well as our words. We should pray for the lost, but we should also do those things that draw them to the Lord and build their faith in him.

While "charity begins at home" isn't Scripture, Paul makes clear that serving others begins in the home. This is an important focus in Ephesians. In 1 Timothy, Paul makes care for one's family a requirement for leadership in the church. Of even greater importance, he is clear that anyone who does not do their best to care for their family has rejected the Christian faith (Gk. *tēn pistin ērnētai*), behaving worse than unbelievers (Gk. *estin apistou cheirōn*, 1 Tim 5:8). Those who neglect their families to serve others are failing to provide an important witness to life in the kingdom of God. Scripture shows that the family is part of God's plan to preserve the faith and to show others how to express love. However, family relationships are not the only ones important for Christian witness.

Relationships, not things, are the most important part of our lives. The only part of life in this age that survives for the redeemed is their relationship

---

1. Wesley, "Use of Money," in *Wesley's 52 Standard Sermons*, 495–501.

with Jesus Christ and their relationship with others who are redeemed—relationships that will last for eternity.

There are basic requirements for relationships that cannot be ignored. The most basic requirement is respect, respect appropriate to each kind of relationship. Jesus taught this when he spoke of giving to God and to the emperor what each had the unique right to expect (Matt 22:15-22). Peter recognized differences in relationship when he wrote, "Honor all people, love the brotherhood, fear God, honor the king" (1 Pet 2:17).

There is a basic respect due all people because they were created in the image of God (Gen 1:26). That image may be marred, and marred badly, but each person is still the target of God's redemptive love (Eph 6:12). Each person is due courtesy and freedom from cruelty. Christians should submit to the leaders of human institutions as long as they aren't trying to impose what dishonors the Lord (1 Pet 2:13-17; Rom 13:1-7). The highest level of respect to people should be given to our parents, spouse, and children (Eph 5:22—6:4). Of course, the very highest level of respect, reverence, goes solely to the Lord (Matt 22:35-38). Mutual respect is the foundation of all good relationships.

The second requirement for good relationships is commitment. The level of commitment must be appropriate to each kind of relationship. Our ability to touch most lives is limited. Our commitment to people we don't know is generally to seek to provide the gospel and to provide whatever aid we can give to those in serious distress—sending financial and other aid to victims of epidemics, floods, earthquakes, and other disasters. Those we know or come into contact with, our neighbors, are people we should do more for—where "neighbor" is defined as Jesus did in the story of the Good Samaritan (Luke 10:25-37; cf. Matt 22:39; Lev 19:18). A commitment to other Christians—the household of faith, fellow children of God, including all the redeemed—is necessarily greater than our commitment to the world (Gal 6:10). Finally, one's family comes before others. And above all, there must be commitment to the Lord himself.

There can be no relationship without mutual commitment. Jesus said that those who intended to follow him would have to carry a cross (Matt 16:24-26; Mark 8:34-36; Luke 9:23-25). This doesn't consist of the problems that are common to everyone, but those burdens that come specifically from our devotion to Jesus Christ. Of course, the Lord requires our deepest commitment. However, some level of commitment is required in all relationships. Any true commitment has a cost. The attempt to avoid commitment destroys relationships.

Legions of people in our time, including some Christians, deprive themselves of the happiness they would have from a good relationship before it starts through lack of commitment. For example, many today who go through a marriage ceremony do not commit themselves to the welfare of their spouse, but to their own happiness. When they cease to be happy, they end the marriage because they were never committed to the other person in the first place. As a result, there was never a true marriage relationship, nor the potential for happiness that brings.

The third requirement for a good relationship is communication. The frequency and kind of communication, again, must be appropriate to the kind of relationship. Communication, of course, is more than speech, it includes our actions, and close relationships require some form of touch. Paul taught that "speaking the truth in love" (Gk. *alētheuontes de en agapēi*) is how Christians should communicate with one another (Eph 4:15). Truth requires honesty, and love requires both courtesy and consideration in the way we speak to others.

Honesty does not mean telling another person everything, but requires not hiding those things that the other person should know. Sometimes this requires difficult conversations that involve confrontation, confession, rebuke, or correction. However the purpose of every communication is to strengthen the relationship. Even difficult communications must take place with respect for the other person—no name calling, no irrelevant comments, no denials of important facts, and no exaggerations. It may be necessary to challenge someone because they are not giving us the respect, commitment, or communication we deserve; but we must always do so with respect for the other person and always in such a way that we encourage the resolution of the problem—even if we have to be frank and firm.

Obviously, there are times when people who have a close relationship must be absent from one another. People who are away in the military, representing their governments, traveling on business, are seriously ill, and so forth, will, at times, have significant absences from loved ones. Relationships can survive absences if there has been communication beforehand and communication is a priority whenever possible. With the Lord, communication means reading the Scriptures to learn from the Lord and speaking to him in prayer regularly. Lack of communication can diminish and even extinguish a relationship.

There are two more requirements for the best Christian relationships, but at this point it is helpful to pause to make several observations. First, there can be no true relationship without mutual respect, mutual commitment, and mutual communication that are appropriate to the kind of relationship. None. There are no substitutes. There is no true relationship with anyone unless all three are present, and mutual.

Further, although we have framed each of these in a Christian context, all human beings are capable of meeting these three requirements, and often do. This is why some people who are not Christians have better marriages, closer families, and more stable personal relationships than some Christians. This is possible because all people were made in the image of God. These three factors can even enable good relationships between people and the higher domestic animals, even though animals certainly aren't capable of relationships on the same level as people.

Genesis teaches that human beings were made to live with animals, so it is not strange that many if not most people love animals. To have a good relationship with pets and domestic animals, they must receive the appropriate respect, commitment, and communication; and they will return these at the level they are capable of. This is because these three requirements are "baked into the universe" if you will. They are part of the basic fabric of relationships because they relate to the character of the Creator.

Where is "love" in all of this? If you do these three, you have the basic ingredients of love. Without them, love is mere feeling—fleeting emotion—which by itself is completely insufficient to bring about a true relationship, though it often seems otherwise, especially to the young.

Moreover, it is foolishness for anyone to think that they can have a good relationship with the Lord if they: don't respect him enough to reverence, seek, or obey him; don't make any commitment of time or resources to serve him; and seldom if ever read the Scriptures or speak to the Lord in prayer. Jesus told the false prophets, "I never knew you" (Matt 7:23). Some people destroy their relationship with God by turning away; many others never really enter into a relationship with God in the first place or let their relationship die by neglect. These three requirements are the bedrock for *any* relationship to be lasting and real.

The fourth requirement for good relationships is to follow the teachings of God's Word with the enabling of the Holy Spirit. Scripture has a great deal to say about human relationships. We have a lifetime to grow in our relationship with others based on these teachings. Christians have something more going for them than those outside Christ; Christians have the love of God in their hearts because of the indwelling Holy Spirit. By keeping up-to-date in our relationship with God and depending upon him, we have the ability to relate to others in such a way that God's purposes in their lives are advanced as well as in ours.

Christians thus have the unique privilege of living in a way that is redemptive. This is, by far, the highest form of morality—of loving our neighbors as ourselves. This is highlighted in the New Testament by the way Christians responded to meat offered to idols. Given the polytheism and lax morality of the time, Paul was concerned that both Christians and non-Christians could be misled by careless behavior. He gave instructions on how to behave regarding meat because meat eaten by pagans often came from animals sacrificed at pagan temples (Rom 14:13–23; 1 Cor 8:1–13; 10:23–33). He taught that even though Christians, themselves, have a great deal of liberty, they should avoid any behavior that might cause others to sin. "Let no one seek his own *good*, but that of his neighbor"; "It is good not to eat meat or to drink wine, or *to do anything* by which your brother stumbles" (Rom 14:21; cf. 1 Cor 10:24). The underlying goal is that others find saving faith (Gk. *hina sōthōsin*, 1 Cor 10:33).

Helping others find faith is more than not creating stumbling blocks. As the people of God, we are charged with revealing God and his nature to others (1 Pet 2:9–10). Jesus taught us to live in such a way that our character and our good works bring glory to God (Matt 5:13–16). In order for that to happen, we need to seek opportunities to make our faith known to others and to witness to his work in our lives. This must always be done in love; with respect for the people we speak with (1 Pet 3:14–16). An air of arrogant superiority or smugness won't do. Our relationship with these individuals is important; people are *loved* into the kingdom of God. It may help to introduce these people to other Christians who strengthen our witness. With this in mind, we should prayerfully seek ways to help others learn and understand the gospel and invite them into fellowship with God through Jesus Christ.

The final requirement for good relationships is related to the fourth, but often missed, and that is to seek God's presence in our relationships. We should bathe our relationships with our families—fellow Christians, and others we are close to—in prayer (Eph 6:18). Jesus promised to be in the midst of those gathered in his name because God can bless in relationships in ways that he can never bless a person alone. There is a subtle but unmistakable difference in marriages, families, and friendships when we honor the Lord and he inhabits our relationships. Even if only one person in a marriage or family seeks God's presence, God is able to bring another factor into the life of the other people, increasing the opportunity for constructive change. However, this should not be limited to our family relationships.

Our relationship to others in the local church will also be more blessed when the presence of God is recognized. As in the family, there are sometimes challenges in our relationships with others in the local church we do not experience with those outside. However, we should meet that challenge with a commitment to make these relationships redemptive for others and ourselves.

Returning Good for Evil

Paul taught, "If possible, so far as it depends on you, be at peace with all men" (Rom 12:18; cf. Heb 12:14-15). With some stubborn, contentious people, the only course of action that leads to peace is to steer clear of them—at least until they demonstrate that they are open to a better relationship (Titus 3:9-11; Rom 16:17-18). This is not the approach we should jump to without good reason, however.

The Holy Spirit is especially helpful when we are wronged or treated poorly. Emotions often cloud our judgment, making us more susceptible to uncontrolled anger. We have the privilege of asking the Holy Spirit to give us self-control, to cleanse us from anger, to help us forgive, to help us use the energy of anger constructively—and to act redemptively, if possible.

Jesus taught us to "love your enemies, do good to those who hate you, bless those who curse you, pray for those who mistreat you" so that you may become "sons of the Most High; for He Himself is kind to ungrateful and evil men" (Luke 6:27-28, 35; cf. Matt 5:38-48). Jesus, himself, is the demonstration that God reaches out to sinners to draw them to himself (Rom 5:7-8). Following Jesus' example, Peter wrote that those "who suffer according to the will of God shall entrust their souls to a faithful Creator in doing what is right" (1 Pet 4:19). Paul exhorted, "Do not be overcome by evil, but overcome evil with good" (Rom 12:21; cf. 1 Thess 5:15).

It is important to understand that nowhere do the Scriptures teach that Christians should accept being victimized. Jesus, Stephen, Paul, and Peter surrendered their lives because of their faithfulness to the Lord and to their ministries. However, they were not careless about their lives. We are never to choose to be victims if we can avoid it and be faithful to the Lord. Jesus' disciples carried swords to protect themselves from robbers (Luke 22:35-38). When arrested, Jesus pointed out that those who arrested him were acting as if they were doing something wrong (Matt 26:55; Mark 14:48-49; Luke 22:52-53). During his trial, Jesus protested that though his accusers asked him to speak, they had no intention of treating him fairly (Luke 22:67, 68; John 18:19-23). Peter resisted the Sanhedrin's attempts to silence him from preaching the gospel (Acts 4:1-22; 5:17-32).

The goal for Christians is not just self-defense, but to try to turn bad situations into opportunities for grace if at all possible. This can be difficult, because sometimes our attackers are so determined to do us harm that they take away from us any opportunity to do other than defend ourselves—sometimes, unfortunately, by the use of force. Nevertheless, we should never stoop to hate and vengeance.

In Romans, Paul recognized that it is right for rulers to use force to oppose evildoers. He made use of the protections afforded to him as a Roman citizen whenever possible (Acts 16:35-40; 21:32-40; 22:22-29; 23:10-35; 24:22-26; 25:6-12). Just as Paul did, when necessary, we should make use of the police and judicial system. If laws have been broken, we should look to society to make retribution rather than to seek our own satisfaction. In extreme cases, we should remember that justice escaped in this age means justice will be done in the next (Rom 12:19).

Beyond this, we should ask God to help us see opportunities to turn situations around, or to at least make a clear witness to Jesus Christ. Stephen could not avoid being stoned for his sermon to the Jews. In spite of this, Stephen's words and actions made an impression on Paul that seems to have prepared Paul to be converted shortly afterward. Paul turned his trials and imprisonment into opportunities to provide his testimony to the work of Christ (Acts 22:1-21; 23:1-8; 24:1-25; 25:13—26:31; Phil 1:12-14; 4:22). In the long run, redemptive behavior brings glory to God by reflecting his character in ways that benefit others—especially with the gospel of Christ.

Abstaining from Evil

Another means of grace is to abstain from all forms of evil. One might think that would be automatic for Christians; however, history teaches otherwise. In his letter to the Romans, Paul had to strongly oppose the ideas that Christians could sin with impunity because they are no longer under the Law of Moses and that grace increases if Christians continue to sin (Rom 6:1-23). Many today think they can judge the morality of their actions by feelings rather than by God's Word.

The New Testament assumes that Christians have been saved from a life of sin (1 Cor 6:9-11; Gal 5:13-21; Eph 5:1-10; Heb 12:1-17; Jas 4:1-10; Rev 22:10-15). John wrote that no one who walks in darkness—who lives a life of sin—is in fellowship with Christ (1 John 1:5-7, cf. 1 John 2:3-6). John recognized that there may be times when Christians do fall into acts of sin. At such times, confession and repentance are necessary. "If we confess our sins," John wrote, "He is faithful and righteous to forgive us our sins and to cleanse us from all unrighteousness" (1 John 1:9; cf. 1 John 2:1-3).

Of course, the best way to keep from temptation is to fill life with positive activities and thoughts. What we focus on eventually affects how we live, so Paul advises us to focus on those things that are good and perfect, which draws us away from that which is unworthy of God (Phil 4:4-9). Today, as in New Testament times, that often means exercising care in the kind of entertainment we allow in our lives. Nevertheless, there will be times we must face temptation or recognize something in ourselves that needs to change.

When the Holy Spirit enters a person's life, he puts a spotlight on areas of that person's life that need to be changed. This enables spiritual growth. When something is recognized that is inconsistent with God's nature, there is the opportunity to confess, repent, and grow spiritually. This process continues throughout life. The redeemed should rejoice that the Lord is active in their lives to make them more and more like Jesus (2 Cor 3:18). Certain habits and even addictions may be of continual concern. God may cleanse these from us or he may help us to deal with them on a day-by-day basis, which is how Jesus taught us to face life (Matt 6:34). Pointing to what God has promised to his people, Paul exhorted, "Having these promises, beloved, let us cleanse ourselves (Gk. *katharisōmen heautous*) from all defilement (Gk. *molysmou*) of flesh and spirit (Gk. *sarkos kai pneumatos*), perfecting holiness in the fear of God (Gk. *epitelountes hagiōsynēn en phobōi Theou*)" (2 Cor 7:1, cf. 2 Cor 6:16–18).

In seeking to avoid evil, we need to be careful of self-justification and of paying too much attention to feelings. All human beings have a tendency to excuse themselves for poor behavior. We should be honest enough with ourselves to admit when we are excusing something we should not excuse. On the other hand, some people are so sensitive that they upbraid themselves constantly in way that promotes depression and hopelessness. Focusing on the divine love and grace with the support of more mature Christians can help here.

There is a redemptive side to this means of grace for others as well as for the redeemed. Paul instructed the Thessalonians to "abstain from every form of evil (Gk. *apo pantos eidous ponērou apechesthe*)" (1 Thess 5:22). He warned the Corinthians that their sins were keeping others from gaining a true knowledge of God (1 Cor 15:34). Walking close to the Lord provides a witness that can draw others to Christ; sinning has the opposite effect.

Life in the Spirit vs. Life in the Flesh

Often when Scripture speaks of "flesh" or "flesh and blood," it is simply referring to human beings as creatures of this world, as in 2 Corinthians 7:1 (Gk. *sarkos*); Romans 1:3 (Gk. *sarka*); and 1 Corinthians 15:50 (Gk. *sarx kai haima*). Sometimes, however, the word "flesh" takes on a theological meaning, as in Romans 8:4. To walk according to the flesh (Gk. *kata sarka peripatousin*) is to live at the level of a creature without any meaningful attention to guidance from God.

The problem here is not that human beings consist of flesh. Jesus became flesh, and he was no less holy. It is not that God is spirit and we are part of a physical universe. Our creaturely humanity is not the problem. The problem is the determination to ignore God and his direction for life. To walk according to the Spirit (Gk. *kata pneuma*) is not only to live with an awareness of the spiritual realm, but to learn from God, and not only to obey God, but to seek to please God by our behavior.

For some Christians, freedom from the requirements of the Law of Moses, and thus freedom in the way the faith is practiced, seems to provide an excuse for carelessness. Paul warned, "You were called to freedom, brethren; only *do not turn* your freedom into an opportunity for the flesh" (Gal 5:13). In other words, don't see this a justification for self-indulgence. "All things are lawful (Gk. *exestin*), but not all things are profitable (Gk. *sympherei*). All things are lawful (Gk. *exestin*), but not all things edify (Gk. *oikodomei*)" (1 Cor 10:23). Paul apparently repeats the phrase "all things are lawful" because this is what the Corinthians were saying to justify unhelpful behavior. Paul reminded them that there were more considerations than just freedom from the Law.

Accordingly, to "live according to the flesh" is to be governed entirely by our inner desires, even if they are destructive to ourselves or to others (2 Pet 1:4; Jas 1:13–15; Eph 2:1–3). To walk by the Spirit is to reject destructive desires and to satisfy our legitimate needs—physical, mental, and spiritual—in ways that please the Lord—in ways that our Creator intended us to satisfy them (Titus 2:11–14; Gal 5:16, 22–25). This is the life that is enabled by the Holy Spirit.

Redemptive Righteousness

To abstain from evil is also to be careful not to cause problems for fellow Christians or to create stumbling blocks that prevent others from coming to Christ. Accusing others of sin without grounds, for example, puts an extra burden on fellow Christians who are often already heavily burdened.

It is always easier to see faults in others than in ourselves. Too often today, it seems, Christians see other Christians facing some difficulty and jump to the conclusion that it is because they committed sin and therefore deserve to suffer. This is clearly against what God expects of us. Scripture makes clear that Christians will face the same difficulties and problems that unbelievers face, so difficulties do not automatically mean the source is sin (John 16:33). There are some exceptions. By living holy lives, Christians avoid the earthly consequences of sinful behavior. Also, there are times when God in his mercy will rescue his people from sickness and suffering.

When the Lord does not take trouble away from his people, the difference for Christians is that God is able to use these problems to strengthen faith, to make us more like Christ, and to provide a testimony to our faith (Rom 5:3–5; 1 Pet 1:3–9; 4:12–19; 5:6–11).

While Christians must always be compassionate toward others, tolerating open sin works against the redemptive goals God has for his church, his *ekklēsia*. Confronting sin in the church is to be done redemptively. Paul wrote, "Brethren, even if anyone is caught in any trespass (Gk. *paraptōmati*), you who are spiritual, restore (Gk. *katartizete*) such a one in a spirit of gentleness (Gk. *praütētos*); *each one* looking to yourself, so that you too will not be tempted (Gk. *peirasthēs*)" (Gal 6:1). The temptation spoken of here is, perhaps, being drawn into the other's sin, being associated with the other's sin, or being tempted to arrogance at not having committed the other person's sin.

Restoration is also in view in Jesus' teaching of how the church should apply discipline. He taught that the sinner should be confronted one-on-one; if the sinner will not listen, the sinner should be confronted by two or more; if the sinner still will not repent, the sinner should be confronted publicly in the church; if the sinner still will not repent, then the sinner should not be considered part of the church (Matt 18:15–17). The goal, of course, is restoration and forgiveness (Luke 17:3–4; 1 Thess 5:14). However, in some cases, people who are undisciplined or contentious may need to have their church membership taken away, as in early Methodism (Titus 3:10–11; 2 Thess 3:6). Even then, eventual restoration is the hope and the goal for those who genuinely repent (2 Cor 2:1–11; cf. Eph 6:12).

Not Putting God to the Test

Putting God to the test is a serious sin. In 1 Corinthians 10, Paul teaches that the redeemed are to learn from the Old Testament (1 Cor 10:6). Among the specific lessons he mentions is that we should not put Christ to the test (Gk. *mēde ekpeirazōmen ton Christon*) the way the Israelites tested (Gk. *epeirasan*) the Lord in the wilderness (1 Cor 10:9).[2] Paul refers to the incident recorded in Numbers 21:4–9, where the Israelites complained about food and water. The Lord sent fiery serpents to punish the Israelites, and those who were bitten died. The Lord directed Moses to make a bronze representation of the serpent and to set it on a pole. Anyone bitten by a fiery serpent who looked upon the bronze serpent would live. By this act, they

---

2. Some ancient manuscripts read *ton Kurion* rather than *ton Christon*, and the NASB reflects this. However, on the basis of the oldest documents and 1 Corinthians 10:4, *ton Christon* is likely the original text.

repented of their unbelief, obeyed the direction of the Lord, and expressed faith in his deliverance. Jesus referred to this incident in his conversation with Nicodemus. He compared looking at his work on the cross with faith as similar to the Israelites looking upon the bronze serpent (John 3:14–15). The incident that led to fiery serpents was not the first time the Israelites committed this sin, however.

Not long after traveling through the wilderness, the Israelites complained because there was no water to drink. If they had simply asked for water, they would not have sinned. Instead, in their complaints they questioned God's existence and provision for their needs (Exod 17:1–7). One might think that after all the miracles they had witnessed they would have trusted the Lord, but they did not. God met their need by bringing water from a rock, which Paul refers to in 1 Corinthians 10:4. In their grumbling and complaining, the Israelites "tested (Hebr. *nassōtām*) the Lord, saying, 'Is the Lord among us or not?'" (Exod 17:7).

When Jesus was alone in the wilderness, Satan challenged Jesus to prove that he is the Son of God. He tempted Jesus to jump from the top of the temple to demonstrate that God would keep him from harm, using a verse from the Psalms to try to persuade Jesus that it was a legitimate thing to do (Matt 4:5–7; Luke 4:9–12). In response, Jesus quoted Deuteronomy 6:16, "You shall not put the Lord your God to the test (Hebr. *lōʾ tᵉnassû ʾet-Yahweh ʾĕlōhêkem*)."

From these Scriptures we learn that putting God to the test is trying to force him to perform some supernatural action either to prove that he exists or to prove how close we are to God. It often occurs when people put themselves in a dangerous situation thinking God is obligated to protect or to rescue them, as Satan tempted Jesus to do. This reverses the Creator/creature relationship, putting human beings in contention with God, seeking to force God to respond to human demands. This is the exact opposite of faith and trust in the Lord.

On the other hand, seeking God for a miracle in dire circumstances is *not* putting God to the test. When we are in danger or someone is gravely ill, we may certainly ask God for a miracle as long as we do so with faith in God's character and we leave the answer to God. This isn't putting God to the test because it respects God's sovereignty and doesn't question his existence or goodness. God often answers such prayers gladly. It is when we try to force God's hand that we cross the line. For example, Paul did not die when a poisonous snake bit him while he tended a fire. He was miraculously delivered from death (Acts 28:3–6). Paul did not then seek to handle other poisonous snakes to prove God was with him!

It is helpful to observe that the temptation to put God to the test is the one recorded temptation of Jesus in the wilderness in which Satan quoted Scripture (Ps 91:11–12). We learn from this that the temptation to put God to the test can seem particularly spiritual. Putting God to the test may seem like an expression of faith, but in reality it is the opposite of walking by faith. We should keep this in mind whenever it seems that we should do something that would generally be considered reckless; most of the time, this is inappropriate. When it comes to working in this world, as we have discussed, God most often uses means.

16

Looking Expectantly

I go to prepare a place for you. If I go and prepare a place for you, I will come again and receive you to Myself, that where I am, *there* you may be also.

JOHN 14:2–3

For now we see in a mirror dimly, but then face to face; now I know in part, but then I will know fully just as I also have been fully known.

1 CORINTHIANS 13:12

Beloved, now we are children of God, and it has not appeared as yet what we will be. We know that when He appears, we will be like Him, because we will see him just as He is.

1 JOHN 3:2

I consider that the sufferings of this present time are not worthy to be compared with the glory that is to be revealed to us.

ROMANS 8:18

Therefore, be on the alert—for you do not know when the master of the house is coming, whether in the evening, at midnight, or when the rooster crows, or in the morning—in case he should come suddenly and find you asleep. What I say to you I say to all, "Be on the alert!"

MARK 13:35–37

Paul called the return of Jesus: "the blessed hope and the appearing of the glory of our great God and Savior, Christ Jesus" (Titus 2:13). Indeed, upon his ascension into heaven, angels assured the apostles that Jesus would surely return physically and bodily just as he rose into heaven (Acts 1:9–11). Peter said not to be worried or to lose faith at the delay of Christ's return because God is giving more time for people to repent (2 Pet 3:3–9).

The Scriptures teach that the natural attitude of Christian believers is one of eager anticipation of Christ's return. For Paul, Jesus' return is a great encouragement and comfort during times of persecution and sorrow (1 Thess 4:13–18). For John, focus and confidence in Christ's return serves to cleanse us from a love of the temporary and worldly (1 John 3:2–3). For Peter, the return of Christ is a powerful incentive to holy living and Christian service (1 Pet 1:13–21; 2 Pet 3:10–18). When, in the Revelation to John, Jesus says that he is coming quickly, John writes, "Amen. Come, Lord Jesus" (Rev 22:20).

The Blessed Hope

The author of Hebrews calls the present time: "these last days" in which God "has spoken to us in His Son" (Heb 1:2). Jesus is referred to in the New Testament as the morning star—the planet we call Venus ([Gk. *phōsphoros*], 2 Pet 1:19; [Gk. *ton astera ton prōinon*], Rev 2:28; [Gk. *ho astēr ho lampros o prōinos*], Rev 22:16). Venus is the brightest object in our sky after the sun and the moon. Because it is closer to the sun than earth and its orbit is smaller, it always appears close to the sun in the night or morning sky. As the morning star, it rises not far from the brightness of the morning, heralding the rising of the sun above the horizon. Jesus, as the morning star, signals the coming of the kingdom of Light and the end of the darkness of sin (Rev 21:22–27; cf. Rom 13:11–14).

In Hebrews 11:1, the author teaches that one aspect of faith is treating what is hoped for in the future as if it is already real. Hope (Gk. *elpis*), as Paul observes in Romans, has to do with that which cannot be seen, otherwise it wouldn't be hope (Rom 8:24–25). "For the things which are seen are temporal," wrote Paul, "but the things which are not seen are eternal" (2 Cor 4:18). Christian hope is not simply faith that an event will take place, but hope in the God who brings about that event and in his Christ. The coming of Jesus, his triumph over sin and death, and his ascension into heaven are therefore seen as a source of hope—especially with the coming of the Holy Spirit at Pentecost indicating that the risen Jesus had come before his Father in heaven. As Peter expressed it, Christians have been "born again to a living hope (Gk. *elpida zōsan*) through the resurrection of Jesus Christ from the dead" and all that follows from that event (1 Pet 1:3).

The author of Hebrews observes that the hope for an eternal kingdom of God is not unique to Christians. He tells us that when Abraham left his home in response to the call of God and lived as an alien in Palestine, he was "looking for the city which has foundations, whose architect and builder (Gk. *technitēs kai dēmiourgos*) is God" (Heb 11:10). He observes that the many people of faith he describes in Hebrews 11 did not receive the reward of their faith during their lives. Their reward has been delayed so that all of God's people throughout time may receive it together (Heb 11:39–40). In making his defense before King Agrippa, Paul stated, "And now I am standing trial for the hope of the promise made by God to our fathers" (Acts 26:6). Paul's hope was based on the promises of God found in the Old Testament (Acts 24:14–15).

The Revelation to John has more references and allusions to the Old Testament than any other New Testament book, showing that it is through Christ that the promises of the Old Testament will be fulfilled. Indeed, the Old Testament speaks of a coming day when God's people are blessed. The return of Jesus will bring about the beginning of a new age. Isaiah foretold that this Son of David would rule with righteousness and justice forever (Hebr. *wᵉʿad-ʿôlām*), and of the increase of his government and of peace there would be no end (Hebr. *ʾên-qēṣ*) (Isa 9:6–7). The New Testament sometimes emphasizes the endlessness of this reign by referring to it as the "ages of ages" (Gk. *eis tous aiōnas tōn aiōnōn*, e.g., 1 Tim 1:17; 2 Tim 4:18; Heb 13:21; 1 Pet 4:11; Rev 5:13; 11:15). Handel's "Hallelujah Chorus" celebrates Christ's return and eternal reign by incorporating many "hallelujahs" that enclose verses from the Revelation to John: "Hallelujah, for the lord God omnipotent reigneth, hallelujah.... The kingdom of this world is become the kingdom of our lord, and of his Christ.... And he shall reign forever and ever.... King of kings and lord of lords, And he shall reign forever and ever ... Hallelujah." (Rev 19:6; 11:15; 19:16).

Sufficient Knowledge

The thirteenth chapter of Paul's First Letter to the Corinthians is famous for what Paul says about love, and rightly so. Though only a brief part of the discussion, equal attention should be paid to what Paul says about our knowledge of spiritual things now versus after the return of Christ, "For now we see in a mirror dimly, but then face to face; now I know in part, but then I will know fully just as I also have been fully known" (1 Cor 13:12; cf. 1 John 3:2). We can know a number of things for certain about the afterlife and the coming kingdom of God. However, there is also much we do not know and we cannot know before Jesus returns.

In the early days of Christianity, a belief system arose called "Gnosticism." Gnosticism taught that it was possible to know certain mysteries about the universe, but that knowledge (Gk. *gnōsis*) was restricted to those who were properly initiated into a special group. Some religious groups today are similar to the gnostics in that they believe they have special knowledge not available to others. However, Christianity is not elitist; it is not a faith restricted to a privileged few. The knowledge of spiritual things, including what is taught about the future, is taught openly in the Bible.

The study of prophecy relating to the end of the present age and the nature of the next fascinates many, and it is an area all Christians are free to explore. At the same time, there are a number of complexities in this topic: the cultures of the ancient world from which this teaching comes, the types of literature it is presented in, and the proper way to understand how various prophecies fit together. As with all other topics, the key is what God expects us to understand from this teaching, and the goal is righteous living in fellowship with God, not cleverness in forecasting the future (2 Pet 3:13–18). For this reason, it is important for both those who make a special study of this topic and those who do not to carefully separate what we know for sure from what we can only render an opinion about. Everyone is entitled to their own opinion on nonessential matters of doctrine, but it is the indisputable teachings that should guide our lives (cf. Rom 14:5).

Those teachings that are without dispute are: the physical, bodily return of Jesus Christ to set up his eternal kingdom; the re-creation of the heavens and earth; the resurrection of the dead; the judgment of all people; the eternal blessing of those who received saving grace through Jesus Christ; and the eternal separation from the Lord of those outside Christ. For each of these events, the knowledge available to us is not comprehensive, but it is sufficient to show the importance of preparing ourselves and to sustain hope.

Paul's statement that we "know in part" recognizes that what we are told about the future is limited because God chooses to reveal only certain things to us. Also, the new creation probably differs so much from the creation we know that there are things we cannot understand before Christ's return. We can understand that sickness, death, and grief will be eliminated (Rev 21:4). However, other things about the age to come must be described by an analogy to things in historical human experience—such as speaking of hell in terms of the Valley of Hinnom or of the glorified body in terms of a dwelling or clothing (Matt 10:28; 2 Cor 5:1–4). In other places, Scripture speaks in highly symbolic terms to describe what the future will be like.

The Revelation to John is an example of apocalyptic literature, which presents thoughts in highly symbolic form. Not everything stated in the Revelation is symbolic, of course. There are teachings that are literally true. However, it impossible to understand what God is teaching if the symbolic nature of the Revelation isn't taken into account.

It is the symbolism that gives the Revelation such strange descriptions of appearance. For example, "a Lamb standing, as if slain" makes no sense in everyday experience because a dead lamb does not stand (Rev 5:6). John is indicating that the Lamb was slain, but is now alive—a reference to the risen Christ. Nor does a lamb have "seven horns and seven eyes" as this Lamb does. John explains that the seven eyes are "the seven Spirits of God, sent out into all the earth." Merrill Tenney observes, "Seven, of course is an important number everywhere in the Scriptures, beginning with the days of creation in Genesis. It is emblematic of completeness or of perfection."[1] Here, the eyes represent complete knowledge (omnipresence and omniscience) and the horns represent complete power (omnipotence)—important themes in John's book. In the Revelation, numbers can carry meaning as well as signify a measure or a count; close attention is sometimes required to determine which.

Like the number seven, the number twelve has significance through much of Scripture. It is the number of tribes of Israel and the number of apostles Christ chose to found his church. In Revelation 4, John tells us of twenty-four elders who surround the throne of God and render worship. The number twenty-four, being the sum of twelve plus twelve, seems to indicate that the elders represent the patriarchs of the twelve tribes of Israel and the twelve apostles. Confirmation of this view is found in Revelation 15:3, where "they sang the song of Moses, the bond-servant of God, and the song of the Lamb," as well as in Revelation 21:10–14, where each of the twelve gates of the New Jerusalem has the name of one of the twelve tribes of Israel inscribed on it and each of the twelve foundation stones has the name of one of the twelve apostles inscribed on it.[2]

The symbolism communicated by numbers may work in a manner that does not depend upon the exact meaning of the numbers themselves. The New Jerusalem represents the dwelling place of God's people for eternity. John tells us that the length, width, and height of the New Jerusalem are equal, making the New Jerusalem a perfect cube. This is a strange shape for a city! A cube makes sense symbolically, however, when we remember that the holy of holies, the innermost room inside Solomon's temple, was a

---

1. Tenney, *Interpreting Revelation*, 37.
2. Alford, *Alford's Greek Testament*, 4:596.

perfect cube (1 Kgs 6:20).³ The shape of this room is not an accident. It is based upon the design of the tabernacle.⁴ Moses had the tabernacle built according to exact specifications given to him by *Yahweh* on Mount Sinai. The New Jerusalem thus takes on the symbolism of the holy of holies.⁵

Access to the tabernacle was forbidden to all but the priests, and the holy of holies was entered by the high priest only once each year on the Day of Atonement. But because of the redeeming work of the Lamb of God, God's people are no longer separated from *Yahweh's* presence. In the form of the New Jerusalem, the holy of holies now *encompasses* God's people, who dwell in the open presence of God (Rev 21:16, 22–23). Richard Bauckham notes, "The radical assimilation of the city to a temple, taken further in Revelation than in its prophetic sources, shows how central to the whole concept of the New Jerusalem in Revelation is the theme of God's immediate presence."⁶ The city as a cube, reminiscent of the holy of holies, is thus the perfect symbolic representation of the words, "Behold, the tabernacle of God is among men, and He will dwell among them, and they shall be His people, and God Himself will be among them" (Rev 21:3).

The size of the New Jerusalem is so enormous (about 1,400 miles long, wide, and tall) that some commentators have sought a different interpretation of the Greek text, principally because the city is so high. This is true even though the Greek text clearly states that the length, width, and height of the city are equal (Gk. *to mēkos kai to platos kai to hypsos autēs isa estin*), and the following verse seems to give the thickness of the wall (Rev 21:16–17). These commentators seem to assume that the city must have some relation to real cities of the ancient world. The symbolism used in the Revelation, however, is often tied to spiritual concepts rather than to present-day realities, so it seems best to see the portrayal of the New Jerusalem as symbolic. We have seen this in John's description of the Lamb with his seven eyes and seven horns. Another example, is the portrayal of Jesus having a sharp, two-edged sword coming out of his mouth (Rev 1:16; 2:16; 19:15, 21).

It is, of course, ridiculous to think that Jesus literally has a double-edged sword that he will manipulate with his mouth to bring judgment. John is referring to the ability of the Lord to bring judgment by simply commanding it (2 Thess 2:8; cf. Isa 49:2; Heb 4:12–13). As the Almighty, he who brought creation into existence by speaking is just as capable to bring

---

3. In 1 Kings 6, the holy of holies of Solomon's temple is referred to as "the Oracle" (Hebr. *hadd^{e}bîr*, 1 Kgs 6:20), which is translated "the inner sanctuary" in the NASB.

4. Durham, *Exodus*, 372.

5. Bauckham, *Theology*, 136, 140–42.

6. Bauckham, *Theology*, 136.

judgment by speaking (Ps 33:6, 9). Martin Luther captures this thought perfectly in his hymn "A Mighty Fortress Is Our God." Speaking of the final judgment that Christ Jesus will bring upon Satan, Luther writes, "One little word shall fell him."

Care must be taken in understanding symbolism. Some parts of the Revelation are notoriously difficult to interpret. There have been many attempts to interpret the number of the beast, 666; so far, there is no definitive answer how to decode it (Rev 13:18). Likewise, the meaning of the millennium in Revelation 20:2–7 is a subject of dispute. Some see it as a literal thousand-year reign of Christ after Christ returns but before eternity begins. Others believe it is the period of time when Christians will bring the world into subjection to the gospel *before* Christ returns. Still others see it as symbolic of Christ's reign in his church from the time of Pentecost until his return. The language used to describe the events just prior to Jesus' return are also open to interpretation. History shows too many examples of Christians jumping to conclusions about the meaning of end-time prophecy and embarrassing themselves when Jesus does not return when they predicted. They also bring the Christian faith into ridicule by skeptics—hardly the best way to win souls to Christ.

The difficulties interpreting yet unfulfilled prophecies, including many in the Revelation, account for the broad diversity of views regarding what will happen at the end of this age and in the eternal age to come. Nevertheless, while many details remain matters of dispute, the information Scripture gives us is sufficient for Christians in this age. The major facts and events of the afterlife and end times are clearly presented in Scripture. It is these that we must focus upon if we wish to be prepared as the Lord has warned us to be.

It seems there is little doubt Christians will be able to recognize when the time of Jesus' return is drawing close. However, Scripture teaches that the most important thing is to be ready. Jesus taught that only God the Father knows the exact time (Mark 13:32). Paul told the Thessalonians that they had no need to know the time or season of Jesus' return because he would come like "a thief in the night," a phrase also used by Peter and stemming from Jesus' teachings (Gk. *hōs kleptēs en nykti*, 1 Thess 5:1–2; 2 Pet 3:10; Matt 24:42–44; Luke 12:39–40). Although the time of his return will surprise everyone, the return itself will be unmistakable. It will be as visible as lightning that covers the entire night sky. Therefore, anyone who claims Jesus has returned secretly is to be ignored (Matt 24:4–5, 23–27).

Speaking with his disciples about the end times, Jesus warned them to be like servants in charge of a household when their master went away (Mark 13:32–37). Since they would not know when their master would return, they needed to be careful to be about their master's business at all times. Likening this to what is required of his followers, Jesus said, "What I say to you I say to all, 'Be on the Alert!'" (Mark 13:37). The language used here is instructive.

Jesus taught that because no one knows the time of his return, his followers should beware (Gk. *blepete*) and keep awake spiritually (Gk. *agrypneite*). He warns that they should not be found asleep (Gk. *katheudontas*) when he comes. Care needs to be taken here, for in the New Testament those who are dead are often euphemistically described as asleep, as by Paul in 1 Thessalonians 4. At other times, as in Mark 13:36, to be asleep is to be careless regarding spiritual and moral realities. Three times in Mark 13:33–37, Jesus commands his followers to "watch" (Gk. verb *grēgoreō*)—to "be on the alert."

Jesus' concern is seen in Peter's teaching. Peter wrote that because the return of Christ is near, Christians should be of sound mind (Gk. *sōphronēsate*) and sober in the sense of not being intoxicated (Gk. *nēpsate*; 1 Pet 4:7; cf. 5:8). In his letter to the Thessalonians, Paul referred to the current age as the night of sin, and reminded the Christians that they are not in darkness (Gk. *skotei*) but are children of light (Gk. *huioi phōtos*), and as such should watch (Gk. *grēgorōmen*) and be sober (Gk. *nēphōmen*; 1 Thess 5:4–11). Similarly in Romans, Paul reminds Christians that the Lord's return is near; Christians should awaken, cast off the ways of a world that is in darkness, and clothe themselves in the Spirit of Christ (Rom 13:11–14). The many words for wakefulness and sobriety indicate that there is a danger in being oblivious to the nature of this world (cf. 1 John 2:15-17; Jas 4:1—5:8). The sobriety required does not eliminate laughter or a good a sense of humor—both of which are indispensable to a well-balanced approach to life. It is, rather, to see everything in its proper perspective, and not make light of those things that deserve caution, respect, or reverence.

Watching, then, means Christians are not to forget that they live in a world in which sin is far too common and the risk of getting drawn into ungodliness is far too real; that the Lord is physically coming to set up his kingdom and hold everyone to account for how they have lived; and that the ways of this world will be banished forever, replaced by the loving and righteous ways of the living God (1 Pet 2:11; 4:12-17; 5:8; 1 John 2:17). While there is effort required to keep watch, it is clear that for those who "love the Lord's appearing," watching is an activity of joyful expectation (2 Tim 4:8; cf. Rom 8:23; Ps 96).

The Resurrection from the Dead

The great privilege of Christians at the time of Jesus' return, in addition to eternal fellowship with Christ, is resurrection from the dead. In fact, it is the occasion of the resurrection that begins unbroken fellowship with the risen Christ himself, whereas before then, fellowship is through the Spirit of Christ—the Holy Spirit (1 Thess 4:13-17).

When Paul testified to the Roman governor Festus and the Jewish king Agrippa, Paul argued that he was on trial because of the promise of resurrection that had been given to the nation of Israel (Acts 26:6-7, cf. Acts 24:14-16). He asked why the concept of God resurrecting the dead was so difficult for the Gentiles to believe (Acts 26:8). Gentiles, of course, had no respect for Jewish culture or beliefs. The real target of Paul's argument, as Paul's words indicate, was King Agrippa, who was familiar with Jewish doctrine and at least seems to have made a show of being a believing Jew (Acts 26:26-27). Resurrection is seen in the Old Testament in Isaiah 25:6-9; 26:19; Daniel 12:2; and Job 19:23-27.

Christians are re-created spiritually at their conversion to be the first part of God's new creation; by resurrection, their bodies are made part of the new creation as well. Paul gives an extended discussion of the glorified, resurrection body in 1 Corinthians 15:35-57 (cf. Rom 8:22-23).

Paul called the resurrection "the redemption of our body" (Gk. *tēn apolytrōsin tou sōmatos hēmōn*, Rom 8:23). He wrote to the Philippians, "For our citizenship is in heaven, from which also we eagerly wait for a Savior, the Lord Jesus Christ; who will transform the body of our humble state into conformity with the body of His glory, by the exertion of the power that He has even to subject all things to Himself" (Phil 3:20-21). This transformation into glorified bodies is necessary because mortal (Gk. *thnēton*), "flesh and blood" (Gk. *sarx kai haima*) bodies are not suitable for eternity (1 Cor 15:50-53). Paul explained to the Thessalonians that upon Jesus' return, the dead in Christ will be resurrected and transformed, then Christians who are alive will be resurrected and transformed—all gathered to Jesus "in the clouds . . . in the air" just before Jesus returns to the earth itself; and from that time on, Christians will never be separate from the Lord (1 Thess 4:13-18). This transformation will take place so quickly that it will be over before the redeemed even realize that it has begun (1 Cor 15:51-52).

Paul's writings show that we may refer to the accounts of the resurrected Christ to learn something of what it will be like to have a glorified body—but a bit of caution is in order here as well. Because Jesus is the eternal Son of God, some of the capabilities he demonstrated may not be given to his followers. Jesus' ability to travel and appear wherever he chose after his resurrection, for example, may be the result of the restoration of his divinity in response to his prayer that the glory he had before his incarnation be restored (John 17:5). On the other hand, Paul taught that Jesus is the "first fruits of those who are asleep" (1 Cor 15:20–23). It seems we are on more solid ground to conclude that Christians will have flesh and bones and will be able to eat (Luke 24:36–43; John 20:19—21:13).

In any case, the risen Christ demonstrates that the future for Christians is not some ghostly existence, but one that is physical and real—though differing in significant ways from the first creation (Luke 24:39). From that point on, there will be no more pain or death for those who are in the Lord, because the new creation has been completed in them, though not yet through all creation (Rev 21:4). This is the joyful hope for the future that Christians may comfort themselves with (1 Thess 4:18).

Between Death and Resurrection

In his Second Letter to the Corinthians, Paul discussed the attitude of Christians toward their future (2 Cor 5:1–9). Paul observed that given the frailty and mortality of the human body, Christians are anxious to be resurrected and glorified at the return of their Lord. Paul knew that he had to address the issue that some Christians would die before the Lord's return. He explained that death holds its own promise for Christians, because when they die, the redeemed pass into a state of blessedness in the presence of the Lord. They are then not only in the presence of Jesus, they are safe from earthly threats to their welfare. This will not eliminate their desire for resurrection and glorification because their existence will be unnatural apart from a body.

In discussing this, Paul uses metaphors for mortal bodies and resurrected bodies. He doesn't use a specific term to identify the portion of a person's makeup that survives death in this passage, but it is clear that after death a person's essence, their self, survives. Even outside this passage, it is difficult to determine a precise term to identify a person's essence that survives death. Just as we use a word in different ways in English, so, too, the Greek words of the New Testament are often used in different ways. The words translated spirit (Gk. *pneuma*, Hebr. *rûaḥ*) and soul (Gk. *psychē*, Hebr. *nepeš*) are used in various ways by the authors of the biblical books. Sometimes they are used to identify a person's essence apart from their physical body; at other times they indicate an individual, including the body. Here again, care must be taken when interpreting Scripture.

Scripture indicates that human beings who are alive have both a spiritual side and a physical side. God is Spirit, and there are created beings such as angels that are purely spiritual beings (John 4:24; Luke 1:8–38; Heb 1:7;

Ps 104:4; Isa 6:1–7; 2 Kgs 6:15–17). It is the spiritual side of human beings that enables full fellowship with God. It is also the spiritual side that enables human life.

In order to create a unified being that has "a foot in both worlds" so to speak, it was necessary for the Spirit of God to give spiritual life to Adam. Adam became a "living soul" when the "breath of life" was breathed into him by God at the time of his creation (Gen 2:7; 1 Cor 15:45). For Adam's offspring, the spiritual nature is passed on as well as the physical body. While animals are also spoken of in Scripture as having a spirit and a soul, the spiritual nature of a human being differs in that human beings are made in the image of God, and that image resides in the intelligent/social/moral nature of human beings (Gen 1:27).[7]

Even when distinguished from the physical body rather than indicating the entire person, the soul is usually seen as closely linked to it (Gen 9:4; Lev 17:11). Body and soul are thus seen in the afterlife only after the resurrection, where the final determination of the whole person is in view (e.g., Matt 10:28). Living as if only the physical creation exists is sometimes described as being natural or soulish (Gk. *psychikos*, 1 Cor 2:14; *psychikoi*, Jude 19). For this reason, it is probably best to refer to the essence of a person that survives death as a spirit rather than a soul prior to their resurrection. The author of Hebrews refers to those Christians who have passed away as "the spirits of *the* righteous made perfect" (*pneumasi dikaiōn teteleiōmenōn*, Heb 12:23). As for the nature of this existence, before the resurrection, Jesus referred to it as Paradise (Luke 23:39–43).

At the resurrection, even the body becomes spiritual. Paul taught the glorified, resurrection body will be: raised in power, imperishable, and glorious, because: "it is sown a natural body (Gk. *sōma psychikon*), it is raised a spiritual body (Gk. *sōma pneumatikon*)" (1 Cor 15:44). However, before the resurrection, what we can know is that those who die in the Lord will be with him in a state of blessedness and will be aware of that state. Although there is no indication they will know anything of what happens on earth, and certainly no indication we should try to pray to them, there does seem to be some indication that they, themselves, will be capable of prayer to God (Rev 6:9–11). This seems a reasonable expectation for those who are in the presence of the Lord.

As for those who die outside of Christ, it is important to understand that they pass away into the hands of a merciful God. Jesus taught that eternal punishment was not created for human beings, but for the devil and his

---

7. Payne, "*rûaḥ*," in *TWOT*, 2:836–37.

angels (Matt 25:41). If people pass into eternity condemned, it is because of the stubborn choices they have made, not God.

Further, it is not our place to determine the eternal destiny of souls. That role has been given to Jesus alone (Acts 10:42; 2 Cor 5:10; cf. Rom 14:10). Far too often, Christians have acted as if they, with their limited knowledge and their personal biases, are capable of determining this. "Do not judge" is Jesus' prohibition against taking a role that is rightly only God's. If "do not judge" meant not evaluating the morality of the certain behavior, he would not have given instruction on how to live (Matt 7:1–2; cf. 1 Cor 4:5; 5:9–13; 6:3). We are expected to be able to determine right and wrong for ourselves and others. We are not to make final pronouncements about others, however, nor to judge them by standards more harsh than we judge ourselves. For those who are truly outside of Christ, as Peter said, "the Lord knows how . . . to keep the unrighteous under punishment for the day of judgment" (2 Pet 2:9).

It seems helpful, at this point, to step back to consider how restrained the New Testament is in describing life after death. There are portions of Scripture that seem to give details, but these, as well as unfulfilled prophecies, are open to differing interpretations. Some may pertain to spiritual realities before the resurrection and ascension of Christ, and their purpose may have been other than to teach us about the afterlife (e.g., Luke 16:19–31; Eph 4:7–10). We do not have an account of what it was like for Lazarus before Jesus raised him from the dead, nor is there any detail from Jesus himself during the time between his death and his resurrection. This, together with biblical prohibitions against the occult, should serve to caution us about stories of people who have near-death experiences. It seems that the Lord did not want to provide us with information that, while it may satisfy some of our curiosity, takes away from the major truths that we should pay attention to about the end of life, the time before Christ's return, and the age to come.

Final Judgment

Divine judgment follows the return of Jesus Christ. At what point, how, and for how long we do not know. However, we do know that it will involve everyone who has lived and has become accountable for their actions. Peter wrote, "*It is* time for judgment to begin with the household of God; and if *it begins* with us first, what *will be* the outcome for those who do not obey the gospel of God?" (1 Pet 4:17). Paul warned, "We must all appear before the judgment seat of Christ, so that each one may be recompensed for his deeds in the body, according to what he has done, whether good or bad"

(2 Cor 5:10; cf. 1 Cor 3:11-15). For those who are part of the household of God, there will be praise or rebuke, but no danger of eternal condemnation. Those who truly love the Lord will not fear such a moment; their faith and their love of the Savior will have cast out fear, and they will be eager to be seen as having lived for their Lord (1 John 4:16-19; John 3:19-21). Faithfulness in this age will bring trust and likely greater responsibility in the next (Luke 12:42-44; 16:10-12; 19:16-19; Matt 25:19-23; Rev 3:21). On the other hand, those who have not been as faithful to the Lord as they could have been will experience shame rather than confidence (1 John 2:28).

Salvation is by faith alone; but true faith results in a changed life (John 14:23-24; 1 John 2:4-6; 3:21-22; 5:2-5). As we have seen, a person's character, and faith or lack of it, is invariably revealed by their deeds (Matt 25:31-46; John 5:28, 29; Jas 2:26; Rev 20:11-13). Jesus is uniquely prepared to be a merciful but righteous Judge. He is omniscient, knowing people's inner thoughts and motivations. He also knows their actions when no one else could see them. If he has a bias, it is a bias toward mercy (Rom 2:4; 5:8; 1 Tim 2:3-4; 2 Pet 3:9). He has lived as a human being and knows the challenges it presents in an evil age. He has the wounds from crucifixion that demonstrate how far he has gone to ensure the salvation of those people who come before him. On the other hand, he also knows when people are self-seeking, evasive, and have resisted having God as Lord of their lives. He will be determined that human history—with all its greed, turmoil, violence, and needless suffering—not repeat itself. While the last judgment will never be thought desirable to those under judgment, it holds the promise of ending human engendered turmoil and violence forever.

The Lord is not cruel. "He does not afflict willingly or grieve the sons of men" (Lam 3:33). The judgment of those who are outside the saving grace of Christ will be necessary to ensure that wickedness is banished forever. This, however, will not diminish the tragedy of wasted and broken human lives. Each will be exposed for their rejection of a benevolent Creator. The true character of each individual will be revealed so completely that it will be obvious that their condemnation is justified. The Lord has withheld his wrath to give time for repentance, but those who stand unsaved before him have not sought his mercy.

At the same time, the punishment of each will be in proportion to the wickedness of their crimes (Luke 12:47-48; Rom 2:5-11; Gal 6:5, 7; Col 3:25; cf. Luke 20:45-47; Jas 2:13; 3:1; Heb 10:26-30; Rev 2:23). Many will be vicious criminals: human monsters, who have indulged their lusts at the pain and expense of others, and richly deserve the recompense they will receive for their wickedness (Rom 12:19; Jas 5:4-6). Among those who receive punishment will be those who persecuted Christians (2 Thess 1:5-10;

Rev 6:9–11). Those who used religion to justify greed and cruelty will be punished for twisting something beneficial and redemptive into something evil and destructive (Matt 7:15–23; Luke 20:46–47; 2 Cor 11:12–15; 2 Peter 2:1). Against such wickedness, the Lord will be righteous in bringing "the wrath to come" (1 Thess 1:10).

The picture Scripture paints of eternity apart from Christ is grim. Just as there is sadness and anger when criminals are sentenced in human courts, sentencing will be followed by "weeping and gnashing of teeth" (Matt 13:42, 50; Luke 13:28). Paul wrote that the wicked will "pay the penalty of eternal destruction, away from the presence of the Lord and from the glory of His power" (Gk. *hoitines dikēn tisousin olethron aiōnion apo prosōpou tou kuriou kai apo tēs doxēs tēs ischyos autou*, 2 Thess 1:9). It is the exclusion from the life-giving presence of God that will be the most important aspect of eternal condemnation. Here, we have largely metaphor and symbolism, but what it indicates is terrifying.

The prison for the devil and his angels, and for those who would rather serve him than the Lord, is called in the Revelation: "the second death, the lake of fire . . . the lake that burns with fire and brimstone" (Rev 20:14; 21:8; Matt 25:41). It is commonly referred to in the New Testament as gehenna (Gk. *Geenna*), which is the Valley of Hinnom near Jerusalem. Gehenna was the site of a massive trash dump at the time of Christ. It included all kinds of filth, including the carcasses of animals and the bodies of criminals who had been executed. For those who witnessed it, gehenna provided a solemn and horrifying picture of what hell would look like. The exact nature of hell, however, is something we cannot know in this age. What we know is enough, however, to warn us that "it is a terrifying thing to fall into the hands of the living God," because "our God is a consuming fire" (Heb 10:31; 12:29).

The Final Destiny of the Redeemed

Details of life for the redeemed in the age to come are sketchy, but communicate great promise. Jesus said he came that his followers "may have life and have *it* abundantly" (Gk. *hina zōēn echōsin kai perisson echōsin*, John 10:10). In Ephesians, Paul said that God gives his people salvation as a gift, "so that in the ages to come He might show the surpassing riches of His grace in kindness toward us in Christ Jesus" (Eph 2:7). To meditate on these passages alone is to know enough about God's plan for his people. However, we can know some more specific facts about this future.

There will be a new heaven and new earth. Everything negative—sickness, death, pain, tears—will be gone. For the first time, God's people will experience a world without the presence of evil influences and temptation. Loneliness will be forever gone because we will be closer to God than we have ever been, and we will be surrounded by people whose main characteristic, reflecting the Lord's, is love.

It seems everyone will be as able to meet Jesus as to meet others. I suspect we will also have an opportunity to meet all of the people we have read about in Scripture. People we have been close to we will grow even closer to, and we will find many more people to be close to. We will know and have fellowship with angels (cf. 1 Cor 6:3).

There will certainly be wonderful times of worship in which we experience the wonder of Trinity with outstanding music and praise; times filled with wonder and awe because "we will see Him just as He is" in all his glory (1 John 3:2; 1 Cor 13:12). It would not seem, however, that this is the extent of human activity in heaven.

When God created Adam, he gave Adam the task of tending a garden. Revelation 5:10 indicates that God's people will somehow "reign" in the new earth. The variety of life and environments in the first creation suggests that there will also be a variety of environments, plants, and animals in the new heaven and earth. Human beings, who have an innate desire to build and create, will find fulfilling work and creativity. It is God himself who will make the new heaven and earth continually fulfilling. It makes no sense that God would take us to himself to be bored, or to give us less than the varied experiences offered by the first creation.

A phrase that appears often in the New Testament, especially in Paul's writings is: "the God of peace" (Gk. *ho theos tēs eirēnēs*, Rom 15:33; 16:20; 2 Cor 13:11; Phil 4:9; 1 Thess 5:23; Heb 13:20). Werner Foerster writes of the New Testament word for peace, *eirēnē*,

> On the basis of OT and Rabbinic usage *eirēnē* thus acquires a most profound and comprehensive significance. It indicates the eschatological salvation of the whole man which is already present as the power of God. It denotes the state of the *kainē ktisis* (new creation) as the state of definitive fulfilment. In this sense salvation has been revealed in the resurrection of Jesus.[8]

As suggested here, because of his Hebrew background, and because of the Hebrew background of the New Testament, it is most likely that Paul had the Hebrew word for peace, *šālôm*, in mind when he referred to the God of peace.

G. Lloyd Carr wrote of the root of *šālôm*, "The general meaning behind the root *sh-l-m* is of completion and fulfillment—of entering into a

---

8. Foerster, "*eirēnē*," in *TDNT*, 2:415.

state of wholeness and unity, a restored relationship."[9] Speaking of the word *šālôm* itself, Carr wrote,

> *Shālôm*, and its related words *shālēm*, *shelem* and their derivatives, are among the most important theological words in the OT.... Implicit in *shālôm* is the idea of unimpaired relationships with others and fulfillment in one's undertakings.... There is also a strong eschatological element present in the meaning of *shālôm*. Messiah, "David's greater son," is specifically identified as the Prince of Peace (*śar shālôm*—the one who brings fulfillment and righteousness to the earth.[10]

The concepts communicated by the biblical words for "peace" surely provide a wonderful description of what the God of Peace has in store for his people in the age to come. The promise of such a future is not guaranteed by some natural process, but by our Creator and Savior (Rev 4–5). The Triune God, himself—Father, Son, and Holy Spirit—is the good news: the reason the coming of Jesus Christ is "the blessed hope."

---

9. Carr, "*shālēm*," in *TWOT*, 2:930.
10. Carr, "*shālôm*," in *TWOT*, 2:931.

Recommended Reading

The following books are recommended for further study in addition to those referred to in the bibliography:

Averick, Moshe. *The Confused World of Modern Atheism: Nonsense of a High Order.* New York: Mosaica, 2016.

Rabbi Averick's work includes both logic and copious information in support of biblical teachings accepted by both Christians and Jews. An appendix explains why a famous experiment in 1953 often cited to support the origin of life without a divine Creator actually supports the opposite.

Axe, Douglas. *Undeniable: How Biology Confirms Our Intuition That Life Is Designed.* New York: HarperOne, 2016.

A highly readable explanation for the nearly universal inclination to believe that the universe has been designed.

Carson, D. A. *The Gagging of God: Christianity Confronts Pluralism.* Grand Rapids: Zondervan, 1996.

Carson shows how secularists seek to marginalize Christians and the Christian message.

Collins, Kenneth J. *The Theology of John Wesley: Holy Love and the Shape of Grace.* Nashville: Abingdon, 2007.

A clear and authoritative source on John Wesley's theology.

Copan, Paul, and William Lane Craig. *Creation out of Nothing: A Biblical, Philosophical, and Scientific Exploration.* Grand Rapids: Baker Academic, 2004.

A comprehensive look at the teaching of creation from nothing (creatio ex nihilo).

Coppedge, Allan. *Portraits of God: A Biblical Theology of Holiness.* Downers Grove: InterVarsity, 2001.

Coppedge unfolds the many aspects of God's holiness in ways that both increase our appreciation of God and help us understand how to respond to his grace.

———. *Shaping the Wesleyan Message: John Wesley in Theological Debate.* Nappanee, IN: Francis Asbury, 2003.

An enlightening study of John Wesley's response to Calvinism.

Green, Michael. *The Books the Church Suppressed: Fiction and Truth in the "Da Vinci Code."* Grand Rapids: Monarch, 2005.

Explains why certain ancient documents that claimed to explain the life and teachings of Jesus Christ aren't included in our Bibles.

Lennox, John C. *Can Science Explain Everything?* Epsom, UK: Good Book Company, 2019.

Written to help Christians understand the relationship between science and Christianity. No background in science or philosophy is necessary to profit from the insights presented here.

———. *Seven Days That Divide the World: The Beginning according to Genesis and Science.* Grand Rapids: Zondervan, 2011.

In my opinion, the most cogent discussion of the correct interpretation of the Genesis creation account available today.

Lewis, C. S. *The Great Divorce.* New York: Macmillan, 1946.

In this fantasy, C. S. Lewis makes the valid point that people who won't spend eternity in heaven are those who don't want to live in God's kingdom anyway.

———. *The Screwtape Letters.* New York: Macmillan, 1961.

C. S. Lewis teaches important lessons for Christians in this fictional account of how demons might work to undermine God's plan of salvation from being effective in the lives of individuals.

Meyer, Stephen C. *Darwin's Doubt: The Explosive Origin of Animal Life and the Case for Intelligent Design.* New York: HarperOne, 2013.

Meyer focuses upon paleontology to show Darwinism's inability to explain the pre-Cambrian explosion. Presents a history of the development of evolutionary views. Lots of helpful information.

———. *Signature in the Cell: DNA and the Evidence for Intelligent Design.* New York: HarperOne, 2009.

Meyer uses information technology to explain why only an Intelligent Designer could have created the DNA code. A good portion of the book is devoted to molecular biology. An excellent resource for those seeking detailed information.

Nicholi, Armand M., Jr. *The Question of God: C. S. Lewis and Sigmund Freud Debate God, Love, Sex, and the Meaning of Life.* New York: Free, 2002.

Based on a college course originally presented at Harvard. A helpful book for those high school age and above who are struggling with how faith affects life.

Oden, Thomas C. *John Wesley's Scriptural Christianity: A Plain Exposition of His Teaching on Christian Doctrine*. Grand Rapids: Zondervan, 1994.

This book is valuable for highlighting John Wesley's unique qualifications to interpret Scripture as well as his teachings on Christian doctrine.

———. *John Wesley's Teachings*. 4 vols. Grand Rapids: Zondervan, 2012–14.

An expansion of John Wesley's Scriptural Christianity. Volumes may be purchased individually if interested in only one area of Wesley's thought.

———. *Systematic Theology*. 3 vols. Peabody: Hendrickson, 2006.

Oden provides cogent insights and copious references to historical Christian writings in his systematic theology. Originally available individually from HarperCollins; reprinted here as a three-volume set.

Oswalt, John N. *The Bible among the Myths: Unique Revelation or Just Ancient Literature?* Grand Rapids: Zondervan, 2009.

Oswalt explains why the Bible should be viewed differently from other ancient literature and exposes bias against Scripture in the academic community.

———. *Called to Be Holy*. Nappanee, IN: Evangel, 1999.

A highly readable and helpful examination of the meaning of holiness in today's world.

Rose, Delbert R. *Holiness: A Theology of Christian Experience; Interpreting the Historic Wesleyan Message*. Salem, OH: Schmul, 2000.

A study of history that helps clarify the Wesleyan message of scriptural holiness.

Shelton, W. Brian. *Prevenient Grace: God's Provision for Fallen Humanity*. Wilmore, KY: Francis Asbury, 2014.

A unique and valuable study of the doctrine of prevenient grace.

Stark, Rodney. *The Rise of Christianity: How the Obscure, Marginal Jesus Movement Became the Dominant Religious Force in the Western World in a Few Centuries*. New York: HarperOne, 1996.

Stark writes as a sociologist. His account of how Christian faith and values enabled it to supplant paganism has insights seldom seen in other accounts of Christian history.

Wells, David F. *No Place for Truth; or, Whatever Happened to Evangelical Theology?* Grand Rapids: Eerdmans, 1993.

Wells examines how modernism undermines evangelical practice and belief. He argues for a restoration of Christian faith and practice based upon the teachings of the Bible.

Wesley, John. *A Plain Account of Christian Perfection*. Kansas City: Beacon Hill, 1971.

A record of John Wesley's growth in understanding of Christian holiness from 1725 to 1777 in his own words.

Bibliography

Alford, Henry. *Alford's Greek Testament: An Exegetical and Critical Commentary.* 4 vols. Grand Rapids: Baker, 1980.
Augustine. *Confessions.* Translated by Henry Chadwick. New York: Oxford University Press, 2008.
———. *On Genesis.* Translated by Edmund Hill and Matthew O'Connell. Edited by John E. Rotelle. The Works of Augustine: A Translation for the 21st Century. Hyde Park, NY: New City, 2002.
Bauckham, Richard. *The Theology of the Book of Revelation.* New York: Cambridge University Press, 1993.
Bruce, F. F. *The Books and the Parchments.* 3rd ed. Old Tappan, NJ: Revell, 1963.
Calvin, John. *Institutes of the Christian Religion.* Translated by Henry Beveridge. Peabody, MA: Hendrickson, 2017.
Copleston, Frederick. *A History of Philosophy.* 9 vols. Mahwah, NJ: Paulist, 1946–75.
Dalman, Rodger. *Is the Bible Really True? Recovering an Ancient Faith with 21st Century Evidence.* 2nd ed. Brooklyn Center, MN: Rodger Dalman, 2015.
Dewey, John. *A Common Faith.* New Haven: Yale University Press, 1934.
Durham, John I. *Exodus.* Word Biblical Commentary. Waco, TX: Word, 1987.
Eliade, Mircea. *The Myth of the Eternal Return; or, Cosmos and History.* Translated by Willard R. Trask. Princeton: Princeton University Press, 1991.
Fletcher, John. *The Works of the Reverend John Fletcher, Late Vicar of Madeley.* 4 vols. Salem, OH: Schmul, 1974.
Green, Joel B. *The Gospel of Luke.* New International Commentary on the New Testament. Grand Rapids: Eerdmans, 1997.
Hoehner, Harold W. *Ephesians: An Exegetical Commentary.* Grand Rapids: Baker Academic, 2002.
Hume, David. "Of Miracles." In *Philosophy of Religion: Selected Readings,* edited by William L. Rowe and William J. Wainwright, 492–99. 3rd ed. Fort Worth, TX: Harcourt Brace College, 1998.
Jastrow, Robert. *God and the Astronomers.* Afterword by John A. O'Keefe and Steven T. Katz. New York: Warner, 1978.
Kant, Immanuel. *Critique of Practical Reason.* Translated by Thomas Kingsmill Abbott. New York: Dover, 2004.
———. *Kant: Political Writings.* 2nd ed. Edited by Hans Reiss. Translated by H. B. Nisbet. New York: Cambridge University Press, 1991.
———. *Religion within the Limits of Reason Alone.* With essay by John R. Silber. Translated by Theodore M. Greene and Hoyt H. Hudson. New York: Harper Torchbook, 1960.
Köstenberger, Andreas J. *John.* Baker Exegetical Commentary on the New Testament. Grand Rapids: Baker Academic, 2004.
Lewis, C. S. "The Grand Miracle." In *God in the Dock,* 80–88. Grand Rapids: Eerdmans, 1970.

———. "Miracles." In *God in the Dock*, 25–37. Grand Rapids: Eerdmans, 1970.
Lindsley, Art. "C. S. Lewis on Miracles." *Knowing & Doing: A Teaching Quarterly for Discipleship of Heart and Mind*, Fall 2004. http://www.cslewisinstitute.org/webfm_send/633.
Oden, Thomas C. *The Rebirth of Orthodoxy: Signs of New Life in Christianity*. San Francisco: HarperSanFrancisco, 2003.
Oswalt, John N. *The Book of Isaiah: Chapters 1–39*. New International Commentary on the Old Testament. Grand Rapids: Eerdmans, 1986.
———. *The Book of Isaiah: Chapters 40–66*. New International Commentary on the Old Testament. Grand Rapids: Eerdmans, 1998.
Peirce, Charles Sanders. *Collected Papers of Charles Sanders Peirce*. Edited by Charles Hartshorne and Paul Weiss. 8 vols. Cambridge: Belknap, of Harvard University Press, 1960–74.
———. *The Essential Peirce: Selected Philosophical Writings; 1893–1913*. Edited and compiled by the Peirce Edition Project. Vol. 2. Bloomington: Indiana University Press, 1998.
———. *Mathematical Miscellanea*. Vol. 3, bk. 1 of *The New Elements of Mathematics*. Edited by Carolyn Eisele. Atlantic Highlands, NJ: Humanities, 1976.
———. *Pragmatism as a Principle and Method of Right Thinking: The 1903 Harvard Lectures on Pragmatism*. Edited, introduction, and commentary by Patricia Ann Turrisi. Albany: State University of New York Press, 1997.
Plato. *Euthyphro, Apology, Crito, Phaedo, Phaedrus*. Introduction by W. R. M. Lamb. Translated by Harold North Fowler. Loeb Classical Library. Cambridge: Harvard University Press, 2005.
———. *Timaeus, Critias, Cleitophon, Menexenus, Epistles*. Translated by R. G. Bury. Loeb Classical Library. Cambridge: Harvard University Press, 2005.
Royce, Josiah. *The Problem of Christianity: Lectures Delivered at the Lowell Institute in Boston, and at Manchester College, Oxford*. 2 vols. New York: Macmillan, 1913.
Schaff, Philip, ed. *The Creeds of Christendom: With a History and Critical Notes*. Revised by David S. Schaff. 6th ed. 3 vols. Grand Rapids: Baker, 1998.
Smith, Ralph L. *Micah-Malachi*. Word Biblical Commentary. Nashville: Nelson, 1984.
Tenney, Merrill C. *Interpreting Revelation*. Grand Rapids: Eerdmans, 1970.
Thompson, Richard P. *Acts: A Commentary in the Wesleyan Tradition*. New Beacon Bible Commentary. Kansas City: Beacon Hill, 2015.
Thompson, Robert J. "Ontological Arguments." In *Philosophy of Religion: Introductory Essays*, edited by Thomas Jay Oord, 59–73. Kansas City: Beacon Hill, 2003.
Turner, David L. *Matthew*. Baker Exegetical Commentary on the New Testament. Grand Rapids: Baker Academic, 2008.
Wesley, John. *Explanatory Notes upon the New Testament*. 2 vols. Kansas City: Beacon Hill, 1983.
———. *Wesley's 52 Standard Sermons with Introductions, Analysis, and Notes*. Edited, introductions, and commentary by N. Burwash. Salem, OH: Schmul, 1967.
———. *The Works of John Wesley*. 3rd ed. Edited by Thomas Jackson. 14 vols. Grand Rapids: Baker, 1978.
Wiley, H. Orton. *Christian Theology*. 3 vols. Kansas City: Beacon Hill, 1971.

Index

ʾăbî-ʿad, 41
ʾahab, 94, 111
ʾehyeh, 29–30
ʾēl gibbôr, 41
ʾĕmet, 142
ʾĕmûnâ, 164

Abraham, 61, 77, 80, 85, 102, 103, 149–50, 164, 212
   promised all familes would be blessed through him, 77, 102, 125, 150
   promised descendants would be delivered from slavery, 101, 114, 150
   promised he would be the father of Isaac by Sarah, 77, 102, 150
   the father of all who have faith, 77, 85
   See also under Kierkegaad, Soren
Adam and Eve
   abused their gift of freedom, 106–8, 171
   and the covenant of works, 106
   brought immediate negative consequences, 108–10
   brought spiritual death, 101–2, 112
   corrupted themselves, 106, 111
   created in the image of God, 101
   displayed a pattern of temptation, 106–8 (*see also under* temptation)
   favored creatures over their Creator, 104–6
   punishment of meant to lead to salvation, 106, 148
age to come, the, 138, 168, 210
   and the endless reign of Christ, 212
   and the God of peace, 224–25
   and the New Jerusalem, 214–15
   and those in Christ, 98–99, 166, 223–25
   and those outside Christ, 223
   sufficient, not extensive knowledge of, 212–17, 221
   symbolism regarding, 213–16
   watching for, 216–17
   See also glorification; Jesus of Nazareth
amemptōs, 171
anagennaō, 168, 169
anointing
   divine commission for specific tasks, 50
   of kings, 51–52
   of priests, 50, 53
   of prophets, 53
   of the craftsmen of the tabernacle, accessories, and garb, 50
   See also under Jesus of Nazareth; Yahweh
anōthen, 168
Anselm, 10
   description of God, 85
aphesis, 130
aphthartō, 89
apolytrōsis, 156, 218
apostles, 74. *See also under* Twelve, the
Aristotle, 16
aseity, 30, 88–89
assurance of salvation, 2, 165
assurance of understanding, the full, 4. *See also* understanding; walking with God
Athanasius, 10, 12, 35
atonement, the
   accomplished through the crucifixion of Christ, 127–29, 133–35

atonement, the (*continued*)
    and the priesthood of the order of Melchizedek, 53, 134–35, 139
    a ransom, 54, 130, 135–36
    a work of God, 132–33
    completed by Christ, 105, 135–36, 139–40, 141, 144
    consequences of, 135–36
    foretold in prophecy, 2, 53, 129, 134
    nature of, 131–36
    purpose of, 127, 129–31
    similar to God's use of Joseph's misfortunes, 128–29
    supernatural events during, 128
Augustine, of Hippo, 10, 12, 24–25, 80
    on hearts resting in God, 86
    on interpreting Genesis, 24–25
    on making assertions about the natural world, 25

baptism
    infants as candidates for, 190
    mode of, 190
    witnesses commitment to Jesus Christ, 189–90
$b^e h\bar{e}ma$, 95
$b^e r\hat{\imath}t$, 115
Berkeley, George, 7–8
Bible, the
    a collection determined by tradition, 34–35
    a collection of ancient documents, 31, 35
    and the Protestant Reformation, 32
    canon of, 35
    each document authoritative in itself, 34–35
    small group study of, 83
    See also Scripture

Christianity
    based on sound tradition, 37, 74–75, 83, 184–85, 188
    bias against, 33–34
    doesn't need rescuing, 7–8
    first called *ho hodos*, 54–55
    not an enemy of science, 21
    rejection of, 5–6, 8, 39–40
    See also under religion
collegia pietetis, 83
coram Deo, biblical basis of, 175–76
covenant
    involved the shedding of blood, 115, 130
    New, 36, 68, 93, 106, 115, 122–23, 124–26, 129–30, 133, 139, 155–56, 170, 179, 197
    of works vs. of grace, 106
creatio ex nihilo, 27–29, 72

Dark Ages, the, 33
Deists, 5–6, 32–33
Demiurge (*dēmiourgos*), 27–28
dikaios, 82, 123, 156, 220
dikaioō, 156
dikaiōma, 144
dikaiōsis, 144
dikaiosunē, 156, 170
discipleship, Christian, 5, 55–58, 184, 195
    requires devotion of the entire inner life, 80–82
    See also understanding; walking with God
doctrine, meaning and importance of, 10, 11, 82–83, 213

eirēnē, 94, 95, 224
ekklēsia, 102, 166–67, 184, 187, 190, 195, 207
elpizō and *elpis*, 164, 211–12
Enlightenment, the, 8, 33–34, 39, 163
    denied the supernatural, 32–33, 39
ethnos hagion, 103
evil, abstaining from, 204–9
    living in the spirit, 205–6
    not putting God to the test, 207–9
    redemptive righteousness, 206–7
    See also Spirit, living in the; flesh, living in the
exēgeomai, 44–45

faith in God, 162–65
    described, 164–65
    does not earn merit, 159
    not a leap, 163–64

INDEX

saving, 2, 162–63
seen in faithfulness, 164
flesh, living in the, 105–6, 205–6
Fletcher, John, 28
   on the scope of redemptive grace, 144–45
foot washing, significance of, 56, 191

gehenna, 223
Genesis
   an ancient document, 26
   correct interpretation of, 25–27
   creation account not myth, 24
   role of, 26–27, 101
ginomai, 168
glorification, 138, 173, 213, 218–19, 220. *See also under* Jesus of Nazareth
gnosticism, 31, 75, 213
God
   aidios autou dynamis, 86
   and anthropomorphisms, 89–90
   Anselm's description of, 85
   calls people to himself, 167, 192
   changeless, 92–94
   communicates with his creatures, 23, 31, 77–78
   Creator of everything else, 24, 28–29, 88, 143, 168
   generally uses means, 72, 177, 178, 183, 209
   ho Pantokrator, 23, 91
   I AM, the, 29–31
   immanent in creation, 26, 91
   is benevolent, 77, 94–95, 132, 143, 180–81,
   is changeless, 92–94
   is holy, 87, 170
   is just, 95–96
   is spirit, 89–91
   is sovereign, 69, 91–92, 128–29, 145, 160, 180, 208
   kingdom of, 52, 111, 122, 159, 166, 168, 179, 180, 192, 198, 212
   not the cause of sin, 106, 107
   of peace, 94, 171, 224–25
   partly revealed in creation, 85–86
   phōs oikōn aprositon, 90
   putting to the test is sin, 207–9
   reaches out to draw sinners to himself, 47, 77–78, 132, 145–46, 203
   reveals himself as he chooses, 77, 86, 90, 213
   seeks a people for his own possession, 98, 102–3, 125, 146, 150, 166, 187, 193, 214–15, 223–25
   self-existence of (see *aseity*)
   supernatural, 17, 27
   theiotēs, 86
   the source of all good gifts and blessings, 77–78, 94, 98–99, 112, 147
   See also under holiness; Holy Spirit; Jesus of Nazareth; Trinity; Yahweh
God-fearers, 69, 119, 154
grace of God
   charis, 94, 144
   common, 146–47
   convincing, 154–55
   election as the, 149–54
   prevenient, 147–49
   providential, 141–43, 191
   saving, 155–57
   universal reach of, 141–43, 144–49
grēgoreō, 217
guidance, direct, personal divine, 183, 185–87. *See also* Scripture; walking with God

hagiazō, 171
hagioi, 169, 171–72, 190
haimatekchysias, 130
Handel's *Messiah*, 51, 212
ḥannûn, 142–43
ḥaṭṭāʾâ, 142, 143, 156
Heber, Reginald, and the hymn "Holy, Holy, Holy," 22
ḥesed, 94, 111, 142
hilastērion, 156
holiness
   defined by the deity or deities it relates to, 87, 170
   the goal for the redeemed, 169–74, 176, 186–87

INDEX

holiness (*continued*)
  See also God; Holy Spirit; means of grace; sanctification
holoteleis and *holoklēron*, 171–72
holy of holies, 54, 130, 134, 139, 214–15,
Holy Spirit
  anointing of makes Jesus the Christ, 48, 50, 52–53, 59–60, 68
  brings benefits of saving grace to believers, 57, 139, 167, 170, 183, 184, 185, 195–96, 201, 203, 205, 206
  brought Scripture into existence, 72
  came with a new mission at Pentecost, 139, 151
  enables Jesus' ministry, 52–53, 57, 59–60, 68
  fulfilled the promise of the Father, 139
  inaugurated the Christian church at Pentecost, 2, 139, 151
  is deity, 97
  is the Spirit of Truth, 2, 71, 167
  witnesses to and exalts Jesus Christ, 64, 71, 74, 155, 211–12
  work of often not revealed in feelings, 7 (*see also* guidance, direct, personal divine)
human beings
  created in the image of God, 90, 100–102
  created wholly pleasing to God, 137
  Creator/creature relationship, 23, 112, 160, 208
  requirements for relationships, 198–202
  spiritual as well as material beings, 17, 19–22, 220
Hume, David, 5–6, 8, 19, 65
  argument against miracles inadequate, 65–70
humility before the Lord, 7, 76, 111, 151, 160–62, 179, 181, 183, 184
hylozoism, 16
hyperperisseuō, 134, 144
hypotypōsis, 4

illumination, divine, 73, 185

individualism, excessive, 6–9
  outside God's plan, 166, 195–97
Irenaeus, 10, 12, 97

Jastrow, Robert, 19, 20–21
Jerusalem Council, 119–20
Jerusalem, New. See *under* age to come, the
Jesus of Nazareth
  always honored the Father, 43–44, 60, 111, 133
  anointed to three-fold mission, 52–54
  ascension of, 56, 60, 139, 155, 211
  baptizes with the Holy Spirit, 49, 139
  becomes the Christ at baptism, 49–50
  Christ (*Christos*, *māšîaḥ*, messiah), 50
  confirmed by works, 48, 60–61, 68–70, 96 (*see also under* miracles)
  foundation of the Christian faith, 38–40, 54–55
  ho logos, 45
  imitation of, 57
  Immanuel, 41, 47, 134
  is deity, 40–43, 45–47, 97
  love of God reaches out through, 47, 58, 203
  priest and intercessor, 31, 53, 139–40
  reaction to is reaction to God, 47, 58, 161
  resurrection and glorification of, 54, 64–65, 69, 136–38, 211–12, 218–19
  return of, 85, 211–12, 216–18, 221
  reveals the Father, 44–46
  savior, 53, 113, 133–135, 141, 145, 211
  sits at the right hand of God, 42–43, 139
  son of David, 40–43, 52, 134–35, 212, 225
  son of God, 40–47, 50, 53–54, 60, 69, 93, 128, 133–34, 138, 167, 181, 208, 218–19

sōtēr pantōn anthrōpōn, 145
    temptation of, 44, 105, 208, 209
    the morning star, 211
    virgin birth of, 41–42, 134, 135
    will judge all souls, 95, 221–22
    without sin, 36, 135, 181
    See also atonement, the; God; Holy Spirit; miracles; Trinity
Jewish Diaspora, 119, 122
John the Baptist
    birth of, 49, 61, 91, 124
    preaches repentance, 49, 66, 74, 109, 124, 154, 160
    witnesses that Jesus is the Christ, 49, 55, 56, 60, 133, 139, 168
Jonah, 77, 95, 137–38, 148–49

kainē ktisis, 169, 224
Kant, Immanuel, 6, 8, 19–20, 33–34, 39, 67
kārat, 115, 130
kardia, 81, 148
kaleō, 166–67
Kierkegaard, Søren, 31, 76, 80, 163
    thinks faith is a "leap," 163–64
    misjudges God, 31, 77
    wrongly evaluates God's test of Abraham, 76–77, 80
kosmos, 18, 109, 133, 145

latreuō and *latreia*, 179–80
lēb and *lēbāb*, 81
Lewis, C. S., 12
    on miracles, 64–65, 67–68, 68–69
liberal progressivism, 5–6, 7, 8–9, 163
life after death, 219–21
Lord's Supper, the, 11, 68, 189, 190

malista, 145
marriage, 31, 200, 201, 202
    ceremony, 190–91
    of God with Israel, 125
mathētēs, 55, 184
means of grace
    ensure spiritual growth, 176–78
    primary identified, 178
    reading Scripture, 183–85

    See also evil, abstaining from; God; prayer; works, good; worship
Melito, bishop of Sardis, 35
Meth' hēmōn ho theos, 41
miracles
    concentrated in four time periods, 61–62
    God always capable of working, 61
    immediate (performed without means), 72, 73, 178
    nature of biblical, 61–62
    supernatural, 61–62
    testify to the work of the Creator, 61–62, 68
    unique and occasional, 67
    witness to Jesus' identity, 64, 66–67
    works that confirm Jesus is the Christ, 59–64
    See also Lewis, C. S.; Hume, David
mišpāṭ, 111
misunderstanding
    causes of, ix, 4–9
    corrective to, 8–9
    instances of, 2–3, 25, 82
    zeal not according to knowledge, 1, 82
    See also understanding
Mosaic law
    a gift of grace, 125–26
    distorted, 35–36, 122–23
    in the history of Israel, 120–23
    logia zōnta, 36, 123
    makeup of, 116–20
    successes and failure of, 123–25
    the covenant agreement between Yahweh and the Israelites, 114–16

natural law, 17, 61

Oden, Thomas, on evaluating new scholarship, 83
orthodox Christianity, 83, 97, 184, 185

ʿābad and *ʿăbôdâ*, 179–80
ʿalmâ, 41
ʿam qādôsh, 103
ʿimmānûēl, 41

ʿôlām, 42, 212

paganism, 11, 16, 18, 21, 28, 29, 32, 105, 141–42, 149, 163, 178, 202. See also under universe, the
palingenesia, 168, 170
pantheism and panentheism, 28
parthenos, 41
Paul, the apostle
   advice to Timothy, 4
   early misunderstanding of Scripture, 4
   schooled in pagan philosophy, 12
Peirce, Charles Sanders
   affirmed divine Creator, 85
   on the ability to understand the universe, 85
   on the orderliness of the universe, 19
   valued medieval scholarly methods, 33
periousios and *peripoiēsis*, 103
perspecuity of Scripture, 185
pešaʿ, 142, 143
Petrarch, 32
philosophes, 32–33
philosophy
   Christian leaders knowledgeable of, 12
   defective can undermine faith, 7–8, 11–12, 34, 39, 65, 92
   defined, 12
   importance of for Christians, 8, 12
physicalism, 16
pietism, 182–83
pistis, 164
Plato, 12, 14–15, 27–28
pleonazō, 134, 144
pneuma. See Spirit, living in the
prayer, 181–83, 200, 208, 220
   in a known language, 181
   intercessory, 152–53, 182
   main parts of, 181
   table grace and prayers of thanksgiving, 191
   without ceasing, 182
   See also means of grace; worship
prophets
   care receiving messages of, 72–73, 186–87
   false, 4, 68, 73, 186–87, 201
   required to be faithful, 7, 72–73, 186
   true, 42, 53, 72–73, 120, 151, 161
proskyneō, 161, 178–79

quod ubique, quod semper, quod ab omnibus creditum est, 83

redemption, 52–53, 62, 130, 135–36, 144, 156, 161
   of the body, 169, 218
   See also atonement, the; salvation
regeneration. See under salvation
relationships, personal, 198–202
religion, 10–11
   characteristic of human culture, 20
   Christianity historically referred to as, 10
   Christianity qualifies as, 11
Renaissance, the, 32–33
repentance, 49, 152, 160–62
   does not earn merit, 159
   God delays judgment to give time for, 77–78, 211, 222
   of believers who sin, 162, 173, 204–5, 207
revelation, 32, 73, 80

sālaḥ, 155–56
šālôm, 224–25
salvation
   adoption, 166–67
   forgiveness for sin, 46, 60–61, 113–14, 129–30, 142–43, 155–57, 162, 204
   from willful sin requires repentance and faith, 160
   justification, 141, 144, 147–48, 156–57, 166
   regeneration, 158, 168–69, 211–12
sanctification
   entire, 171–74
   initial, 169–71
sarx. See flesh, living in the
Satan
   a liar, 73, 104, 187

a murderer, 104
and his workers eternally
   condemned, 145, 155, 216
and his workers the enemies of
   human beings, 96, 136
background of, 104, 105
opposes God, 128, 177
oppressor, 96
ransom not paid to, 135–36
restricted by God, 105
the tempter, 44, 104–7, 173–74,
   208–9
science, description of, 16
scientism, 16
Scripture
   apocalyptic symbolism in, 214
   divinely inspired, 34–35, 72–73, 123
   first rule of interpretation of, 26
   freedom interpreting non-central
      teachings, 12, 185
   inerrancy and infallibility, 78
   interpretation dependent on divine
      intention, 75–78
   lessons not hidden, 31, 213
   tradition guides interpretation of,
      83, 184
   validity of in contemporary culture,
      31–32
   See also Bible, the
second coming. See under age to come,
   the
secular materialism, 16
sin
   as *anomia*, 111–12
   as *hamartia*, 111, 123, 144
   universal, 108–10
Socrates, 14–15
Spener, Phlipp Jakob, 82–83
Spirit, living in the, 205–6. *See also*
   guidance, direct, personal
   divine; walking with God
spiritual growth. *See* means of grace

tabernacle, 29–30, 50, 87, 103, 116, 120,
   130, 134, 179, 215
ta panta, God the Creator of, 28–29,
   87, 88
temptation

Christians not exempt from, 81, 122,
   162, 173, 204–5, 207, 209
nature of, 81, 106–8, 110–12
theology, x, 21, 27, 82, 83, 85, 101, 138,
   205
errant understanding of, 10, 11–12,
   92
meaning and importance of for
   Christians, 9–10, 97
thrēskeia, 11
ṭôb mᵉʾōd, 137
tradition
   and the interpretation of Scripture,
      83
   beneficial vs. harmful, 35–37
   paradosis and *parathēkē*, 36–37
Trinity, 96–97
   baptism in the Name of, 189
   best described by Cappadocian
      fathers, 97
   eternal, 97
   key to understanding some Old
      Testament passages, 42–43, 97
   mutual love of Father, Son, and Holy
      Spirit, 98
   roles of in creation and in salvation,
      133
   the source of social relationships,
      97, 201
   three equally divine Persons in
      perfect harmony, 132–33, 225
truth, 2, 23, 31, 73, 99, 112, 142, 145,
   153
   all truth is God's, 80
   conveyed by Scripture, 12, 22, 24,
      25, 40, 42, 74, 78, 183–84
   walking in, 2, 9, 54, 65, 76, 82, 167,
      194, 200
   See also under Holy Spirit; Scripture;
      tradition
Twelve, the
   choice of, 74
   unique witnesses to Jesus and his
      teachings, 2, 64, 66–67, 72,
      74–75, 184, 214,

understanding
   full assurance of, 4

understanding (*continued*)
    hindrances to, ix, 5–9, 12
    importance of, ix, 2–4, 11, 12, 75, 79, 85, 173
    See also misunderstanding; walking with God
universe, the
    ability of to cause events, 17, 21, 61
    ability to understand is God-given, 85–86
    and the supernatural, 10, 17, 27
    big bang theory of origin, 16, 20–21
    created from nothing, 27–28, 72
    God separate from, 17, 26, 86
    God sovereign over, 17, 22–23, 86, 88, 91–92, 97, 105, 145
    naturalistic explanation of origin inadequate, 19–23, 97–98
    natural stuff as creator of, 16, 17
    orderliness of the basis for science and technology, 18–19
    pagan concepts of, 15–18, 21, 27–28
    pagan gods and, 15, 17, 26–27, 88, 141–42, 150
    paganism and cycles of, 16, 88, 141–42, 149
    platonic understanding of, 15, 27–28
    Scripture true in what it affirms regarding, 25–26
    Steady State theory of, 16
    theory of multiple universes, 18
    thought to be oscillating, 16
    transformed into new heaven and earth, 91

Vincent of Lérins, canon of, 83

walking with God, 111, 124, 131, 164, 179, 192
    a witness to Christ, 205
    enabled by the Holy Spirit, 170, 206
    rebelled against, 125, 194
    requires understanding, ix, 2, 82
    works prepared for, 175, 193, 196–97
    See under guidance, direct, personal divine; Holy Spirit; means of grace; Spirit, living in the; truth; understanding; works, good
watching. *See under* age to come, the
Wesley, John, x, 10, 12, 83, 110
    early misunderstanding of Scripture, 1–2
    on divine guidance, 185–86
    on expecting the end without the means, 178
    on the use of money, 197–98.
works, good, 193–204
    and giving, 197–98
    and spiritual gifts, 195–97
    and the redeemed, 193–95
    in relationships, 198–202
    returning good for evil, 203–4
worship, 28–29, 87, 120–21, 141–42, 161, 178–91, 224
    and service, 179–80
    Christian ceremonies of, 189–91
    corporate, 187–91
    first subject of human conflict, 131
    of false gods, 28, 87, 141–42, 150
    personal, 181–87
    See also baptism; foot washing; Lord's Supper, the; marriage ceremony; means of grace; prayer; universe, the

Yahweh, 29–30, 41–42
    anointed servants chosen by and responsible to, 50
    defines details of the tabernacle, 116, 214–15
    name known to Abraham, Isaac, and Jacob, 30
    name related to creation, 30–31
    nature of revealed to Moses, 117, 142–43
    See also anointing; God; Mosaic law
yeled, 41

zōē, 55, 89, 103, 167, 168, 223

www.ingramcontent.com/pod-product-compliance
Lightning Source LLC
Chambersburg PA
CBHW050849230426
43667CB00012B/2212